SAMS
PUBLISHING

M T W T F S S **24**

Using the *Teach Yourself in 24 Hours* Series

Welcome to the *Teach Yourself in 24 Hours* series! You're probably thinking to yourself, "What? They want me to stay up all night and learn this stuff?" Well, no, not exactly. This series introduces a new concept in teaching you about exciting new products: 24 one-hour lessons, designed to keep your interest and keep you learning. By breaking the learning process into small units, you will not be overwhelmed by the complexity of some of the new technologies being introduced in today's market. Each hourly lesson has a number of special items—some old, some new—to help you along.

10 Minutes

In the first 10 minutes of the hour, you will be given a complete list of all the topics and skills you will have a solid knowledge of by the time you finish the hour. You will be able to know exactly what the hour will bring, with no hidden surprises.

20 Minutes

By the time you have delved into the lesson for 20 minutes, you will know what many of the newest features of the software application are. In the constantly evolving computer arena, knowing everything a program can do will aid you enormously—if not right now, then definitely in the near future.

30 Minutes

Before 30 minutes have passed, you should have learned at least one useful task, oftentimes more. Many of these tasks will take advantage of the newest features of the application. These tasks take the hands-on approach, and tell you exactly the menus and commands you need to step through to accomplish the goal. This approach is found through each lesson of the *24 Hours* series.

40 Minutes

As you will see after 40 minutes, many of the tools you have come to expect from the *Teach Yourself* series are still here. Just a Minutes and Time Savers offer you quick asides into the special tricks of the trade to make your work faster and more productive. Cautions give you the knowledge to avoid those nasty time-consuming errors.

50 Minutes

Along the way, you may run across terms that you haven't seen before. Never before has technology thrown so many new words and acronyms into the language, and the New Terms elements you will find in this series will carefully explain each one.

60 Minutes

At the end of the hour, you may still have questions that need to be answered. You know the kind—questions on skills or tasks that may come up every day for you, but weren't directly addressed during the hour. That's where the Q&A section can help. By asking and answering the most frequently asked questions about the topics discussed in the hour, Q&A might not only get your specific question answered, but also provide a succinct review of all that you have learned in the hour.

Teach Yourself
PCs
in 24 Hours

Teach Yourself
PCs
in 24 Hours

Greg Perry

SAMS
PUBLISHING

201 West 103rd Street
Indianapolis, Indiana 46290

Between long writing streaks, my dear friends Harley and Frannie Hollan encouraged me. Thanks for your patience but most of all for your friendship!

Copyright © 1998 by Sams Publishing

FIRST EDITION

International Standard Book Number: 0-672-31163-1

Library of Congress Catalog Card Number: 97-68006

01   00   99   98   4   3   2

Interpretation of the printing code: the rightmost double-digit number is the year of the book's printing; the rightmost single-digit, the number of the book's printing. For example, a printing code of 98-1 shows that the first printing of the book occurred in 1998.

Composed in AGaramond and MCPdigital by Macmillan Computer Publishing

Printed in the United States of America

President   Richard K. Swadley
Publisher and Director of Acquisitions   Jordan Gold
Director of Product Development   Dean Miller
Executive Editor   Lorna Gentry
Managing Editor   Tom Hayes
Director of Marketing   Kelli S. Spencer
Product Marketing Manager   Wendy Gilbride
Associate Product Marketing Manager   Jennifer Pock
Marketing Coordinator   Linda B. Beckwith

Acquisitions Editor
Kim Spilker

Development Editor
Brian-Kent Proffitt

Production Editor
Karen A. Walsh

Copy Editors
Kim Hannel
Lori Lyons
Julie McNamee
Tom Stevens
Colleen Williams

Indexer
Tim Tate

Technical Reviewer
Jim Grey

Editorial Coordinators
Mandie Rowell
Katie Wise

Technical Edit Coordinator
Lynette Quinn

Editorial Assistants
Carol Ackerman
Andi Richter
Rhonda Tinch-Mize
Karen Williams

Cover Designer
Tim Amrhein

Book Designer
Gary Adair

Copy Writer
David Reichwein

Production Team Supervisor
Brad Chinn

Production
Marcia Deboy
Michael Dietsch
Cynthia Fields
Maureen West

Overview

Contents

Acknowledgments

During the end of this book's authorship, I had the fortunate experience to spend a day with the editors and production staff of Sams Publishing. What a pleasure! I want all readers to know that nobody cares more for getting the right books into the right hands than the people at Sams. It is an honor to work for Sams and to be a part of such a loyal staff.

I too often take for granted Mr. Richard Swadley, President (of Excellence), who single-handedly can take a book concept and turn that concept into a success. Thank you, Richard, for letting me write for you again and again.

As always, I'm thankful to Mr. Dean Miller for providing me with this writing opportunity. You are just one of the editors who are a friend to me first and an editor second. In addition, although I've only worked with Brian-Kent Proffitt on a couple of books, I learned quickly that Brian is the premiere Development Editor in the publishing business. Brian is able to transform my efforts into material that the reader needs.

Extending the best of the best, Kim Spilker somehow managed to make my writing meaningful, proving that even the unthinkable can occur. As I've already indicated, the editorial and production staff at Sams is the cream of the crop. In addition to putting a great Technical Editor on this book, Jim Grey, the rest of the staff made this book good and I want to thank Karen Walsh, Kim Hannel, and Julie McNamee for their efforts.

My lovely and gracious bride stands by my side night and day. Thank you once again, precious Jayne, as you are everything that matters to me on earth. The best parents in the world, Glen and Bettye Perry, continue to encourage and support me in every way. I am who I am because of both of them.

—*Greg Perry*

About the Author

Greg Perry is a speaker and a writer on both the programming and the application sides of computing. He is known for his skills at bringing advanced computer topics to the novice's level. Perry has been a programmer and a trainer since the early 1980s. He received his first degree in computer science and a master's degree in corporate finance. Perry is the author or co-author of more than 45 books, including *Teach Yourself Windows 95 in 24 Hours*, *Absolute Beginner's Guide to Programming*, *Absolute Beginner's Guide to C*, and *Moving from C to C++*. He also writes about rental-property management and loves to travel.

Tell Us What You Think!

As a reader, you are the most important critic and commentator of our books. We value your opinion and want to know what we're doing right, what we could do better, what areas you'd like to see us publish in, and any other words of wisdom you're willing to pass our way. You can help us make strong books that meet your needs and give you the computer guidance you require.

Do you have access to the World Wide Web? Then check out our site at http://www.mcp.com.

JUST A MINUTE

> If you have a technical question about this book, call the technical support line at 317-581-3833 or send e-mail to support@mcp.com.

As the team leader of the group that created this book, I welcome your comments. You can fax, e-mail, or write me directly to let me know what you did or didn't like about this book— as well as what we can do to make our books stronger. Here's the information:

Fax: 317-581-4663

E-mail: Lorna Gentry
          lgentry@mcp.com

Mail: Lorna Gentry
          Comments Department
          Sams Publishing
          201 W. 103rd Street
          Indianapolis, IN 46290

Introduction

If you scan the computer bookshelves today you'll find all sorts of low-level books that introduce you to PCs. Why is this book different? First of all, this 24-hour tutorial is just that; each chapter comprises a single hour of study so that you can sit down and easily cover a chapter in a single sitting. In addition, unlike the *PCs for People Who Can't Spell PC* books out there, this tutorial respects your intelligence and realizes that you want a no-compromise, straight-to-the-point, introduction to PCs without a lot of cartoons, jokes, and wisecracks taking up space.

At the same time, you want a book that talks at your level without talking down to you. You've got the right book. By the time you finish just the first few hours of lessons, you'll know more about PCs than many people who sell them! In addition, you'll understand the roles that PCs play in our world. You'll learn all about PCs and how to operate and upgrade them. The world of PCs is full of surprises, gimmicks, seeming miracles, and fun, and it even offers some tools that help you get work done.

Who Is This Book For?

The book was written specifically to these people:

- ☐ Those who have never used a PC or who have used one on a limited basis
- ☐ Those who use a PC but who want to understand how PCs work
- ☐ Those with older PCs who want to know what's in store for upgrading their computers
- ☐ Those who want a PC but don't know how to buy the right one
- ☐ Those PC and non-PC users who keep hearing about the Internet but who have never jumped on board the online bandwagon

Can This Book *Really* Teach PCs in 24 Hours?

Yes. You can master each chapter in an hour or less. (By the way, the chapters are referred to as "hours" in the rest of this book.) The material is balanced with mountains of tips, shortcuts, and traps to avoid that will guide you through the purchase, use, and upgrade of your PC and extend your knowledge from *user* to *pro* in 24 hours or less.

Conventions Used in This Book

Each hour ends with a question-and-answer session.

This book uses several common conventions to help teach the PC topics. Here is a summary of those typographical conventions:

☐ Commands, computer output, and words you type appear in a special monospaced computer font.

☐ If a task requires you to select from a menu, the book separates menu commands with a vertical bar. Therefore, this book uses File | Save As to select the Save As option from the File menu.

This book defines new terms when you first see them. A glossary at the end of the book reviews all the terms in case you forget something later on.

In addition to typographical conventions, the following special elements are included to set off different types of information to make them easily recognizable:

Just a Minute

> Special notes augment the material you read in each hour. These notes clarify concepts and procedures.

Time Saver

> You'll find numerous tips that offer shortcuts and solutions to common problems.

Caution

> The warnings warn you about pitfalls. Reading them will save you time and trouble.

Don't Hesitate!

Stop letting the PC industry pass by. In just 24 hours, you can master every major concept required by PC users. Turn the page to see how.

PART

I

PC Fundamentals

Hour

PART

1

Hour 1

Get Started Now!

Don't panic! You'll understand everything that's really important about PCs before the day is up. *PC* stands for *personal computer*. The computer industry just loves abbreviations and *acronyms* (letters that stand for words and sound like a word themselves). To a newcomer, the biggest computer challenge is understanding what all the acronyms mean. You've no doubt seen *RAM*, *CPU*, *SCSI*, and many others in the computer ads and on store shelves. Don't be swayed from your goal of learning about PCs because of terms. If you happen to forget a term, check the glossary in the back of this book any time.

Computers are simple. They are not simple only for the computer experts—the experts are the ones who often make things difficult! After you master the terms, you'll see that everything else falls into place. Your computer is a tool that you can use for beneficial work and fun.

The highlights of this hour include

- ☐ Why PCs are not smart without people
- ☐ When is the best time to learn PCs
- ☐ What programs do
- ☐ Which categories of PC programs can benefit you
- ☐ What you can expect after you purchase a PC

The Original Myth: Computers Are Smart

Computers are not smart; people are smart. Computers are electronic circuits that sit on desks until someone tells them what to do. If you have never used a PC, or if you use one only on a limited basis such as for order entry, you might have the idea (as many do) that you can type the following question into a computer and the answer displays immediately:

```
What year was George Washington born?
```

Although programs exist that can make a computer answer such questions, computers are not just repositories of data that spew out answers to the questions you type. Rather, computers work best when they can process and analyze data, as you'll learn throughout this book. Computers will repeat the same action on scores of data values without complaint. Computers don't get bored, but they don't get smart either.

Your car cannot drive without your turning the wheel and pushing the pedals. Your calculator cannot compute without your clicking the buttons. Your phone cannot call someone on its own. Your hammer cannot drive a nail without you. Your PC cannot do anything and *will not do anything* until you tell it to do something.

CAUTION

Perhaps the most important thing of which to be aware is that your PC has little discernment. If you tell the PC to do something incorrectly, the PC will try to do it. Your PC is your slave.

Different Computers for Different Tasks

PCs are small; they are sometimes called *microcomputers*. In offices, people often connect PCs to other PCs through a cabled *network* connection. Larger computers also exist, such as *minicomputers*, *mainframes*, and *supercomputers*. The most expensive supercomputer in the world acts much like your PC. Companies, universities, and governments buy larger computers because the larger computers often are faster and store more information than can PCs. Nevertheless, the weather bureau's most powerful supercomputer that costs millions of dollars is no smarter than the PC on your desk. When specifically told what to do, though, supercomputers and mainframes can do a job faster (and more expensively) than your PC.

1

Every few months, computer companies make their computers faster, smaller, and less expensive. Today's PCs are faster and hold more information than yesterday's mainframes. (Well, mainframes from 15 years ago, to be more accurate, but you get the picture.)

JUST A MINUTE

Two fundamental kinds of PCs exist today: The Macintosh (made by Apple) and the PC-compatible (named after IBM's first entry into the PC arena, the *IBM-PC*). Although both kinds of PCs do similar work, their hardware differs and so does the way you use them. The large majority of PCs in use today are the PC-compatible kind. This tutorial primarily discusses the PC-compatible PCs due to their overwhelming popularity in the marketplace. The Macintosh is a great machine, but 24 hours is not enough time to give both kinds of PCs the attention they require. A good beginner's guide to the Mac is *Teach Yourself the Macintosh in 24 Hours* (Sams, 1997).

Don't Be Afraid of PCs

Some people do not actually fear PCs so much as they are hesitant to begin using them this late in the game. After all, PCs in one form or another have existed since the 1970s. Surely, these people think, anyone learning about PCs this close to the millenium is so far behind the learning curve that it's too late to begin.

Don't you believe it! Here's the good news that some PC pros might not want you to know: PCs are easier than ever to learn, not harder. Instead of needing to attend math classes where they used to teach beginning computer users how to write a program to factor a polynomial equation, today's PC newcomers can sit down at the keyboard and make the PC do a lot of work with very little preliminary help.

JUST A MINUTE

You cannot physically harm the PC from the keyboard. You could erase an important file and reorganize the PC's setup, but you cannot damage the computer's components by typing the wrong thing. Don't be afraid to go to the keyboard and move and click the mouse. PCs give instant feedback if you do something they don't understand, so you'll quickly learn what works and doesn't work.

Instead of taking several years of college to learn how to use PCs effectively, you can now learn quickly (within 24 hours, actually) how to operate today's PCs. The *last thing* computer companies want to do is make their products difficult for newcomers! The easier a PC is to use, the more likely you and others will learn to operate PCs and buy PC products.

You don't have to be good at math to be good at computers. PCs streamline many tasks. Today's electronic age puts more and more PCs everywhere, including homes, cars, offices, watches, televisions, and just about anywhere that automated control over some device benefits people and simplifies lives. If you think you can't learn PCs because you cannot program a VCR, keep in mind that many VCRs are not equipped to include the helpful icons, descriptions, and hand-holding help that most PCs provide as you use them.

Bottom line: Now is the best time to learn about PCs.

PCs Don't Help with Everything

Even computer novices have some idea of a computer's power. Often, however, the mystery that surrounds PCs escapes a large majority of people who have never touched a PC. Throughout this 24-hour tutorial you will learn all about PCs and how to buy the right PC for your needs. You first need to understand with what a PC can help you, though, so you'll know which of your needs a computer can solve.

Although it's rare these days, some people buy a computer and then realize it's not at all helpful. Let's assume that you manually balance your checkbook at the end of each month, and you wonder if a PC can help you eliminate that chore completely or at least make the balancing easier. If you write only a handful of checks each month to pay utilities, the mortgage, and other common household expenses but you do not run a small business out of your home or own rental properties for which you also pay bills, a PC might *increase* the time it takes you to balance your checkbook! To balance your checkbook accurately, your PC will need to know every check's amount and date. Therefore, you'll either have to manually enter all the checks you've written at the end of the month or you'll have to print each check, as you need one, from the computer. The latter task requires that you purchase expensive computer printer checks.

PCs can be cumbersome; probably the *last thing* you want to do when your paper carrier knocks on your door to get paid is to turn on a computer, load check paper into the printer, start a checkbook program, enter the information, print the check, tear off the check, and turn off the computer! The trouble and expense of printing checks just wouldn't justify the savings of a few minutes at checkbook-reconciliation time.

1

JUST A MINUTE

This is a lot of talk about checkbook programs! You'll find, however, that one of the first benefits anyone lists for a PC is a checkbook program. "A PC can help you with your checkbook!" is a phrase often heard in PC stores. As with anything, the PC is a tool that benefits different people in different ways. You might never put your simple checkbook on a PC, yet that same PC might help you make millions of dollars in the stock market by analyzing good stock buys. (One can wish.)

Don't throw away this book just yet if you wanted to automate your checkbook! Just understand that different PC applications benefit certain situations more than others do. In fact, you won't finish this hour without seeing a screen from a popular financial checkbook program because such programs do benefit so many people.

So What *Can* PCs Do?

The previous section's checkbook story illustrates that a PC can be overkill. Nevertheless, millions of PCs would not be in all the homes and businesses today if they did not offer numerous benefits. A PC might very well help with your checkbook—and automate many other tasks in your life as well. Despite the hassle involved with printing checks, a computerized checkbook does come in handy when you write a large number of checks each month. Perhaps you are the treasurer for a Little League team, you own rental properties, you sell cosmetics out of your home, or you simply write more checks than "normal." One of the benefits of a PC checkbook program is that at the end of the year, you can click a button to obtain a printed list of tax categories showing the totals you accumulated over the year of check writing.

Before looking at a survey of PC benefits, you should understand what a PC is really doing. At its simplest level, a PC processes data. Look at Figure 1.1 to see the standard data-processing model. Your PC processes *data* (raw facts, figures, and commands) and produces *information* (meaningful output). Your company's weekly work hours might be the data, and the computer might process that data and turn the data into paychecks. The paychecks would be the informational output.

Figure 1.1.

PCs turn raw facts and figures into meaningful information.

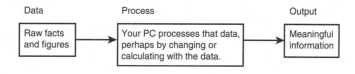

Data → Process → Output

Data	Process	Output
Raw facts and figures	Your PC processes that data, perhaps by changing or calculating with the data.	Meaningful information

The input data might come from your telephone if you have phone access to another computer elsewhere, perhaps via the Internet. You might type the input at your keyboard. Your input might only consist of controlling the program as you might do in a game. The input might come from a mouse attached to your PC.

The PC takes its input and does something with it using the program you have given the computer (see the next sidebar). The output might appear on your screen, on the printer as a report or as checks, or it might even be some kind of sound and video presentation. Today's PCs work with a variety of data sources and produce all kinds of output, including *multimedia output* composed of sound, color, and video.

Programs Do Work

Perhaps you're one of the many people who don't know exactly what's being talked about when someone mentions a computer program. Just as a printed program tells a theater audience the order of the show, a computer program tells your PC exactly what work to do and the order in which to do it.

A program is a set of instructions that adds some "smarts" to your dumb PC. Remember that your PC is nothing more than a set of electronic components that can do nothing on its own. After you load a program into the PC, however, the PC can follow that program's step-by-step instructions and do a requested job. A checkbook program tells your PC how to manage a checkbook. An encyclopedia program tells your computer how to retrieve information that you request from a data source such as a CD file.

Often you will not be able to see the instructions within a program. When you purchase a color graphics program, for example, the program's internal instructions let you draw colorful pictures, but you will not be able to see the instructions that comprise the program. Programs are *compiled* into a encrypted, compact form to save space and to help eliminate accidental changes.

TIME SAVER

By the way, the PC industry uses the terms *programs* and *software* interchangeably.

1

A Survey of PC Uses

Surely you've heard of the famous (and infamous) *Windows*. Windows is the name applied to today's most popular PC *operating system*. The operating system is the traffic cop that controls the many tasks going on inside your PC. Windows almost always comes preinstalled on new PCs. When you turn on your PC, Windows will automatically start. As you can see in Figure 1.2, the name *Windows* is appropriate because the computer's screen contains several windows in which you can do many different tasks.

Internet Explorer window   My Computer window

Figure 1.2.
Your PC does different things in different windows; having too many windows gets confusing.

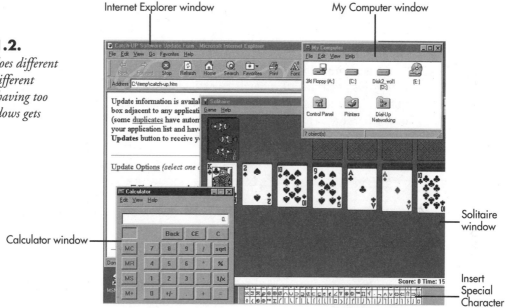

Calculator window

Solitaire window

Insert Special Character window

When you first begin to learn about PCs, the multiple windows can be confusing. Even PC gurus often work within a single window at a time, expanding that window to the size of the entire screen to see the work better. For now, just understand that Windows is a controlling environment that lets you work within one or more windows. Windows does not do anything on its own, but exists to help you communicate with and control the other programs you run.

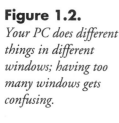

JUST A MINUTE

You'll see the term *run* or *execute* used with computer programs. When you start a program, such as a checkbook program or a graphics drawing program, you are *running* or *executing* the program. Therefore,

> if you ever see instructions that tell you to "run the program," you'll know
> that those instructions want you to start a certain program. How do you
> run a program? Some programs run automatically while you use a PC, but
> for others you must trigger the program execution yourself. You'll learn all
> about programs and how to manage them throughout this 24-hour tutorial.

Lots of Windows versions exist—Windows 3.1, Windows for Workgroups 3.11, Windows 95, Windows NT, among others. For now, don't worry about the differences because they all provide your PC with an operating environment that lets you run the programs you need to run.

Although understanding Windows is vital to mastering your PC, Windows is not an answer to anyone's computing needs because Windows is a *system program* and people are interested in *application programs*. If you only had Windows, your PC would look nice and you could spend a lot of time learning how your PC works, but that's it. You need the applications to do specific work. The applications help you create graphics, analyze sales, interact on the Internet, manage a business, and play games.

Lots of Program Categories Exist

When you walk into a computer store, you won't see two sections labeled "System Programs" and "Application Programs." Although all programs do fit within these two broad categories, the stores attempt to make shopping easier with more descriptive sections.

Utilities, sometimes shelved as *System Tools*, are system programs that help you manage a particular setup in your PC such as the fine-tuning of storage, managing the information inside your PC, making backups, extending your system's capabilities, and checking for errors. *Programming Languages* are software tools that you use to create new programs from scratch (programming is fun but requires much training). The *Games* category is self-explanatory (and is a serious impediment for computer book authors who need to get their real work done). In addition, you'll find all kinds of other categories such as *Children's Software*, *Research Tools*, and *Educational Programs*.

A survey of the PC's common uses requires that you look at various programs on the market because, as you learned in the sidebar titled "Programs Do Work," the programs make your PC perform specific work such as playing a game. The following sections give you glimpses into the kinds of things programs can do.

1

Part III, "Software Drives the PC," explores programs in more depth.

JUST A MINUTE

Word Processing

Certainly one of the most common uses of PCs is *word processing*. You might have seen electronic typewriters in stores or offices that have small display screens and are called *word processors*, but those machines are little more than simple computers that have only one program in them. If you load any of today's PCs with a word processing program, that PC will not only become a word processor rivaling those dedicated machines, but you'll still have a computer that can do other tasks as well.

Figure 1.3 shows a typical word processing screen. Notice the graphics embedded with the text. The word processor will help you enter, edit, and print documents of any kind. You can write letters, book manuscripts, newsletters, notes, faxes, reports, invoices, announcements, and more.

Figure 1.3.

A word processor can help with virtually any writing or publishing needs you have.

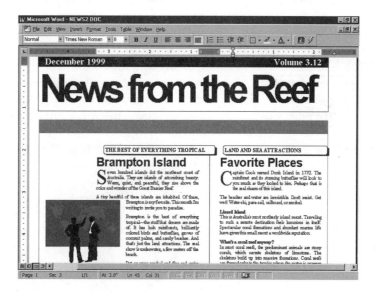

Word processors do not make you a better writer, but they do help you write with less effort.

CAUTION

As Hour 8's lesson ("Creating with Your PC") explains, the word processor's strongest power is in its capability to correct mistakes. Not only can you easily make corrections to anything you write, but the word processor can help you format the text to look nice; arrange graphics, lines, borders, footnotes, headings, and titles; and even check your spelling and grammar.

JUST A MINUTE

Another software category called *desktop publishing* exists that was originally designed to help you create published fliers, newsletters, and other documents that require a tight integration of text and graphics. You'll learn more about desktop publishing programs in Hour 8's lesson, but as you can see in Figure 1.3, today's word processors have the power to produce most desktop-published documents without requiring that you purchase and learn a separate program.

Games

A few years ago, games would not have deserved second place in a list of software uses. Despite the fact that many children now grow up more comfortable with PCs than their parents are because of the games the kids play, games now comprise a tremendous amount of the software sales in the world, and those sales are to all age groups. The reason is that the PC's powerful multimedia hardware makes it a fantastic platform for games nobody could have dreamed of a few years ago. As you can see in Figure 1.4, the graphics and animation take the player into a seemingly real confrontation in which he can play against a computerized opponent. In other words… PC games are fun! (They're not just for children anymore.)

Figure 1.4.

PC games put you in the middle of a multimedia world.

Despite that lead-in, many readers of this book will never want to play a PC game and might never do so. Nevertheless, for anyone to get a true grasp on PCs today, he must understand the important role that games play in the sales of PCs and software. Walk into any computer store these days and you won't see the latest word processor on the shelves closest to the doors; instead, you'll see the latest line of games.

Financial Programs

Financial programs aren't just for accountants anymore. Although you already know that a financial program won't necessarily solve all your financial organization skills or make everyone's checkbook management easier, many people who use their PC on a daily basis like to put their finances on the PC. Many programs, such as *Quicken* (shown in Figure 1.5), not only help manage a checkbook but also help organize records, track mortgages and investments, and help with year-end tax recording.

Figure 1.5.

Quicken is a personal financial-management program.

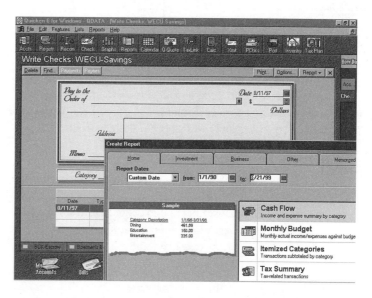

In addition to dedicated financial programs, a special class of programs exists called *electronic worksheets* (sometimes called *spreadsheets*) that work somewhat like a word processor for numbers. You can arrange all kinds of numeric data along with textual descriptions and easily embed calculations to produce summary sheets, accounting reports, expense-tracking lists, Little League statistic-analysis papers, schedule resources, and just about anything else that involves numeric information.

Figure 1.6 shows an example of *Excel*, one of the most popular electronic worksheet programs today. Unlike dedicated financial programs such as Quicken, electronic worksheets let you design your own forms and numerical analysis to fit exactly the way you do business. Hour 8's lesson describes worksheets in more detail.

Figure 1.6.

Organize your financial information in the format you need with an electronic worksheet program.

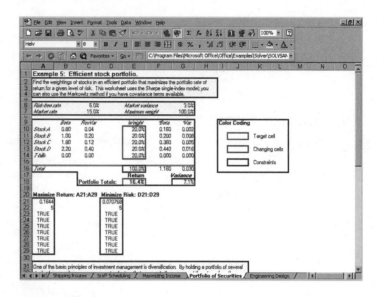

Other financial programs exist that help serious investors track their investment portfolios. If you're connected to an outside service via the phone lines, you'll be able to get up-to-the-minute stock and mutual fund pricing sent directly to your PC. You can then analyze that data in your electronic worksheet as done in Figure 1.6.

Online Services

This book talks a lot about the Internet and online services that give you access to the Internet, such as America Online, CompuServe, and others. Just a few years ago, such coverage would not be justified because not enough people had access to online services. Today you can book plane and hotel reservations, shop for automobiles, read the news, play games, update your software, and contact people in remote parts of the world by running a program that connects your PC to the phone lines.

Figure 1.7 shows an online travel service called *Expedia* that offers photos of travel destinations, lets you track planes in flight, books cruises, and checks weather and foreign exchange rates over an Internet connection. Hour 2's lesson, "Hardware's Easy, Not Hard," describes the equipment you need to go online, and Part VI in this 24-hour tutorial, "Connecting to the World," teaches you how to get started exploring online universes.

The Rest

Trying to describe every software category is a little like trying to describe every book in the bookstores. Many more kinds of programs exist; the chapters in Part III of this 24-hour tutorial explain how you can take advantage of many of the popular programs in use today.

Figure 1.7.

Online services offer just about anything you'd ever want.

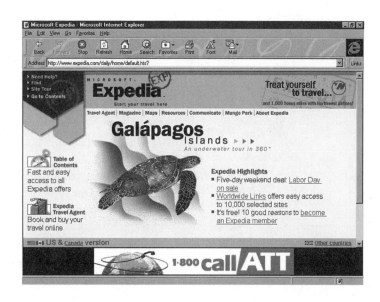

Although so many more software categories exist that a quick overview cannot do them justice, take a few moments to peruse Table 1.1 to learn other ways a PC can help you, your family, and your business.

Table 1.1. Several program categories exist that you can explore.

Category	Description
Database	Organizes large amounts of data into manageable sets of information such as inventories, catalogs, and personnel and customer records.
Educational	Teaches children and adults all kinds of multimedia-based subjects such as math, science, reading, and even foreign languages.
Graphics	Lets you design colorful graphic pages for publication on paper or to the Internet. With the combination of photo- and video-capturing PC equipment, you can embed and embellish art from outside sources in your creations.
Integrated	Combines two or more programs into a single, massive application you can use to share data between, for example, a spreadsheet and a word-processed document.

continues

Table 1.1. continued

Category	Description
	With Windows, however, such data sharing between non-related, non-integrated programs is often still possible even if the programs are not integrated with each other.
PIMs	*Personal Information Managers*, such as *Outlook* (shown in Figure 1.8), let you track your contact names and information, schedule, personal phone books, and calendar; manage to-do lists; and organize messages—all from within a single location.
Reference	Contains sets of easy-to-access repositories of data such as dictionaries, encyclopedias, phone books, bibles, political data, art museum exhibit tours, and historical documents that you can display.
Utility	Helps you manage your PC by providing backup services, fine-tuning memory (the PC's, not yours), and checking your system for errors.

Figure 1.8.

Organize your schedule, contacts, faxes, and other messages with a Personal Information Manager.

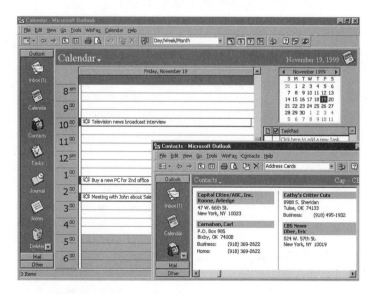

The Work Begins *After* the Purchase

Please know that when you purchase a PC your work has just begun; selecting and buying a PC is the *easiest* part of using a PC. Some small businesses make the mistake of thinking that if they just purchase the computer, everything else will fall into place and they'll be automated in no time.

In addition to the PC hardware itself, you must consider the following factors:

- ☐ Programs
- ☐ Data
- ☐ Procedures
- ☐ People

You will continually add programs over the life of your PC just as you add videos and audio CDs to your collection after you purchase an electronic entertainment center for your family room. As programs get more advanced, you'll be updating the programs you own to get the latest features.

You must determine the source for your PC's data if you use the computer for any kind of routine work. For example, if you want to computerize your business's inventory, you'll not only need the PC (the hardware) and the program (a database program), but you'll also need to get your current inventory information into the PC. If you've used an outside inventory service you'll want to find out how to transfer the data to your PC. If you've used a card-filing system, you'll need to get that data from the cards into the database program in an appropriate format.

Even if you don't plan to use the PC for your business, you'll need to determine how much home-based information you want to store. If you computerize your finances, do you want to include your checkbook only, or do you also want to computerize all your tax and investment information? If the latter, that data-entry takes planning and time and is rarely a trivial task.

The procedures surrounding your PC are critical whether you use your PC solely for the home or for business also. You'll need to protect your data adequately with backup procedures. If you use your PC in an office setting, you'll need procedures in place that describe the routine tasks you and others do with the PC so that someone else can take over if the primary operator is away.

You must be sure to adequately train the people who will use your PC so they know the proper backup methods and understand how to use the software. If your business is short-handed already, a PC will require *even more* people-hours, not fewer (at least at the beginning), because of the program installation, data-entry, procedure-writing, and training required at start-up. Putting a new computer system in place *always* takes more time than you first expect. To avoid the disappointment, expect problems and surprises. PCs are fun; you'll learn why in the remaining hourly lessons. If PCs were not worth the trouble, millions and millions would not be selling all over the world.

CAUTION

> Not only does setting up and organizing a new PC take time and effort, you'll sometimes spend *more* money, not less, during your PC's lifetime than you did on the PC itself. Expect that. If you were to total all the money you've invested in CDs and video rentals, you would probably see that you've spent far more money for those items over the years than you ever spent on the original hardware to watch and listen to that entertainment. The cost of programs, data, procedures, and people, especially for PCs in a business setting, also adds up over time, but the benefits of owning and using the PC also add up considerably.

Summary

This hour has introduced you to the world of PCs. Perhaps you are less intimidated and more interested than you previously were. Perhaps you want to get to the meat and quit messing with an overview! Either way, you've now seen a glimpse of how a PC can and cannot help you. The rest of this 24-hour tutorial fills in the details and explains all you need to know about PCs.

In today's electronic age, many people feel as if they're too far behind the curve to learn PCs now. If you are one of those people, please understand that PCs are getting easier to use every day, and you are starting at the best point to learn as much as possible about computers.

The next hour gets to the nitty-gritty. You'll learn those foreign computer terms, such as *CPU* and *RAM*. When you master the next hour's material, you will be able to walk into any computer store and describe almost every bit of hardware you see there.

Q&A

Q Do I need to be able to type to use PCs?

A In spite of the science-fiction movies that have shown people talking to computers for decades, voice-activated PCs are still over the horizon and don't work extremely well today. Although you can control a PC through several different kinds of devices, the keyboard is still the most direct route.

1

If you don't type well, you will certainly need to improve your typing skills to use a PC efficiently. Nevertheless, as a newcomer, you will not need to type quickly at first because everything will be so new that you'll be slow until you familiarize yourself with the PC's operation.

Any PC user would admit, however, that having better typing skills *does* lead to better and more efficient PC usage. Fortunately, you can find many multimedia-based interactive typing tutorial programs that will help you master the keyboard. Use your PC as a tool to improve your typing; don't look at the PC as a stumbling block to those who type slowly.

Q Should I fear these PC viruses I hear so much about?

A Yes and no! The truth is that a virus will *never* affect the vast majority of PC users. A PC virus is a program that not only damages your files but also replicates itself over all your computer's storage, making eradication difficult.

You can help insulate (and vaccinate!) your PC from possible virus attack, however, by adding a virus-protection program to your PC that monitors all programs, checking and correcting for virus problems. Generally, if you install programs written by reliable software companies, you install programs from online services only from trusted sources, and you put into place the electronic mail security options available in almost every program that let you send and receive messages to other users over the phone lines, you'll never be troubled by viruses.

Like terrorist attacks, virus problems are few and far between, but their risk justifies preventive maintenance. Fortunately, today's virus-protection programs work well to eradicate viruses from your computer.

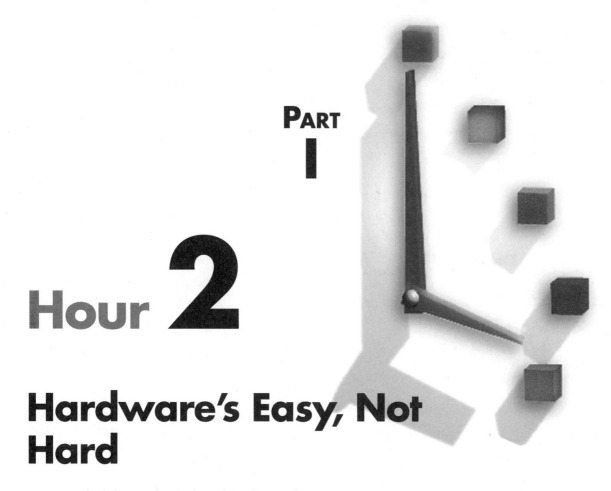

Hour 2

Hardware's Easy, Not Hard

You don't have to know the technical name for every component in your PC system, but you should take this hour to learn some of the more common hardware devices that comprise your PC. After you learn the basic terms, you'll better understand the ads you see for PCs and will be better informed when you make a PC purchase.

The word *hardware* refers to the physical parts of the PC. A computer is more than just hardware, but the hardware is the best starting point to learn how your PC operates. A computer is a *system*, and a system is a collection of interrelated parts that work together to do something. Therefore, your PC system is not just one box but a collection of several components that operate together to analyze finances, play games, connect to the Internet, and manage a business. This hour covers an overview of hardware; the rest of your 24-hour tutorial will fill in the details.

The highlights of this hour include

☐ What comprises a standard PC

☐ Why the system unit is so important

☐ How to measure memory

☐ Which types of memory should concern you

☐ What distinguishes between various monitors, printers, and storage devices

The Basics

Figure 2.1 shows you what a typical PC looks like. The word *typical* is suspect, however, as more and more companies are beginning to change the style of PCs that remained constant (including their drab color) for so long during the industry's startup years.

Figure 2.1.

Most PCs today contain these common pieces.

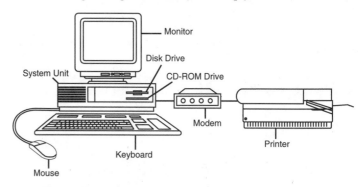

JUST A MINUTE

One of the reasons for the price differences among computers today is that the speed and storage capabilities vary among PCs. Almost every PC sold today, including the less expensive types, has the standard hardware you see in Figure 2.1. The speed and storage of the internal components cause the price differences you see. The faster and more storage a PC has, the higher the price will be.

Many components reside inside the PC's *system unit*, the box that holds the disk drives and into which you plug the keyboard. The majority of the PC's memory and storage devices reside inside the system unit. Of course, a laptop computer houses virtually *all* its components in the system unit, including the video display. It's difficult to distinguish a laptop from its system unit because the video screen raises up from the system unit; in a desktop PC, the system unit and monitor are usually separate devices.

The next few sections walk you through the hardware components that make up a typical PC. If you are brand-new to PCs, you will see many new computer terms as well as some you've no doubt read and heard over the years. Before this hour ends you will realize that PC hardware is simple to understand.

The System Unit

The *system unit* is the box where the brains are kept. The system unit houses the computer's memory, circuit boards, expansion slots, power supply, and the all-important *CPU* (which stands for *Central Processing Unit*). Technically, the CPU (sometimes called the *microprocessor*) is the actual computer, and everything else that makes up your PC helps the CPU get data and send output to other places. It's your PC's CPU that processes all the data that flows through your computer. The faster your CPU is and the more computing power your CPU has, the better (and more expensive) your PC is.

If you were to open the system unit and look inside, you'd see a lot of space. Not many components are inside a system unit because so many of a PC's system unit components are miniaturized. Perhaps you've heard of an *integrated circuit chip* (also called an *IC* for short). Figure 2.2 shows one such chip. Your PC's memory and CPU are integrated circuit chips. Many times a PC contains several rows (called *banks*) of these chips. When you add memory to your computer, you add additional memory ICs to the PC.

Figure 2.2.
An integrated circuit contains many thousands of parts.

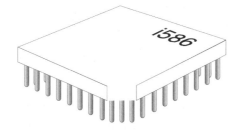

Thank You, NASA

Computers play a vital technical and safety role for rockets launched into orbit. In the early days of space travel, our computers on Earth were so large and heavy that rockets were unable to lift off the ground with on-board computers. Therefore, computers controlled the early rockets by radio from Earth to the ships' controls.

When ships began going farther out into space, however, a problem began to show itself. The computer-controlling radio waves took longer and longer to reach the ship. If a split-second correction were needed, the Earth-bound computers could not radio to the ship in time to make the correction.

> At that point, NASA saw the need for lighter and smaller computers. In the early 1970s, NASA developed the integrated circuit chip to make on-board computers viable. The ships then had their own computers, and the people back on Earth had a new creation that made PCs possible.

Types of CPUs

One of the most telling factors of a PC's speed is its CPU. The faster your PC's CPU can process data, the more quickly your PC can do its job. The PC's CPU also comes in various models. Each model has a name that distinguishes the models from each other. Perhaps you've heard the terms *386*, *486*, and *Pentium*, which are model names of the CPU inside your computer. These names are the originals given by Intel Corporation. (Intel Corp. designed the original PC's CPU, called the *8088*.) Following are the names of the CPU models as they progressed in capabilities and speed over time:

- [ ] 8088
- [ ] 8086
- [ ] 80286 (more commonly known as the *286*)
- [ ] 80386 (more commonly known as the *386*)
- [ ] 80486 (more commonly known as the *486*)
- [ ] Pentium (sometimes incorrectly called the *586*)
- [ ] Pentium Pro
- [ ] Pentium II

This list is not exhaustive. Different versions of each model have come and gone, such as the *486-DX* and the *386-SX*. Usually Intel will modify the name if the speed of the CPU increases, but the internal makeup of the chip does not change much. For example, the *486-DX* was a 486 chip that was twice as fast as the original 486. Intel did not change the internal design of the CPU enough to warrant a completely new model name, so it added the letters *DX* to distinguish it from its predecessor.

Recently Intel added multimedia capabilities directly onto the CPU and added the letters *MMX* to CPUs with that feature. Before the Pentium MMX arrived on the scene, PCs stored this advanced multimedia circuitry in hardware located in the system unit away from the CPU. By placing the multimedia components directly inside the CPU, Intel helps ensure compatibility among the various add-on multimedia hardware makers and improved multimedia performance.

Intel Corporation owns most of the PC's CPU market. Competition constantly nips at its heels, however. You'll see competing CPUs from companies such as Cyrix, AMD, and others when you go to look at PCs in stores and catalogs. The competitors do not always get to the market with a faster CPU, but they often sell for less money than computers with the Intel CPU inside. These competing CPU makers have gotten so good that you need not concern yourself too much with compatibility. No matter which company's CPU your PC has in it, all programs should work with your PC.

The CPU's Speed

As stated earlier, the speed of your CPU directly influences the speed of your entire computer system. If you have a PC with a CPU that's twice as fast as your neighbor's PC, and everything else is equal, your computer will calculate and perform much faster than your neighbor's. Although you will not always see a twice-as-fast performance due to external factors such as disk drive speed, you might sometimes see *more* than twice-as-fast performance depending on the task you are doing.

The CPU's speed is measured in *megahertz*, often abbreviated to *MHz*. This is one of those technical jargon words that indicates the number of instruction cycles your CPU can perform in a single second. *Meg* (or *mega*) always means million, so a 200MHz CPU can process 200 million instructions per second. These instructions are internal CPU codes that execute when you issue a command from the keyboard. The megahertz measurement gives the industry a fairly consistent yardstick to measure and compare CPU speeds.

Today's PCs run at hundreds of millions of instructions per second. Even a 200MHz CPU is considered virtually outdated now, but the very first IBM-PC that started the entire PC-compatible market contained a CPU that ran at a whopping 1.7MHz! The industry thought it had found nirvana when that 8088 CPU arrived on the scene. We've come a long way, baby.

JUST A MINUTE

Every couple years, the speed of CPUs doubles. Nobody knows how long that trend can maintain its pace. Eventually the physical speed of light will become a factor in limiting the speed because electricity cannot travel down a wire faster than the speed of light. For the time being, however, CPU manufacturers have a way to go before they come up against the speed-of-light wall.

CAUTION

Don't wait to buy your first PC until they get faster! You'll never get one because they'll *always* get faster. It's best to purchase the fastest PC you can afford today and learn about and use that PC immediately. Sure, it will be out of date in a year or two, but you'll get the benefit of using it during that time.

The Memory

Your PC system actually contains several types of memories. Some are ICs, whereas others are physical devices. Following are just a few kinds of PC memories:

☐ *ROM* (pronounced "rom" and stands for *Read-Only Memory*), which contains commands you cannot change

☐ *RAM* (pronounced "ram" and stands for *Random Access Memory*), which holds your running programs and their data as you use the PC

☐ Disks

☐ Online (via the phone) services

☐ CD-ROMs (similar to audio CDs)

In addition to these memories, new devices arrive on the scene all the time.

The first two kinds of memory listed, ROM and RAM, are integrated circuit chips (ICs) that are often smaller than your PC's CPU. The CPU is often the largest IC inside your system unit because of the number of internal circuits the manufacturer must pack into it. ROM is memory with burned-in information; you cannot change ROM. When you first turn on your PC, the ROM memory dictates what the computer does first. Usually your PC will perform a self-test of its basic hardware; the instructions for this self-test reside in ROM. You never need to add more ROM than your PC comes with.

JUST A MINUTE

> Often, computerized modules in non-computer equipment, such as automobiles and televisions, store all their instructions in ROM. ROM is less important in PCs than in those standalone devices that are made for one specific purpose. Your most important computer memories will be RAM and the memory-storage devices because those are the memories where you can store information.

Although ROM used to be more important in early microcomputers, today's PCs don't utilize ROM except for start-up testing. Rarely will computer manufacturers tell you how much ROM is inside your PC, and you'll never need to know. RAM, however, is a different story. One of the most important things to know about your PC, other than the model and speed of its CPU, is how much RAM it has.

As the role of your PC grows, the more complex your programs become and the more RAM your computer needs. When someone refers to your computer's "memory," that person is almost always referring to the amount of RAM you have. Although today's computers have a physical limit to the amount of RAM they can hold, that limit is so large that users rarely fill their PCs to capacity. As you'll learn in Hour 4's lesson ("What Do I Buy First?"), you'll almost always want to add RAM to the PC you purchase. Although you can never have too much memory, 16 *megabytes* (a megabyte is one million characters of storage) is generally the lower limit for today's PCs.

Have a Byte

A *byte* is a computer term for one character of storage. For example, the word *computer* requires eight bytes, or characters, of memory. Today's PCs contain so much memory that you'd get tired of writing the actual memory amount because of all the trailing zeros.

Computers use terms such as *kilobyte*, *megabyte*, and *gigabyte* for memory measurements. A kilobyte represents approximately 1,000 characters of memory. A megabyte (abbreviated as M or MB) represents approximately 1 million characters of memory. A gigabyte (abbreviated as G or GB) represents approximately 1 billion characters of memory. Instead of writing *640,000 bytes* of memory, you can write *640K* or *640KB*. Instead of writing *16,000,000 bytes* of memory you can write (and say) *16 megabytes* or, for short, *16 meg*.

By the way, you get more memory than you really ask for. Because of the way PCs store information, 1KB of memory is exactly 1,024 bytes, not an even thousand. As the memory size grows, those extra 24 bytes per thousand add up so that instead of 16MB being 16,000,000 bytes, the exact amount is 16,384,000 bytes. Isn't it nice to get *more* than you're promised for a change?

RAM memory is short-term PC memory. RAM holds your data and programs as well as system-controlling programs such as Windows. As you type text into a word processing program, both the program and the text you type reside in your PC's RAM. RAM memory is *volatile*, meaning that its contents stay only as long as the PC's power remains on. If you turn off the PC before you save the text from RAM to a disk drive or other long-term storage device, you'll lose everything you typed because the PC clears the RAM memory when you turn off the PC. The more memory you have, the more your PC can process at one time and the faster your PC works. Throughout the rest of this book, the generic term *memory* will always refer to this short-term, volatile RAM.

JUST A MINUTE

As you work at your PC, it constantly moves data to and from memory. As Figure 2.3 shows, you always have more external disk, CD-ROM, tape, and inline storage space than memory. Therefore, the more memory you have, the less time your PC must take to transfer data to and from those devices.

Figure 2.3.

Your PC transfers data to and from memory from disks and other storage devices.

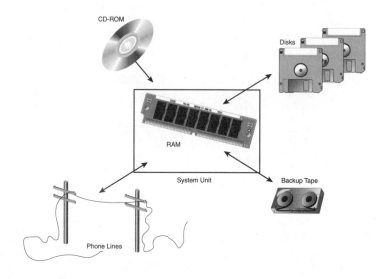

System Unit Expansion

Most PCs you buy today can be upgraded to hold additional hardware such as extra memory, storage devices, and advanced sound and graphics boards. Some of these components go inside the system unit, whereas others connect to the outside of the computer. These devices (other than RAM memory chips) are often called *peripheral devices* because they work on the periphery, or around, the CPU, both inside and outside the system unit.

JUST A MINUTE

> The PC industry never uses a short, common word when a long one will confuse more people.

Some peripheral devices go either on the inside or the outside of your system unit depending on the model you purchase. For example, if you want to connect your PC to another one via the phone lines, you need a *modem*. A modem tells your PC how to talk to other computers over a telephone. You can purchase an external modem or an internal modem. If you get an internal modem, you'll have to remove the cover from your PC and install the modem or have the store do it for you. You only need to plug external modems into the back of the system unit. (You'll learn more about modems in the later section, "Modems Connect to the Outside World.")

Your PC's system unit will contain *expansion slots* into which you can insert *expansion cards* that add functionality to your PC. These slots contain *ports* that stick out the back of the system unit into which you can plug cables that connect to devices such as printers.

2

Most PCs come with six to eight expansion slots, although some may already be in use depending on what your PC contained when you purchased the machine. You can add or upgrade an internal modem, replace the existing graphics board with a faster one, or add new devices that arrive on the market such as extra-large tape drives.

Figure 2.4 shows an expansion board that drops into a PC slot. Several kinds of expansion boards exist, as you'll learn in Hour 15, "Why and When to Upgrade." In Hour 15 you will also learn how to access your PC's system unit internals. You must be sure to match the right type of expansion board with the kind of expansion slots your PC supports. Although adding and replacing expansion boards require that you open your PC's system unit, doing so will *not* violate your PC's warranty in virtually all cases. The expansion slots are there for you, the user, to access.

Figure 2.4.

You will not violate your PC's warranty if you add or replace expansion boards.

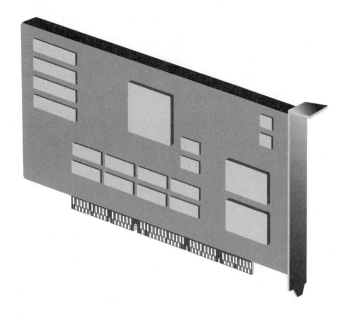

Caution

Always unplug the system unit from the power source before you plug or unplug a cable or open the case.

When you want to expand your PC's RAM memory, you will probably *not* drop an expansion board into the PC. More often, extra memory comes on small circuit boards that contain at least nine integrated circuit chips. As Hour 16, "Upgrading Your CPU and Memory," explains, you'll need to read your PC's owner's manual to learn the type of memory your PC needs for expansion.

TIME SAVER

Most of today's computer stores provide a service department that will upgrade your PC for you. Although you will save a little money if you upgrade your system yourself, you can be sure that the store will upgrade with the correct components and will repair anything that might go wrong with the upgrade.

If you want to connect your PC to a *network* (a network is, at its foundation, little more than two or more computers connected by wires) for data and program sharing, each PC on the network will need a network card in one of your expansion slots. Hour 5, "Setting Up Your New PC," explores more about networking hardware.

Many exciting expansion boards are now available for your PC that combine the PC's regular operations with the outside world. For example, you can install a PC/TV board and receive cable, satellite, and airwave television transmissions right on your PC screen. As Figure 2.5 shows, you can watch the broadcast in a small window or, when something really exciting comes over the TV, you can expand the TV window so that it consumes the entire monitor. (You can quickly hide the window when your boss comes in the door!)

Figure 2.5.

With a PC/TV expansion board, you can watch television while you write a report!

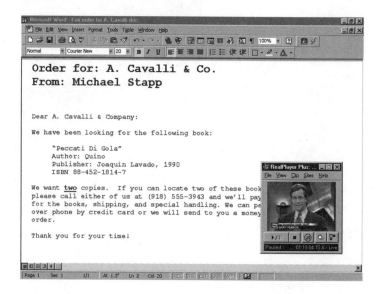

You'll use FM radio cards if you want to listen to FM radio while you compute. The PC has all the entertainment bases covered: television, CD audio, and radio. When you install one of these entertainment boards (Hour 17, "Upgrading Your Disk and CD-ROM Storage," explains how to install expansion boards into your PC's expansion slots), you'll control the hardware with programs that let you change channels and control the volume.

2

Disks and Other Storage Devices

Disk drives (sometimes called *disks* for short) hold the long-term memory storage for your programs and data. Disks come in all sizes. Most of the time, a PC's disk drives reside inside the system unit. Lights appear outside the disks when the PC reads from or writes data on the disk that's in the drive.

Most disks fall into one of the following categories:

☐ Removable disks (sometimes called *floppies* because they used to be bendable) or high-capacity removable disks such as Zip disks

☐ Hard disks (also called *fixed disks*)

Although removable disks generally hold less data than hard disks, you can keep as many removable disks as you need, which gives you virtually unlimited storage. The drawback is that the computer can access only a single disk in the drive at a time. A hard disk often holds far more data than a removable disk.

TIME SAVER

Some of today's hard disks are huge, and many PC newcomers think they won't need as much hard disk space as even the most basic PC contains. Disk space fills up fast! Do not skimp on hard disk or memory size. If you need to save money, buy a smaller monitor but get as much hard disk space and memory as you can afford. No matter how much hard disk space you buy, always purchase at least one removable disk drive so that you can share data and programs with others and install new programs that you buy.

The most common removable-disk drive is a 3-1/2" disk drive. Surely you've seen disks lying around offices. Figure 2.6 shows a 3-1/2" disk drive and a disk that you insert into the drive. Most disk drives contain a button that pops out as soon as you insert a disk. To remove a disk, push the button and the disk will eject. The 3-1/2" disk drive has been around for many years. Generally, a 3-1/2" disk holds 1.44 megabytes of data (although some 3-1/2" drives still exist that write to less efficient disks that hold only 760KB of data).

New kinds of removable disks are beginning to appear, although none have become as standard as 3-1/2" diskettes. The advantage to these newer removable disks is that they hold much more than the typical 3-1/2" disks. You'll see removable drives that hold from 100 megabytes to over a gigabyte with trade names such as *Jaz* and *Zip*. Many PC users use these extra-large removable disk drives for backing up their non-removable disks in case something happens.

Figure 2.6.

You can transfer
information to other PCs
with a removable disk.

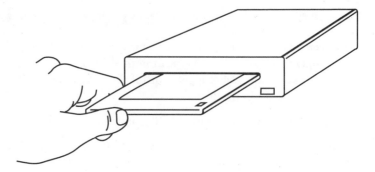

Hard disks hold much more information (the disk capacities can reach several gigabytes of storage) and are usually much faster than removable drives. All PCs sold today have at least one hard disk, and if you have a chance to add a second hard disk when you purchase a PC, do so. Most of the day-to-day work you perform on a regular basis will utilize your hard disk due to its speed and storage capacity. You'll primarily use your removable disks for backing up your system and for transferring data and programs to and from your PC.

CAUTION

One of the problems with hard disks being so much larger than removable drives is that *backing up* (making a copy of your data) is tedious because it often takes many removable disks to hold your entire hard disk. Hour 14, "Protecting Your PC," explores some of the ways you can protect your data.

CD-ROM drives have become extremely popular within the past few years because of these two facts:

☐ CD-ROMs hold more than 600 megabytes of storage, which is much more than the largest disk drives in existence at the time the first CD-ROMs were distributed. Their large size let PC users experience multimedia long before disk storage supported such massive amounts of data.

☐ CD-ROM drives are capable of playing regular audio CDs.

You can both write and read data to and from a disk drive, whereas you can only read from CD-ROM drives. (You'll recall that *ROM* stands for *Read-Only Memory*). As with disk drives, PC-based CD storage is changing rapidly. New CD drives exist that let you write to blank CD-ROMs so you can create your own CD-ROMs (these are called *WORM drives* for *Write-Once-Read-Many*), and the computer industry is also perfecting CD drives on which you can write and read to CD media just as you can with hard drives.

2

Although CD-ROMs are slow, their rather large storage capacity and ease of use continue to make them popular despite the competing and more advanced storage products arriving on the markets these days. When you insert a CD-ROM into your PC, the program on the CD-ROM automatically installs itself in most cases, or begins executing if you've already set up your PC to work with the CD-ROM. If you put an audio CD into that same PC CD-ROM drive, the music begins automatically (and you can use onscreen controls to control the volume, track, and other CD information), as Figure 2.7 shows. In addition, some CD-ROM makers produce a CD-ROM changer that works like a jukebox, making one of several CD-ROMs available without requiring that you insert a CD-ROM every time you need to access a different one.

Figure 2.7.

You can play and control audio CDs in your PC's CD-ROM drive.

JUST A MINUTE

DVD (*Digital Video Disks*) drives are becoming popular in both the computer and the entertainment industries. DVDs are removable drives into which you can insert DVD media that hold enough storage (several gigabytes) to view full-length movies as well as hold a lot more data than regular CD-ROMs.

Monitors

The majority of the time you sit in front of your PC, you work in front of the PC monitor. The monitor is sometimes called a *video screen* or *CRT* (for *cathode-ray tube*, the name of the big glass tube that displays the output). Although some monitors, such as *touch-screen monitors*, both display information and accept instructions from the PC user, most monitors only output information. (Touch-screen monitors often appear in mall and airport kiosks where a keyboard is overkill for the information required.)

When companies first produced PCs, you had the following choice of monitors: green letters on a black background, yellow letters on a black background, or white letters on a black background. No graphics were available. These were called *monochrome monitors* because of the single color they displayed. The first color monitors excited the PC market, but they were expensive and displayed limited colors and graphics.

JUST A MINUTE

To produce video output, your PC requires both a video card inside the
system unit and a monitor plugged into that card.

Today we are fortunate because most PC monitors sold are high-quality, color graphic
monitors capable of displaying broadcast-quality output. Just a few years ago, PC buyers had
to decide between various color graphics options named with all sorts of acronyms such as
CGA, EGA, VGA, and SVGA. Almost every PC sold today contains *SVGA* graphics, which
stands for *Super Video Graphics Array*, a fancy name for "great graphics."

Burn-In is Out

Monochrome monitors and early color monitors had a problem that you'll often
still see on automated teller machines. The characters, if left on too long, burned
into the monitor and stayed on the screen even if the screen went blank. These
shadow characters appeared slowly over time and eventually made the monitor
harder to read.

To guard against this character burn-in, *programmers* (people who write programs)
wrote *screen-saver programs* that displayed moving text and graphics during the PC's
period of non-use. No character would remain on the screen long enough to burn
in that character at that place on the screen.

Modern monitors don't have the burn-in problem, yet more screen-saver programs
are sold today than ever before! Go to your local computer store and you'll see an
entire wall of screen-saver programs! Programmers got so creative with their screen-
saver programs that we often want them even though our PCs no longer require
them.

Input Only: Keyboards and Mice

You'll give your PC instructions most of the time through the keyboard or mouse. Both the
keyboard and mouse are *input devices* because your PC receives your input from these devices.
The keyboard is great for entering text and controlling several kinds of tasks, whereas the
mouse is good for pointing to and moving objects on the screen. Figure 2.8 shows a typical
PC keyboard.

PC keyboards contain the following sections:

    ☐ **Alphanumeric keys**: Letters, numbers, and special characters

2

☐ **Function keys**: Labeled F1 through F12 (sometimes only to F10), they add functionality to many programs

☐ **Numeric keypad**: A 10-key keypad on the side of the keyboard with numbers arranged in a calculator fashion, along with some extra controls and math operators such as plus and minus signs

☐ **Ctrl, Alt**: Keys you combine with other keystrokes, as you'd do with the Shift key, to perform certain tasks (otherwise there would not be enough keys to do everything one needs to do on the PC)

☐ **Arrow keys, PageUp, PageDown**: Move items around your screen, often duplicating mouse functions

☐ **Esc**: A key you can often use to back out of certain tasks you've begun

Figure 2.8.

A PC's keyboard contains common text keys as well as controlling keys.

Today's PCs work in *graphical environments*, which simply means that you'll often see text as well as graphics on the screen while you work. A keyboard was not quite enough to control the graphical elements, so computer designers introduced the mouse, shown in Figure 2.9. Some mice have two or three buttons that you can click to select certain items on the screen. Generally, you'll never use more than two buttons.

Figure 2.9.

The mouse controls on screen operations.

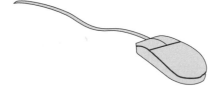

TIME SAVER

Shop around for mice and try them before you choose one. Some will work better in your hands than others. One thing of which you can be almost sure is that the mouse that comes with your PC will not be extremely high quality. Try a *trackball*, which works like an upside-down mouse, if you have limited desk space because the base remains in one place and you roll the trackball with your hand. You might find that you prefer the trackball to a mouse. Hour 19, "Upgrading Your Peripherals," describes more kinds of mice you can try.

Oh, one more thing. Neither the Pause key nor the SysReq (for *system request*) works these days. Nothing, nada, big zero. The Pause key actually *used* to pause scrolling output and games, but Pause does nothing inside today's Windows environments. When the PC world first saw the SysRq key on the *IBM-AT* (the first 286 PC), IBM promised everyone that the key would play a vital role in the future. That future has still not arrived.

Printers

Through the life of PCs, printers have fallen in price and gained features. Your printer options are numerous, but most printers sold today fall into one of these two categories:

- ☐ *Inkjet printers*, which produce printed output by shooting ink onto the paper
- ☐ *Laser printers*, which produce printed output by burning toner (as a copier does) into the paper

Of the two, inkjet printers are much less expensive to purchase, but you do need to buy ink cartridges quite often, and the cost of those can add up. A laser printer is often faster than an inkjet and generally less trouble to use and maintain. Laser printers do require expensive *toner cartridges*, small storage bins full of the laser toner that produces the output, but toner cartridges are much larger than inkjet cartridges so you have to change them much less frequently.

Both kinds of printers produce high-quality output. Both inkjet and laser printers are available that print in color, but color lasers are still rather expensive. You can get an inexpensive color inkjet printer for as low as a couple hundred dollars as opposed to three thousand and up for high-quality color laser printers.

You'll learn in Hour 4 how to decide which printer is right for you. If you have children, a color printer will come in quite handy for birthday invitations, report covers, and all sorts of projects. Some of today's color inkjet printers even create T-shirt iron-ons.

JUST A MINUTE

Perhaps you've heard of the *dot-matrix printers* that were so popular a few years ago. Dot-matrix printers produce printed output by striking a series of dots against a ribbon onto the paper. Inkjet and laser printers produce such better quality than dot-matrix printers that very few dot-matrix printers are sold today.

Faxing from Your PC

Don't worry about connecting a fax machine to your PC. All PCs sold today come with faxing capabilities as long as you plan to hook your PC to the phone lines (as described in the next section, "Modems Connect to the Outside World"). You can type a document into your PC and, instead of printing to a printer, you can send that text as a fax right from your keyboard to any fax machine or fax-receiving computer in the world.

Some printers come with a built-in fax machine; if you think your office warrants such a purchase, you can get one. Be warned, however, that combination printer/ faxes are expensive. It is generally better to purchase a *scanner* (a scanner reads printer material into your computer) to scan into the PC any paper-based information that you want faxed and then send the fax via the modem. Unlike a dedicated fax machine, you can use the scanner for tasks that don't involve faxing such as saving an art image in a file.

Modems Connect to the Outside World

This 24-hour tutorial's final part, "Connecting to the World," teaches you scores of ways you can benefit from hooking your PC to your telephone lines. Not only can your PC send and receive faxes, but you can also connect to online services such as CompuServe and America Online for late-breaking news, weather, sports, and entertainment. You can also access the Internet, send and receive e-mail, and even play online computer games with someone in another part of the globe.

JUST A MINUTE

> Most online services, such as America Online, require that you subscribe to a provider of that service for a monthly fee, as described in Part VI.

You need only a modem and a phone line (and a modem cable if you use an external modem) to wire your PC to the world. Most of the PCs sold today come with a modem included, and that modem is usually internal. An internal modem means you'll need less desk space for your PC, and you won't need an outlet to plug the modem into because internal modems get their power from your system unit. An external modem is often more expensive than an internal modem (to pay for the case and power supply), but external modems have signal lights that help you troubleshoot problems that you might have connecting to some remote systems. In addition, some systems contain so many expansion boards that no room is left to install an internal modem. Given that external modems are easier to install than most internal modems, you should consider purchasing an external modem if you're adding to or upgrading a PC you already own. If an internal modem comes with a PC you purchase, you'll be happy with it.

Where the Word *Modem* Came From

Modem is actually a combined version of two words: *modulate-demodulate*. Your computer needs a modem to communicate directly over most phone lines because the PC uses a signal called a *digital* signal, whereas your phone uses a special electronic signal called an *analog signal*. A modem demodulates the PC's digital signal into an analog signal so your data can travel over the phone lines. The receiving PC's modem then demodulates that analog signal back into a digital signal so the remote PC can understand what you sent.

You'll use your modem to connect to other computers, for Internet access, and for fax sending and receiving. Although you might have heard horror stories about computers being infected with a bad program from the modem, you have full control over your modem and can easily control whether someone communicates with your PC. Hour 14 explains more about the security ramifications of owning a PC.

Don't Forget Laptops!

Figure 2.10 shows a laptop computer. A *laptop* often contains all the components that a desktop system contains. Today's laptops have monitors, memory, disks, often a CD-ROM drive, multimedia sound, and places for printers, external keyboards, and monitors. Although laptops are generally more expensive than desktop counterparts with the same features (the miniaturization is costly), a laptop can often do exactly what a desktop can do, except in a smaller area and at a remote location.

This 24-hour tutorial does not devote a lot of material to laptops simply because you'll purchase and operate a laptop using the same parameters as you use for desktop systems. In other words, when you purchase a laptop and it's time to determine how much RAM you want to purchase, you'll be making the same kind of purchase decision that you would make with a desktop system.

Figure 2.10.

Laptops aren't limited by their size.

One of the only hardware characteristics that distinguishes laptop hardware from desktop PC hardware is that laptops often employ a *PC card slot* into which you can plug a *PC card*. A PC card is a credit card–sized expansion board that you can take in and out of the side of your laptop. PC cards come with memory, extra disk space, modems, and network connections. PC cards are simpler to install and remove than a desktop's expansion board because you don't have to remove the system unit case to insert or remove a PC card. Your laptop, however, will not have as many PC card slots as your desktop PC has expansion slots.

PC cards used to be called *PCMCIA cards*. Aren't you glad they shortened *that* name!

JUST A MINUTE

Summary

This hour introduces you to the PC's hardware. Although you still might have many questions if you're new to computers, the mystery that surrounds PCs should be beginning to fade. If you are reading this text for a refresher course, you no doubt read about some new technology that you might want to add to your system, such as a PC/TV expansion board.

As you read through the rest of this tutorial's lessons, you'll learn more details about the hardware introduced in this hour. You will learn how to purchase and install the hardware so you can keep your PC up-to-date with today's and tomorrow's technology. The nice thing about PCs is that you can add to them as new devices come out.

The next hour takes an introductory look at *software*, the programs that make the hardware do work.

Q&A

Q I have a PC that's about 10 years old. What can I use it for?

A Sadly, not much. Despite the fact that PCs are so easily upgradable, a PC older than four or five years will have such outdated hardware (often called *legacy hardware*) that today's components will not work well with it.

You might be able to benefit from a tax write-off if you donate the PC to a school (and if you have not already depreciated the PC). Many of the private schools that don't get government funding have few or no PCs, so old computers are better than none at all for those students.

Q Now that I know more of the terms, what's the best place to buy a PC?

A Have patience! Hour 4 describes all the decisions you'll face as a PC purchaser.

Q This hour taught me a lot of terms. How can I possibly learn everything I need to know in the next 22 hours?

A Although you won't learn *everything* you need to know in the next 22 hours, rest assured that this hour was extremely top-heavy on new terms. Most of the PC terminology deals with the various hardware devices, and you covered much of that ground here.

Subsequent hours will not have to introduce so many terms. Now that you are familiar with the hardware names, you will better understand the store ads and will feel more comfortable in front of a PC. One of this hour's objectives is to give you confidence that you can master the PC. As with most subjects, after you learn the terms, the skills come much easier because you are comfortable with the tools you use.

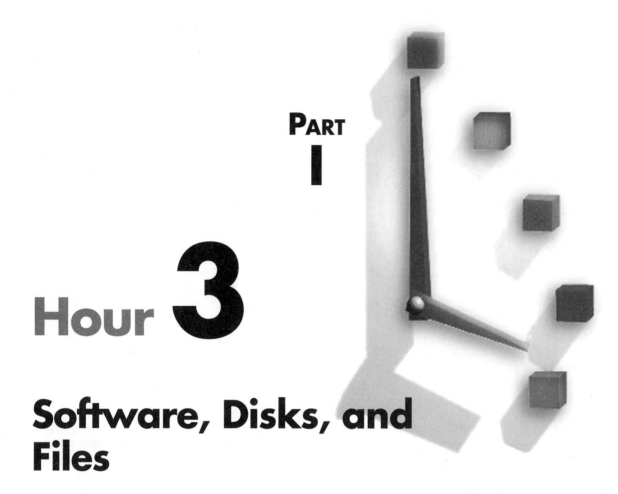

Hour 3

Software, Disks, and Files

The word *software* refers to the non-physical elements of computing. Software consists of programs, data files, and controlling system programs. In addition, PC users often loosely use the term *software* to refer to disks, although all disks are really hardware. The programs and data stored on the disks make up the actual software.

This hour's lesson explains how programs and data reside on the PC hardware. You'll learn how software interacts with the hardware to do the computing job at hand. In a way, disk storage often seems to cross the border between hardware and software, and you cannot fully understand software until you learn how disks hold their data.

The highlights of this hour include

☐ What comprises software

☐ Why so many versions of Windows exist

☐ Which commands PC users use for working with programs and files

☐ How to locate a file on a huge disk

☐ How folders and subfolders help you organize your disk storage

What Exactly Is Software?

To review, software includes your PC's operating system, programs, and data. In the three lessons that follow this one, you'll learn tips to help you purchase the right PC and set it up correctly. In addition, you'll see many traps to avoid in the process. Part of purchasing and setting up your new PC requires an understanding of software. Although you won't fully understand software until you begin using your PC regularly, a brief introduction here and in the lessons that follow will help ensure that you make the right purchase and setup decisions.

The Operating System

If you already have a PC, you might already have one of the following operating systems installed:

☐ Windows 3.1

☐ Windows for Workgroups 3.11

☐ Windows 95

☐ Windows NT

Windows 3.1 was the first release of Windows that truly made Windows a de facto standard among operating systems. Technically, Windows 3.1 and Windows for Workgroups 3.11 are not operating systems; they are *operating environments*—along with these Windows versions you must also have an operating system installed such as MS-DOS, the text-based forerunner of *GUIs* (*graphical user interfaces* such as Windows).

JUST A MINUTE

> Many refer to both Windows 3.1 and Windows for Workgroups 3.11 generically as *Windows 3.x.*

The primary difference between Windows 3.1 and Windows for Workgroups 3.11 is that Windows for Workgroups 3.11 provides more support for networking in small office environments. Windows 3.x was such an improvement over other operating environments that most companies began producing programs exclusively for Windows. These companies began using Windows exclusively, forsaking MS-DOS and other graphical operating environments that came into use about this time (such as IBM's *OS/2*). Windows makes it possible to manage today's PCs graphically instead of from the tedious text-based perspective users had before.

Windows 95 was the next major release for the mass PC market, and many people have now replaced Windows 3.x with Windows 95 because of 95's improved operations and error avoidance. This book uses Windows 95 for all figures and descriptions because the majority of people who read this book will use Windows 95 for their operating system. When you turn on your PC, the ROM self-tests the PC and, if everything checks out okay, automatically loads Windows 95 into your PC's memory. Windows 95 then takes over and remains in memory until you turn off the PC. As Figure 3.1 shows, the operating system sits at the bottom of memory (RAM memory) at all times, but programs that you load, as well as data, come and go as you use the PC throughout the day.

Figure 3.1.

Windows always resides in memory and controls the programs and data you load as you work on the PC.

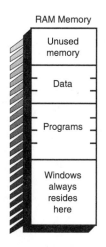

RAM Memory

Unused memory

Data

Programs

Windows always resides here

3

Multitasking in Windows

Figure 3.1 shows that more than one program may be running at the same time. If this is the case, some or all of those running programs will be in memory together. Depending on your memory size, Windows might have to keep only the active part of a program in memory. The more memory you have, the less Windows has to swap parts of programs to and from the disk drive. Each running program has its own data area.

The capability to run multiple programs at the same time is called *multitasking*. The reason the windowed concept works so well is that you can see the results, the *output*, of each running program in its own window on your screen. In addition, you can move, resize, and close those windows (and, therefore, stop running the program) easily by navigating and adjusting the windows with your mouse and keyboard.

Windows NT is becoming extremely popular in companies that rely on heavy PC networking and on the PCs that serve as Internet repositories that others remotely access. NT is not as popular in the home and small business market as is 95 because of its complexity and cost, but basically, the user will not notice a lot of difference between NT and 95 because in general, it's the programs that users care about, not the operating system. Generally, people who network PCs prefer NT over Windows 95 due to NT's superior networking management software. Unlike Windows 95, NT does not require a fully compatible PC because NT runs on a variety of computers.

Future operating systems will keep improving upon the original Windows standard. As time goes by, the goal of operating-system developers (primarily Microsoft, which owns most of the operating system market) will be to incorporate the online world into every PC so, whether you want to look at a file on your own hard disk or on a PC across the globe, the interface will be consistent.

Programs and Data

This book's first lesson explained the major program categories you'll run across as you use your PC. The programs do the work and, depending on what you want to accomplish, you'll run one or more programs on your PC every time you turn on your computer. Actually, Windows and every other operating system are nothing more than gigantic programs that interact with and control other programs on your PC.

Following is the typical life of a program:

1. You run the program. In Windows terminology, you'll *open* or *load* the program. You can open any file within Windows and, depending on the file type, Windows runs the file if it's a program, displays the file if the file contains displayable text, or issues an error if Windows does not recognize the file's data type. When you run a program file, Windows always starts the program.

2. You use the program to do the job you want, such as creating a word-processed document. You *save* that data document to one of your disk drive areas before you leave the program if you ever want to reuse the data subsequently.

3. You *close* the program. *Close* is a Windows term for stopping the program. Because a program runs inside a window, if you close the window you also close (stop) the program.

TIME SAVER

You don't have to be a huge company to write programs! If you know of something you want to do on your PC but you cannot find any programs out there that do it, write your own. First, however, you must learn a programming language, and that takes a little time. This book teaches you how to work with programs but not how to create them. For a great introduction to programming, check out Sams Publishing's *Absolute Beginner's Guide to Programming*.

This lesson is going to look at the data that the programs process. Just how do the programs you run locate and save data on disks? That question requires a fairly complex answer, and that answer is one of the few complexities a PC newcomer must face.

Organizing Disks

This section provides a high-level overview of disk storage. All disk storage devices, from disks to hard drives to CD-ROMs, use the same methods to store information. All these storage devices have one thing in common: They offer long-term, non-volatile storage. When you turn off your PC, the information stays on the disks. When you want, you can erase data on those disks just as you can tapes (except on CD-ROMs, though). The differences are that you must rerecord the entire tape if you want to insert something between what's already recorded there; removing precise information (such as a single word) from a tape is difficult, but removing data from disks is simple.

Of course, you cannot erase data stored on CD-ROMs because CD-ROMs are burned using a special CD device that creates them. Nevertheless, you'll access CD-ROM information in the same way you'll access disk information when you work on your PC.

Disk Names

The storage devices on your PC have special computer names. To your PC, the name of the first (and possibly only) disk drive is called *A*. Often you'll see a colon (:) after the disk drive name, so you might see drive A's name written A:.

Rarely do PCs in use today have two disk drives. The older ones have two disk drives, and the second drive name is *B*. If you have only one disk drive, your PC will not have a drive with the name *B*.

JUST A MINUTE

> The reason PCs don't have two disk drives today is because that extra slot can house another hard disk that holds so much more and faster storage than a second disk drive could offer.

The first (and possibly only) hard disk on your PC system will be named *C*. If you have a second hard disk, it will be *D*, the third *E*, and so on. Sometimes, a hard disk is *partitioned* (divided) into multiple disks called *logical disks*. Therefore, you might have only one physical hard disk, but that disk might be set up to act like two separate disks. You'll treat such partitioned disks as if they were two separate drives. If you have a CD-ROM drive, as many computers have today, the CD-ROM drive will typically be named with the letter that follows your last hard disk.

Here's a scenario: If you have one disk drive, two hard drives, and one CD-ROM drive, their names will be

A	Disk drive
C	First hard disk
D	Second hard disk
E	CD-ROM drive

If you have two disk drives and only one hard disk, their names will be

A	First disk drive
B	Second disk drive
C	Hard disk

If you have one disk drive, two hard disks, and two CD-ROMs, their names will be

A	Disk drive
C	First hard disk
D	Second hard disk
E	First CD-ROM drive
F	Second CD-ROM drive

JUST A MINUTE

The drive names go with the physical drive, *not* the medium within the drive. In other words, no matter which CD-ROM title you insert into your CD-ROM drive, the CD-ROM drive always has the same name.

As you use your PC, you'll refer to these drive letters often. If it helps to label the drives with taped labels until you get used to their names, that's just fine—and it could keep you and others who use your PC less perplexed about which drive name goes with which drive. (If your PC has a tape drive, the tape drive is a special drive for backing up your computer disks. The tape drive does not manage data in the same way as a disk does, so a tape drive has no name because you'll never access the tape as you access a disk.)

The hard drives reside inside your system unit. Of course, the disk drive does too, but you cannot see your hard disks in most cases. The front of your system unit shows one or more slots into which you insert disks into their drives. You don't insert or remove anything from hard disks, so you don't see them from the front of the system unit. You will, however, likely see a red or green light flash as you use your hard disk. When you read or write to a hard disk, the system unit's drive light flashes to let you know a disk operation is in process. Never turn off your PC as long as the light is flashing. (Hour 6, "Starting Your PC," describes the PC's proper power-up and power-down processes.)

CAUTION

Virtually every PC in existence will follow the drive-naming conventions described here. A very few, however, might have external hard drives or multiple disk drives for special reasons. In addition, the new larger-capacity disk drives, such as the Jaz drives, might *follow* your CD-ROM drive name, especially if the large-capacity drive is external.

Disks and Floppies

The most common disks, as you learned in the previous hour's lesson, are 3-1/2" disks. These disks replaced the 5-1/4" disks used in the early PCs. Figure 3.2 shows these two kinds of disks.

The 5-1/4" disks (often called *floppy disks*) were more fragile than the hard-shelled 3-1/2" disks. The 3-1/2" disks' smaller size and larger capacity made them an instant success, replacing 5-1/4" drives.

Both the 5-1/4" and 3-1/2" disks have two versions: a *low-density* version and a *high-density* version. The low-density 5-1/4" disks hold 360KB, and their high-density counterparts hold 1.2MB. The low-density (sometimes called *single-density*) 3-1/2" disks hold 720KB, whereas their high-density counterparts (sometimes called *double-density*) hold 1.44MB. The name *double-density* or *high-density* often appears on the high-density disks. In addition, all 3-1/2" disks have two square holes that you can see from the front if they are high-density.

When you purchase disks, look for the correct size. In almost every instance you'll purchase 3-1/2" disks in packs of 10 or 12 (or more). If you have a special, large-capacity disk drive, you'll need to check the labels carefully to match up the disks you purchase to your drive. Write on the disks with a felt-tip pen or fill out the supplied stick-on labels before you stick the labels on the disks. If you keep your disks properly labeled with the data they hold, you'll save yourself time trying to determine what's on a particular disk when you need something.

Figure 3.2.

The 3-1/2" disk is sturdier and holds more than its 5-1/4" predecessor.

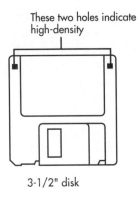

These two holes indicate high-density

3-1/2" disk

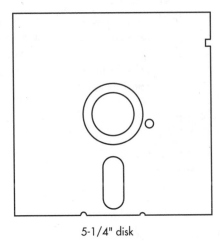

5-1/4" disk

TIME SAVER

Look for disks labeled *Formatted*. A new disk is either formatted or not. When a disk is formatted, magnetic tracks in the disk, not unlike a race track, keep data properly in its place. You cannot write to or read from an unformatted disk. Although you can format disks yourself by using a utility program found on all PCs, save yourself some time and trouble by looking only for formatted disks. The formatted disks are generally verified for error-free storage.

Although disks are fragile, the hard-cased 3-1/2" disks and the newer large-capacity disks can take some punishment. Drop them on your desk or slip them in a pocket, and they'll probably be fine. Remember, though, that magnets are the enemy and can scramble a disk's contents. Keep the disks away from speakers, telephones, screwdrivers, and anything else that might be magnetized.

Hour 7, "Your PC's Software" explains how you insert and remove disks from their drives.

Files Group Data

The disks and hard disks (the rest of this book calls both kinds *disks* unless otherwise qualified) hold data. Of course, your PC might turn that data into meaningful information as you learned in Hour 1, "Get Started Now!," but to your PC, all the information on a disk is just data that the PC reads and writes. Your disks hold both programs and the data that the programs process.

Disks can hold a lot of data. Those storage megabytes require some kind of organization. As you work through this book, as well as learn more about your PC through using it, you'll learn how to organize disks in a way that makes access easiest for the way you work.

Just like in a file cabinet, a disk holds *files*. A computer file is a collection of related information. Following are just some of the things that you might store as a file on your disks:

☐ Programs

☐ Data files

☐ System programs (operating system-related files)

☐ Word processor documents

☐ Graphics files

☐ Multimedia files such as files that contain sound and video

☐ Setup files that control how a program loads

Other kinds of files exist, and you'll run across them as you work on your PC. Unless a file contains a special form of compacted information, each file holds a single program, a single data file, or a single word-processed document.

Each file resides on a disk at a particular location. That location is often called the file's *path* (or *pathname*) and *filename*. As operating systems get more complex, and as hardware gets more interconnected to other computers both locally and remotely through networks and online services, the exact location of a particular file must be very specific indeed so that you can find that file when you need to work with it.

CAUTION

> Keep in mind this is an overview only! You'll be working hands-on with files soon enough, but this introduction will make that work go *much more smoothly*!

The goal of Windows is to make your PC as easy as possible to use (so you'll buy more PCs!). With that simplicity comes a little complexity as well. Perhaps someday all PC complexity will be gone, but the industry's not there yet.

Windows considers your PC screen to be your *desktop*. Obviously, your *desk*top is your desktop, but Windows doesn't know anything outside of the PC environment. Therefore, consider that anything you view, at any time, is generically known as your desktop. Your PC's universe, therefore, is called the desktop. Figure 3.3's screen is a desktop, and if a word processing program were running, its screen would be part of the desktop.

Figure 3.3.

*To Windows, your screen
is the desktop.*

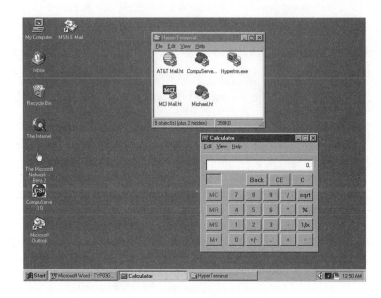

The reason for the desktop analogy is that Windows connects you to so many things—your PC's memory, the disk drives, and other people's computers (which may be in the next room or in another country)—that your screen really does provide the portal to every piece of information you'll ever access on your computer.

Actually, the desktop analogy is not really one of the wisest names Microsoft Windows coined. The term is confusing because your desktop accesses so many other computers these days. For simplicity's sake, the rest of this book ignores the location technically known as the desktop, although you'll see the name floating around some figures and within parts of Windows.

Within your desktop, you can access your PC and possibly other PCs via a networked cable or the phone lines. Your PC also has one or more printers attached, as well as several disk drives. For the time being, we're only concerned with your PC and your files. The parts of your computer that you access are stored in a desktop location called *My Computer*. What a name! You'll actually select the area labeled My Computer when you need to access a particular location inside your PC's storage area or within the system's setup.

JUST A MINUTE

If a file resides on one of your disks, it always resides within your area called My Computer. Obviously, if you access a file over the network, that file will not be part of the area on your PC called My Computer. (All this *really will* make sense before you finish this hour's lesson!)

3

The next level of storage is the disk drive name. Therefore, inside the location called My Computer are all your disk drives. As you'll learn in Hour 6, Windows describes the My Computer location on the desktop with the window shown in Figure 3.4. As you can see, the My Computer window is not too difficult to understand. Figure 3.4's My Computer window describes a PC that has four disk drives (a disk, two hard drives, and a CD-ROM), as well as at least one printer, a modem connection inside the Dial-Up Networking area, and a special Control Panel from which the PC's system settings can be adjusted.

Figure 3.4.

The My Computer window helps you see your PC's physical organization.

Getting More Specific

Let's recap: All files are stored somewhere. Your PC's files are located in the My Computer area (as opposed to someone else's PC!). Within the My Computer area, your files reside on your disk drives. Therefore, the My Computer location describes all your disk drives. See how Figure 3.4's graphical representation simplifies things? Without Window's graphical nature, nobody would be able to keep track of everything inside their PC.

After you've narrowed down the location of a file to a disk drive, you still have to find the file. With multi-gigabyte disk drives these days, structured disk organization is required to find anything. All your disk's information is stored in *folders*. All disks are said to contain a *root folder location* in which you add one or more levels of folders and subfolders. All this sounds rather confusing, but with Window's graphical interface, you'll learn that things make a lot of sense when you begin using the PC.

The icons in Figure 3.4 labeled *Control Panel, Printers*, and *Dial-Up Networking* graphically represent folders. These pictures (called *icons*) appear throughout Windows and represent a grouping of related files and devices.

A folder used to be called a *directory* in pre–Windows 95 versions of Windows (and sometimes within parts of Windows 95 as well). Folders can reside inside folders. These are called *subfolders* (but used to be called *subdirectories*). The folder analogy on a disk drive is not unlike a folder in a particular drawer within a file cabinet. Folders can hold one or more files.

You are in charge of many of your PC's folders and files, but many folders and files will already be on your PC's disk drives because of Windows and the other programs you've installed.

If you create a new folder, you'll have to assign a name to that folder. The same is true for files that you create because you'll have to name your files as well.

Follow these file-naming *conventions* (guidelines) to name folders and files:

☐ Names can contain letters, numbers, spaces, and certain special characters. The following special characters are *not* allowed, however: <, >, *, ?, :, /, \, and ¦. To avoid confusion, stick to letters, numbers, and spaces.

☐ Make your names descriptive. For example, Sales Figures is a better name for your sales figures file than X39349, although both will work and your PC just won't care which one you use. When you search through a long list of folders and filenames later, however, you'll be glad you gave them decent names that somewhat describe what they contain.

☐ Don't use too long of a name because you can too easily make a typing mistake if you ever have to type the name. Names can range from 1 to 255 characters.

☐ Filenames often contain a *filename extension*. (Don't use extensions for folders.) The extension is a three-letter abbreviation that follows the filename, separated by a period. For example, almost every word processor now automatically appends the filename extension .doc to all documents you create. (The program won't add a second extension if you type the extension when you first enter the name, though.) The extensions let you look at a list of files and determine (much of the time) at what kind of file you are looking. Windows now places an icon to the left of most files in listings, and the icon is usually taken from the program that created the file. The icons make the file extensions less important because you can see at a glance that a file is a database file or a graphics file without looking at the extension and trying to remember which program supports that filename extension.

CAUTION

> If you still use Windows 3.x, your file and directory names are much more limited than with Windows 95 and later. You'll need to keep all file and folder names at eight or fewer characters (not counting the extension) and avoid using spaces.

Why All This Now?

Scan through this 24-hour tutorial's table of contents and you'll see that this lesson comes *before* the PC purchase and installation section! Why worry about files and folders now when you might not have even bought a PC yet?

You'll need to understand something about the way your files are grouped on disks during the installation of your PC and its initial software setup. This overview makes you more ready to face terms such as *folders* and *root folders* when they pop up at you during your PC's setup. Rest assured, you'll have a chance to do some hands-on work with files and folders soon enough, and this background will make that upcoming chore much less tedious.

Reviewing It All Backward

Going from the detailed to the general, suppose that you just wrote a letter to Aunt Sally by using your word processor. Before you turn off your PC, you know that you must save the letter so that you can edit the name later and send it to Aunt Jane.

All you want to do is save the file, but you're going to have to make an immediate decision, when prompted by the word processor, about what name you want to give the file and where you want to save it. Suppose that you want to call it MyAunt.doc (a good name for a word-processed document written to an aunt). You also must tell the word processor where to save the file.

You'll have to select the disk drive (remember, you don't want to save the file on a CD-ROM because you cannot write to a CD-ROM). Suppose that you have free space on C, so you want to save it on the hard drive named C. Now, *where* on C do you save it? You'll have to select a folder, and possibly one or more folders within that folder, before you get to the exact point on that disk, within your PC (the My Computer icon area), on your viewable desktop, where you want to save the file! You might be saving it to this location (called a *pathname*) and file:

C:\Word\Data\Personal\MyAunt.Doc

Now that's a unique location! Reading from right to left, a file named MyAunt.doc stored in the Personal folder located within the Data folder located within the Word folder located on drive C located on your computer! (Fortunately, as you'll see in Hour 6, you'll rarely if ever have to type pathnames such as this one.) Long pathnames were the bane of pre-Windows MS-DOS users. With Windows, you'll now follow these basic steps to locate a file:

1. Issue the proper command so that your program knows you need to access a file. The program will open with a list of folders not unlike Figure 3.5's window of folders.

2. Use your mouse to point to an appropriate folder, and then open that folder by clicking the mouse (you'll learn how to work the mouse in Hour 6).

3. If you must select a different disk drive, you can do so before you begin opening folders and subfolders to find the location where the file resides.

4. After you've gotten to the right location, type the name of the file (just as a file folder within a file cabinet drawer contains a name on its label); the program will then load the file at that location.

Figure 3.5.

Your program often provides a list of folder icons from which you can select.

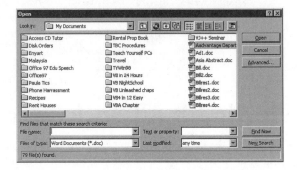

Come to think of it, even *that* sounds tedious, and it actually is. Most of the time, you don't even have to search through folders to find a file. Programs often remember where you last stored a file. If you use your word processor to write letters, the word processor will remember the location where you saved the previous letter. When you subsequently save a new letter, the *default* folder (the folder the word processor first opens) will be that same folder, and most of the time you'll save the document there or in a folder not too far away.

To simplify folder-traversal, Windows offers a graphical, icon-based folder organization called *tree-structured folders*. You can access these tree-structured folders in different areas of Windows and from the programs you run. Figure 3.6 shows an example of a tree-structured folder window. When you use your mouse or keyboard to open and close the folders, they will expand and collapse to show whatever detail you want to see.

CAUTION

This book does not go into Windows in great depth. It focuses on the PC itself more than on its operation because you must first learn quite a bit of a PC overview before you begin advancing your Windows skills.

TIME SAVER

Windows includes powerful file-searching capabilities. Although two files with the same name cannot reside in the same folder on the same disk drive, you could possibly have two files on your PC with the same names in different folders. Nevertheless, such duplication actually occurs very rarely. If you don't remember where you stored a file with which you need to work, you can always ask Windows to search for the file. Windows will return with the file's location (or multiple locations, if you've given two files that same name in different parts of your PC), and you can select that location by simply clicking the mouse's pointer over that found filename.

Figure 3.6.

The Windows tree-structured folders graphically show the disk's structure.

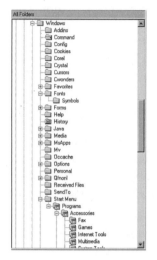

Summary

This hour introduces you to your PC's software. Software includes your operating system, programs, and data. This lesson describes the theory behind your software's storage and will help ease the mystery of such storage locations when you're ready to begin setting up a PC in the next hour's lesson.

Given that hard disks are very large and can hold billions of characters of data, Windows helps you organize your disk information into files, folders, and drives. A PC could easily have tens of thousands of files available to it at any one time. By using the folder analogy that Windows offers, you'll find that locating the correct files when you need them is streamlined greatly.

It's time to get serious and select that PC you need so desperately! The next hour walks you through the PC-selection process and explains how to buy the best PC for your budget. If you already have a PC, read the next hour's lesson anyway because you'll need to replace your PC as technology outdates it. (It happens to all of us!)

Q&A

Q I'm going to start out on an old PC. How can I determine which disks are inside?

A One way to determine what's inside a PC if you cannot easily locate someone who has used it before is to turn on the computer and open the My Computer window. (You'll learn how to do this kind of thing over the next two hours' worth of lessons.) If, however, the PC uses Windows 3.x (or, even more difficult, MS-DOS without Windows), the job isn't so easy. *Look very hard* for a manual that came with the PC! Lacking that, you might have to open the system unit and look inside to see how many drives exist inside the system unit. You'll be able to see the disk drives from the outside, but the inside will tell the story on the number of physical hard drives. You learned in this lesson, however, that a physical drive might be partitioned into multiple logical drives. Perhaps you will have to get an MS-DOS guru (they still exist; look in dark basements) to run a special MS-DOS command called CHKDSK on all possible drives to determine how much storage is available.

Q How do I know what extension to give a file?

A Generally, you don't have to worry about coming up with a filename extension in Windows because almost every Windows program takes care of the extension for you. In fact, many file listings you see throughout Windows will not put the filename extensions on the filename. The file's icon gives you clues that describe the file type.

Q Should I care how much free space is left on a disk drive?

A Windows provides all kinds of tools that tell you how much space is already consumed and how much is left on your PC's disk drives. Today's PCs have large storage capacities, but today's programs are large as well, so you'll need to monitor your disk space as you use your PC.

3

Hour 4

What Do I Buy First?

Buy, use, and be merry, for tomorrow your PC will surely be obsolete! The PC industry is racing to get faster and more powerful products out the door more quickly than one can buy them. Know that. Today's latest and greatest PC will be cheaper tomorrow and obsolete next week. Okay, hyperbole aside, know that today's PC purchase will always include two opposing results: You should buy the most powerful hardware that you can now comfortably afford, and you should expect to see that same hardware for less money soon afterward.

This lesson takes you to the PC store and helps you pick out the PC that's right for you. If you must cut back in one area, this lesson will tell you where.

If you already have a PC and you're ready to get started with it, you can skip this hour for now, but remember: Soon you'll upgrade or replace your PC equipment. It might pay dividends to browse through this hour's lesson quickly to get ideas that might help you decide to upgrade sooner.

The highlights of this hour include

- ☐ How to read the PC ads
- ☐ When to shop by mail and when to shop in the store
- ☐ Which PC hardware and software is most important

☐ Why some PC systems are not as inclusive as you need

☐ What extras to buy with a PC

Making Sense of the Ads

What on earth are you getting in this ad's PC system?

Limited Time!

Model M-SST244X, 244MHz Pentium MMX

32MB EDO RAM (SDRAM available)

512K cache

Full Plug-and-Play support

PCI 64-bit video

4.3GB EIDE or SCSI 12ms

32-bit wavetable stereo sound

Internal 33.6 fax modem (fully upgradable to X2 or K56Flex)

104 keyboard

12x CD-ROM

12" Non-Interlaced (.28 Dot Pitch) MPR Compliant

Fully loaded with all the software you need today, including Windows, SoftSys's All-In-One word/data/PIM suite, and the latest in 16-color graphic games

Mouse and pad

Call for pricing today!

Although you understand some of this better now that you've mastered basic PC terms, some of an ad's details that you must parse (*parse* is a $10 computer term meaning to shift or sort through; the more of those you know, the higher salary you can command!) can confuse you. The rest of this lesson explains all those cryptic codes and describes the most important buying decisions you must make to get a PC that works best.

Mail-Ordering Versus Store Buying

Look in any PC magazine these days and you'll wade through page after page of ads before you get to the first article. People all over the world want to sell PC products to you!

4

You'll learn a lot about PCs from the magazine ads. Don't skip the ads. You'll learn which PC speeds are most commonly available, familiarize yourself with current prices, and learn about warranties and service.

Almost every month, more than one PC magazine contains an article for first-time buyers. With such an ad you'll learn about new products recently introduced that you might need. In addition, you'll learn which companies are the major hardware vendors and will become acquainted with name-brands quickly.

You can purchase PCs through the mail or in a store. Following are some advantages of mail-order buying:

- ☐ Mail-order prices are often lower than in the stores because of lower overhead.

- ☐ Mail-order shipping and handling for a computer is generally much less than your local sales tax would be for the same sale.

- ☐ Mail-order requires only a toll-free phone call and a credit card. You don't have to leave your home.

- ☐ Mail-order is not just for voice phones anymore. You can shop over the Internet and with online services such as Prodigy. (Of course, if you don't have a PC you can't do that!) Nevertheless, if some of your friends have Internet access, ask if they can sit down with you and glance through the name-brand mail-order PC companies. (They'll know how to search for them.) You'll learn a lot about PCs just by sitting there.

These advantages weigh in heavily, but consider some mail-order drawbacks:

- ☐ You cannot see what you're buying before it arrives.

- ☐ After-sale service and support might be inconvenient. The only thing harder than getting a PC out of its original box is getting it *back in* the box to return it.

- ☐ Mail-order companies have been known to go out of business quickly.

Okay, so *now* you're convinced to go to the store in spite of the cost savings. Before you do, please remember that hundreds of thousands of people are extremely happy with their mail-order PCs. Rarely will anything be wrong with your PC when it arrives. The reputable mail-order companies seem to go out of their way to fix whatever might be wrong with an order. Many major mail-order companies let you take your PC to a local service center for repair instead of shipping it back to the company.

As long as you feel comfortable with mail-order in general (and you should, as long as you shop with the better-known mail-order companies), you'll be okay making your PC purchase through the mail. Also, consider that if you have a quick question, your mail-order company might be an inconvenient place to call to get answers, but your local computer store's staff probably knows little more than you do (after you've read this book!) about PCs, and they will often refer you to the manufacturer or software publisher for technical questions.

JUST A MINUTE

If you are brand-new to PCs, as many readers of this lesson will be, and if you have qualms about mail-order PCs, the extra cost of in-store buying is worth the extra sleep you'll get at night. Many of today's PC megastores offer prices that come close to those of mail-order companies even though you'll often pay more because of the sales tax alone.

Consider these in-store shopping advantages:

- You'll learn a lot about PCs from browsing the stores and reading the shelf ads.
- You'll get many software ideas so you will know where to spend that extra money you always seem to have floating around.
- Before you purchase a model, you can try it out.
- Returns and repairs are often very convenient.
- You'll help your local economy.
- You'll get to interact with others in the traffic jams that seem to pile around today's PC megastores.

(Perhaps that last one is a disadvantage. Who knows, you may be an extrovert and like such encounters.) You've now seen the term *megastore* twice. Large PC-store chains are popping up all over the world. Smaller stores simply have too much relative overhead to compete in today's market, so the smaller PC stores are becoming more specialized, offering services and special hardware not always found in the larger stores.

For quantity and prices, nothing beats the large PC stores. They will often match a competitor's pricing, and you, the PC buyer, often come away not only with a PC but with a handful of rebate coupons that help ease the sales tax pain.

Brand-new PC buyers should probably stick to the in-store buying for their first purchase. Most of the mail-order companies are great, but you can shop them for your second PC. In addition, the mail-order companies are fantastic places to buy software after you get the hardware home.

If you go with mail order, stick with a company that advertises a lot (showing they have a big budget), has been in business for several years (showing they are loyal to customers), and that offer simplified return and service policies that you are comfortable with. PC manufacturers also sell their products by mail. Such companies are able to answer questions about their products and are well equipped to repair their computers.

4

Home-Brew PCs? Stick to Coffee

Perhaps you've heard of people who successfully bought the parts for their PCs and assembled their own computers. These are sometimes called *home-brew PCs*. You don't have to be an electronics wizard to put together today's common PC parts... but it helps!

Today's PCs are sold in such great volumes at such low profit margins that, unless you like the challenge, strongly consider buying the PC fully assembled (except for the routine setup described in the next lesson). You can save as much as 50% on a computer if you assemble the parts yourself, but that kind of thing just isn't recommended for the average PC newcomer.

Name Brand or Not?

You'll save money if you go with an off-brand, but you'll save headaches if you stick to the name-brand companies that have sold PCs for 5 to 10 years or more. If you relocate, you'll want to be able to find service wherever you go. If you need technical assistance, you'll want a number that's available during reasonable hours.

When you narrow down your PC purchase to a handful of products, ask the salespeople how long those companies have been making PCs. Although any PC could fail the moment you turn it on, the long-term companies are long-term for good reason: Their PCs work well, and their customers are generally happy.

What You *Must* Buy

Your goal, before leaving the store or hanging up from the mail-order salesclerk, is to purchase the following items:

- ☐ System unit (all popular PC system units will come with a CPU, a disk drive and hard disk, and some memory)
- ☐ Monitor (you have to see the results your PC displays)
- ☐ Keyboard
- ☐ Operating system
- ☐ Mouse
- ☐ All the proper cables to connect everything (rarely will a printer cable come with the printer, but most other peripherals come with their required cable)

JUST A MINUTE

Although a mouse is not technically required, you cannot work well with Windows-based programs without one.

Rarely is a PC sold today without including everything in this list. Therefore, you don't have to worry too much about receiving these items, but make sure you're getting them before you leave the store. In addition to these must-haves, you should consider the following extra items if they are not already bundled with the PC (as many are):

☐ Printer

☐ Modem

☐ Speakers and microphone

☐ Tape drive or large-capacity removable disk drive

☐ Joystick

Your own PC needs might dictate other items, such as a scanner if you want to bring into your PC images and text from paper-based sources.

A Word About Bundles

Vendors sell a huge number of bundled PC/software combinations these days. The new PC buyer is almost always better off buying one of these "complete" systems, but hardly any one package is right for everybody.

If almost everything you want in a PC comes in one of the bundled packages, ask the store or mail-order company if it will swap or trade certain components that may be more suitable for you. For example, many PC bundles come with a small monitor measuring 12 to 14 inches of diagonal viewing area. If you plan to work several hours in front of your PC each day, a larger screen will be easier on your eyes and will let you see more work on your screen at one time. Ask for the actual viewing area size because the screen's physical dimension often measures more than the picture area.

The following section explains how to make an appropriate buying decision. As you read through the text, consider which PC components are most important to you; when you are actually buying, ask the store if it will let you upgrade parts of the package to accommodate your needs.

Important Buying Considerations

The decision-making process for the must-haves and might-wants can be messy. The following sections will help you know what to look for so that you can decipher the codes and terms you've yet to see.

4

System Unit Specs

Every kind of PC out there has a different model name and number, such as *Q/200 SL-8x* and *XM 233X32*. Sometimes the model name might give a clue to the CPU and speed, and sometimes it might just be confusing. *Q/200* might refer to a CPU speed of 200MHz, and *SL-8x* might give a hint that an included CD-ROM drive is an *8x*-speed drive (see the later section named "Storage" for details). The *233X32* in a model named *XMI 233X32-b* might indicate that the CPU is a 233MHz CPU with the special internal multimedia processing called MMX included on the CPU chip. (Hour 2, "Hardware's Easy, Not Hard," explained MMX in more detail.)

As you can tell, the model name and the numbers with the name often only hint at the CPU, so you have to look further in the ad for the details. If the system unit contains an Intel CPU, you'll almost always see Intel listed in the ad's details because, for many, the Intel brand is an advantage because Intel has routinely been the first out with the next generation of CPU chips for PCs. If you don't see the Intel name (companies often fly the "Intel Inside" logo somewhere in the ad), look for *AMD* or *Cyrix*. Another CPU manufacturer might be listed instead. A non-Intel CPU is often less expensive but still compatible with Intel.

The higher the CPU speed, the higher the MHz value. 133MHz is much slower than 266MHz. Within a small range, the speed will vary depending on other hardware; a 250MHz CPU might run as fast or faster than a 266MHz, depending on the disk drive speed and type of memory.

4

BIOS Means More Than Life

Besides being Greek for *life*, the term *BIOS* stands for *Basic Input-Output System*. Although not inside your CPU, the BIOS is a kind of ROM included in your PC that determines how the system components interact with each other.

Different manufacturers make PC-compatible BIOSs. Phoenix has probably been around the longest, but you'll also see AMI, Award, and others. Today, don't worry about the distinction. The ads often include BIOS information just to look technical.

System units often come in three kinds of boxes:

☐ *Desktops* are rectangular boxes that sit on your desk.

☐ *Mini-towers* are small, upright boxes that sit on the floor, or possibly on your desk if you have adequate vertical room. Mini-towers sometimes offer more expansion room than do regular desktop systems. Mini-towers have a smaller *footprint*, meaning that less room is needed for them than the regular rectangular deskspace-eating system units.

☐ *Towers* are taller than mini-towers (often as tall as three feet high) and provide the maximum expansion room possible. Although towers don't necessarily contain more expansion slots than desktop units, towers do offer more *drive bay space* for extra disks, CD-ROMs, and backup tape drives.

Memory

The more RAM, the better. You'll need a minimum of 16 megabytes (16MB), but 32 is better, and Windows knows what to do with even more. If you are watching a budget, do your best to move to 32MB and, if money is not such a factor (memory is inexpensive), move up a little higher.

CAUTION

Purchase as much memory as you think you'll need when you buy the PC. It's much harder to add the memory later because, if you have the store install it, you'll have to do without the PC for a while during the installation. Many people never get to the memory upgrade later, even if they need it, because of the hassle.

Most memory today is either *EDO* (*Extended Data Out*) or *SDRAM* (*Synchronous Dynamic RAM*). SDRAM is newer, a little more expensive, and offers faster access than EDO because all the memory is immediately available to the CPU. A slight memory wait occurs with EDO. A *cache* (as Figure 4.1 shows), pronounced *cash*, is a temporary storage location between the RAM and the CPU. A cache gets data to and from RAM, and the larger the cache size (if one exists), the better.

Figure 4.1.

A cache stores up data for the CPU's quick retrieval.

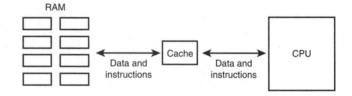

Hardware Issues

Over time, you will add new hardware to your PC. Perhaps a fast new modem will come out that you want to use in place of your old one, or you might replace a black-and-white printer with one that prints color. Installing new devices offers challenges because, even though the hardware might be called *PC compatible*, not all pieces work well together and almost all can be difficult to set up initially. If you purchase your PC in town but then purchase upgrade equipment from a mail-order company, you will have to perform the installation yourself.

4

You'll somewhat simplify future expansion if your PC supports *Plug and Play*. In theory, your PC will automatically recognize and configure itself to support new hardware if your PC is Plug-and-Play compatible and your added hardware is also. Unfortunately, not all Plug-and-Play devices install so easily, but almost all of them are simpler than devices that are not Plug and Play. If you think you'll upgrade your PC often, look for one that supports Plug and Play. As you add additional hardware over the PC's life, make sure that hardware is Plug-and-Play compatible as well.

The more expansion slots the PC has, the better. Most of today's PCs combine *PCI* (*Peripheral Component Interconnect*) with *ISA* (*Industry Standard Architecture*) expansion slots. PCI slots are newer and support more devices (including more complete Plug and Play support). Internal tape drives, CD-ROMs, and video cards now are PCI-based, so be sure you get some PCI slots. Ask the salesperson how many slots are already taken and how many are free. The disk drives, video board, and internal modem might already consume three slots, and other devices might be taking additional slots.

Getting the Picture

Video cards drive the monitor. The better the card, the easier your monitor will read (and the more catchy PC games will look). Video cards have on-board memory to build the image you see, and the more memory you have, the more colors appear, the crisper the picture looks, and the faster the video appears. The video memory is called *VRAM*, for *Video RAM*, and differs somewhat from the RAM that goes in your system unit.

Probably the minimum on-card video memory today is 1MB of 32-*bit* video. (A *bit* is one eighth of a byte. The more bits you have, the wider the video data path will be.) If you can get a video card with at least 2MB (4 or more is better if games or graphics are really important) of 32-bit RAM, do so. If you can get 64-bit RAM, you'll be even better.

TIME SAVER

> If money is tight, you can replace the video card later; whatever comes with today's PCs generally offers adequate video.

Read the fine print. The ads with seemingly outstanding PC prices often don't include the monitor, so you might have to buy one separately. The larger the monitor, the better the viewing—but the more costly your system will be. At least a 14-inch viewing area (measured diagonally) is imperative. To save money up front, you can purchase an inexpensive monitor and then replace it later. You don't have to open your system unit to replace a monitor, so the replacement is simple.

The better monitors have a *dot pitch* (the width between the dots on the screen that form pictures and text) of .28 or less. A problem arising, though, is that those monitor vendors are getting smart and changing the shape of the dots from circles to squares. The upshot is that dot pitch is no longer a reliable indicator of monitor quality, but it's a place to begin. (Some manufacturers use a different measurement system altogether different from dot pitch.) The monitor's *non-interlaced* measurement (which refers to a special way the dots overlap one another) makes for smoother pictures than monitors that aren't labeled as non-interlaced. To really choose the best monitor look at *each one* hooked to a PC running the same program (the stores often have most of their monitors hooked to PCs) and select the one that looks best to you. The higher cost monitors don't always look better than the less expensive ones.

JUST A MINUTE

Most monitor makers now include power-saving features, sometimes indicated by the words *MPR compliant* or *Energy Star compliant*. These monitors have the capability to turn themselves off after a preset period of non-use.

Storage

Purchase a PC with at least one hard drive that's 1.6 gigabytes or larger. Sometimes a vendor will fool you by advertising *unformatted* disk capacity, as in *2 gigabytes unformatted storage*. When you format the disk, as you'll have to do, you'll lose some of that space, and a 2GB disk might drop down to 1.6 or 1.7 gigabytes.

Access time refers to the speed of the disk, and the difference between 8, 12, or 15 milliseconds (stated as *ms*) is trivial for most users. The smaller the access time, the better.

Most disk drives will be billed as *EIDE* (for *Enhanced Integrated Drive Electronics*) or *SCSI* (for *Small Computer System Interface*). EIDE drives do not require an internal disk controller card that takes up one of your expansion slots. In addition, EIDE drives are less expensive than SCSI drives and easier to set up. SCSI, however, lets you chain up to six more SCSI devices (such as additional disks or any SCSI device such as a tape drive or large removable disk) without changing anything inside your PC.

JUST A MINUTE

One of the problems (and advantages) to SCSI is that the manufacturers are always improving the standard. SCSI turned into SCSI-2, which turned into SCSI-3. Make sure your SCSI card matches the SCSI device you want to plug into it. If you're purchasing a new PC that has already has a SCSI drive, the SCSI card and SCSI disk will be compatible.

Rarely will any but the most advanced new PCs come with a SCSI interface. If your PC is EIDE, you'll be happy with that purchase.

4

The CD-ROM you get will likely be listed as a *12x*, *16x*, or *(something)-x* drive. Those values represent the drive's speed as the number of times faster than the first CD-ROM sold. Speeds vary! All 16X drives are not the same speed. Even the fastest CD-ROM drives are much slower than hard disk drives, however, and if you get a PC that contains a CD-ROM drive of 10x or faster you'll be fairly pleased with the performance.

I Want my DVDs

Some newer and more expensive PCs come with a *DVD* (*Digital Video Disc*) drive built in that stores seven times the amount of information that a CD-ROM stores, letting you watch feature-length films from your PC.

The first-time PC buyer will rarely get a DVD, although this new feature might become more common as software publishers begin writing giant programs that take advantage of the new DVD technology. To add a DVD later, you'll have to have the proper DVD adapter. The adapter might be on an expansion board, or the back of your PC might have a place for a DVD device.

Don't fret too much if the PC you want to buy is not yet DVD-ready. Until more companies support DVD, you will rarely, if ever, realize it's missing.

4

Multimedia

Even if you don't think you want multimedia, you'll probably get it. Hardly a PC is sold without some kind of sound card, microphone, and speakers. Generally, the microphone and speakers are low quality, but they are adequate until you need better multimedia.

The PC's sound card will almost always be touted as being *SoundBlaster compatible*, meaning that it is (probably) compatible with the industry-standard sound card produced by the original SoundBlaster's company, Creative Labs, Inc. Creative Labs still leads the sales in sound cards, so you might even get one of their low-end cards in pre-packaged PCs.

The low-end sound cards offer stereo sound and fill most needs adequately. The standard is *16-bit*, which describes a two-byte data path throughout the card. If you want better quality, look for a *32-bit* card. You may see the term *wavetable*, which indicates that the sound card is capable of advanced sound reproduction.

Connecting with a Modem

Most PCs are sold today with internal modems because internal modems cost less than external modems. All modems today send and receive faxes. The most important statistic to look for is the modem's speed. The speed refers to the amount of information that can travel to and from your PC and phone line.

The higher the speed, the better. 28.8Kbps is the bare minimum, but many modem manufacturers now offer 33.6Kbps. This speed measurement indicates the *baud rate*, or the maximum number of bits transmitted over the line in a second. 28.8K, therefore, means 28.8 kilobits travel across the modem per second (a bit is one-eighth of a character of memory). Speeds close to 56Kbps are possible, but a standards battle is still raging; you'll get a 56Kbps standard labeled either *X2* or *K56Flex*. If you already know which online service to which you want to subscribe, find out which standard the service supports before you make the final PC decision because the two 56Kbps standards are not compatible. If you are unsure which standard you'll need, you can run either standard at a lower speed such as 28.8Kbps; at that speed they will both be compatible with any service you dial.

The Keyboard and the Mouse

When it comes to the keyboard, take what they give you and then decide if you need to replace it later. The ads will almost always brag about a *104-key keyboard* or something like that, but the truth is that most PCs come with all the keys anyone would ever use. Also, most PCs are sold with really cheap keyboards. Fortunately, even cheap keyboards usually last as long as you'll keep the PC.

Obviously, the quality of the keyboard is critical if you type all day. Test the keyboard in the store to make sure you like its typing feel. Some prefer a loud strike, whereas others want a soft touch. Some keyboards are *ergonomic*, such as the one shown in Figure 4.2, and (for many people) offer more a natural typing arrangement that should help lighten your hands' workload.

Figure 4.2.
Some funny-looking keyboards exist that can ease typing stress.

JUST A MINUTE

To save desk space, many users prefer the keyboards that include trackballs in them. The *trackball* takes the place of a mouse; instead of moving a mouse over your desk you'll roll the trackball's ball with your fingers. Another option is a touch keypad area that measures about 3 inches square. You can drag your finger over this pad to simulate moving a mouse.

Figure 4.3 shows a mouse and trackball. The trackball might come separately from the keyboard, just as a mouse does. You might have the option in the store of picking out your own mouse. Although 3- and even 4-button mice exist, two buttons are all you need. Some mice and trackballs now come with a roller button that lets you navigate some programs more easily; if you have the roller option, get the roller.

Figure 4.3.
You might want a regular mouse or a trackball.

Don't make a mouse decision based on looks. Try all mouse options to get a feel for the best one for you. Be sure to try the separate ones before you opt for the keyboard version over the separate and more standard mouse.

Then There's the Software

Almost always, PC companies pack software that you'll never use on a PC. Make sure you get Windows and then hope that whatever else they throw in is usable. If you get a major software package such as Microsoft Office, you have software you will potentially use, but a lot of software that comes packed on PCs takes space that better (albeit costly) software should replace as soon as you can afford to do so. Look for low-power versions of several software programs. You'll be able to try these test versions to see if you want to purchase the full-scale program. Often, limited versions of high-end games come on new PCs sold today.

Need a Printer?

You probably need a printer. You can get by without one if you just want to learn more about PCs for right now, but a printer becomes a requirement when you want to print checks, reports, and letters from your PC.

Color printers are fun and work well for business graphics and published reports you might want to distribute. The quality of even the least expensive printer these days is not too bad. If you get an ink jet, the difference in cost between color and black-and-white is trivial, but remember that the price of color ink cartridges does add up quickly if you print a lot in color.

Laser printers are the cream of the printer crop. If you can afford one (and if you don't need color, unless you're willing to spend several thousands of color-laser dollars), you'll be happy with a laser's quality and speed.

The two printer specifications for which to look are speed measured at *pages per minute* and *resolution*. The higher the speed, the more pages the printer can print. More complete printer descriptions will compare a full page of graphics versus a full page of text because most printers take longer to produce a page with heavy graphics than a page with text. Resolution refers to the number of dots per inch that make up the dots, shapes, text, and lines your printer produces. The low-end measurement is *300 dpi* (dots per inch). Anything higher simply makes your output even nicer, and many of today's inexpensive printers can output at 600 dpi.

Save Money for Extras

Don't spend all your money on the PC itself, or you'll regret not having a few extras when you get home. You'll need a box of disks, backup tapes (if your PC has a tape drive), and printer paper. Consider where you'll put your PC. Do you need a desk? Do you need a printer stand? If you plan to do heavy printing, now is the time to purchase an extra packet of ink jet cartridges or a spare laser cartridge.

One of the best extras you can purchase is a *power strip* so that you can plug all your computer power cords into a regular outlet. Most power strips sold in PC stores and catalogs have some form of *surge protection* so that power spikes in your electrical system aren't as likely to affect your PC. PCs are fairly sensitive to power surges, and you don't want your PC restarting right before you save your work because you'll lose your work. (Remember that RAM gets erased as soon as your PC powers down or resets.) Some power strips offer very little surge protection, so ask the salesperson which strip offers good protection.

TIME SAVER

For real protection, consider getting an *uninterruptible power supply* (*UPS*). UPSs store energy, so your PC will remain on for a few minutes if the power goes out of your home or office. With that extra time, you can save your work before your PC loses power. The UPS will beep loudly if the power goes out to warn you that you have a few moments to save your work.

CAUTION

No PC surge protector in the world will protect against a direct or close lightning strike. Unplug your PC if a lightning storm begins.

4

A PC system does not consume a lot of power. The monitor consumes more than all the other PC components combined in most instances. You can leave your PC on 24 hours a day without worrying too much about power, although you should power-down your monitor if you'll be away for a few hours or more.

Walk through the software aisles to see if anything strikes your fancy. (By the time you finish Part III, "Software Drives the PC," you'll have a good understanding of which software you should get.

If you or someone in your family is a game player, get a joystick. Joysticks generally run less than $100 and often sell for much less. The joysticks with a heavy base generally cost more but have a better feel. Some joysticks include support for flying controls, and some work well for race-car games. Specialized rudder controls and steering wheel–based joystick controls exist, but the better ones can get costly. As with keyboards, if you take your games seriously you should try all the joystick options in the store before you purchase one.

Summary

This hour went to the PC store with you and helped you pick out a computer. Decisions abound, but research pays dividends. You now know on which components to concentrate and which are less important for a first-time purchase.

The mail-order versus in-store purchase decision is not always easy to make. You can get great deals and high-quality PCs through the mail, but many people prefer to shop in a store and purchase there in case problems arise later. You'll learn a lot about PCs and current prices if you study the ads in your local paper and in the current computer magazines.

The next hour takes you past the purchase to the setup; after you buy your PC, what do you do? You must assemble the PC's components and make sure everything works as expected. The next lesson shows you how.

Q&A

Q How much should I spend on a PC?

A An old PC industry saying goes something like this: "I can live with a $2,000 PC, but the one I *really* want is $5,000." If you look at the price of the most powerful PCs today, and then look at the average PC sold, you'll see that this range still holds true.

There's no way to determine how much you should spend because you have a budget that's unique to you. Of course, whatever your budget is, you'll want the best PC for the money. This lesson has explained how to filter through the purchase decision. You can learn from this lesson which components to pay more for and which to get by without until a later time when you might want to upgrade.

Q How do I shop for a laptop?

A Many of the same specification ranges work for laptops as for desktop systems. For example, today's laptops come with sound cards, CD-ROM drives, and hard disks. Laptops do offer some unique differences for which to look. The more the laptop can do and the less the laptop weighs, the easier you can tote the laptop with you when you're on the go. Any laptop over 10 pounds is considered fairly heavy by today's standards.

Find a laptop with an *active matrix screen* so that you can easily read the display in bright light. Be sure to get a laptop with at least one credit card–sized PC card slot (at least one should be called *type III*) so you can expand the laptop. If the laptop has a *lithium ion* battery, you'll be able to keep the battery charged more easily. Get a sturdy carrying case for those runs through the airports!

If the laptop supports an *infrared interface*, you'll be able to transfer files to and from your desktop PC without wires. Expect to pay more for a laptop than for a similar desktop, and remember that a laptop is more difficult to upgrade than a desktop in many cases. Therefore, buy more laptop than you think you'll need.

4

PART
II

What to Do First

Hour

Hour 5

Setting Up Your New PC

You've decided on the best PC purchase and bitten the bullet. The credit card's not due for a month, so you have some time to enjoy your new PC. After you bring the PC home or to your office, expect some initial hardware and software setup. You must connect the hardware components and, after turning on the PC, set up software before you can use your new PC.

This lesson helps take the mystery out of the PC's initial setup. You'll save time if you follow some guidelines laid out here. In addition, proper PC setup will improve the enjoyment you subsequently have with the PC.

The highlights of this hour include

- ☐ Which environments make for happy PCs
- ☐ How to unpack the computer
- ☐ How to determine where the cables go
- ☐ What safety precautions to take
- ☐ How to manage electrical outlets

The Room's Environment

Your PC is susceptible to heat and cold. If the components get too hot, your PC will malfunction. If your PC is cold, the circuits might not work consistently until they warm up. If you bring in a new PC from the cold, let it warm to room temperature before you connect anything because the possible condensation could cause problems. Fortunately, only extreme temperatures affect PCs, and most of the time you don't have to worry unless you house the PC in a strange location, such as in a shed or inside a cold storage location. If you're comfortable, the PC is probably just fine. Make sure that your PC has room to breathe and that all its air vents will have adequate space for proper air flow.

Your PC is somewhat allergic to smoke, so you might need an air filter. Today's PCs are fairly rugged, so they're rarely affected by smoke and dust as long as you keep their areas clean. Dust regularly, keep the cola drinks off the keyboard, and keep things off the air vent holes and your PC will be happy in its new home.

TIME SAVER

> Plan ahead! Your PC will have cables coming out the back of it. You'll need writing space next to the keyboard, and you'll need to have access to the back of the PC from time to time. Some PC users prefer a long table for their machine so they have access all around the PC and plenty of desk space for other items, such as a phone. (Is a phone jack nearby?) Look around the room where you'll put your PC and think about these placement issues before you decide on the best location.

Your printer will need paper. Leave enough room for the printer along with its paper feed tray. Some printers leave a large *footprint* (meaning they require a lot of desk space).

Where will your keyboard go? If you purchased a desktop system unit, the monitor will probably sit on top of the system unit, and you'll place the keyboard in front of it. Many PC stores and mail-order houses sell slide-out keyboard holders that fit under your desk. The lower keyboard makes typing easier for many and leaves more desk area for papers and all the Sams books you'll want to get.

A tower unit often sits on the floor. Whatever kind of system unit you bought, place it within easy reach of your keyboard's area. As you use your PC, you will be inserting and removing CD-ROMs and disks.

Is your chair comfortable? Most people don't think about the chair until they spend 13 hours straight on the Internet. Office-supply stores and furniture companies sell surprisingly comfortable and sturdy desk chairs inexpensively. An adjustable office chair lets you sit comfortably at a proper height for the keyboard and at the best position to reduce monitor eye strain.

5

A close bookcase holds extra paper, disks, and CD-ROMs without your needing to leave the PC. Consider also your planned expansion. If you become the PC power user you want to become, are you going to be getting a scanner, an external removable disk drive, a tape drive, a second or third printer, or an amplifier for the sound card? Think about this possible expansion when you first put your PC in its place. By organizing around probable expansion, you'll more easily adjust to the new equipment and have room for it when the time comes.

| Planning is best done in advance! |

TIME SAVER

Opening the Boxes

Your PC arrives at your doorstep or at the PC store's doorstep the same way: by vehicle. Trucks deliver the PC to mail-order customers and the stores. The PCs are packed well to handle the truck delivery. Therefore, the packing is somewhat overwhelming when you begin opening the boxes. Some companies put recommended unpacking instructions directly on the box. Try to keep the boxes and packing material in their original state in case you need to repack the PC for service or repair.

The best box to open first is the one for your system unit, although some PCs come with both the system unit and the monitor in the same box. The system unit is the center of your setup work (that's where all the cables go), so place the system unit on the table before you put other items there.

Expect to find all kinds of manuals, papers, and cards as you unpack the boxes. Save everything! Look especially for pages that say, *Read this first!* and then read those first. Such notices often inform you of critical unpacking instructions (such as, "Do not open this end first"). This probably means the manufacturer has had too many complaints about pieces falling and breaking when the purchaser dumps the contents onto the floor.

| If you're like most people (including PC-book authors) you won't read the instruction manuals—you'll want to dive right in. That's fine, but put all the manuals in a safe place because you'll need them eventually if you have a problem. |

JUST A MINUTE

Separate the registration cards as you find them. Make a pact with yourself that before the day is over you will fill out every one of them. You must register your hardware and software, and the best time to do that is the day you buy them. If you don't, you might forget until the registration deadline expires 10 or 20 days after the purchase.

What Do They Really Want?

You know that many companies offer bogus registration cards that are little more than data-gathering resources for their marketing departments. These cards seem to care much more about your age and family pet than the $2,000 system unit you just brought home.

In most cases, the store or mail-order location where you purchased the PC stands behind the product. You'll take or mail the PC back to them if you have a problem, not back to the original manufacturer (unless you ordered directly from the manufacturer). Therefore, the registration cards do not add a lot of warranty protection in many cases. (Check the fine print, though.)

Almost always, registering your software is critical because you'll want to know if an update comes out that fixes a *bug* (error) your software might have. If you don't want the companies to distribute your information to other companies, the cards often have a checkbox you can mark to indicate you want your privacy.

As a new PC user, consider mailing all the cards and getting on all the lists. You'll find out about many new products through the mail, and you'll keep up with prices as well.

Open all the cables and unwrap all the small pieces. Be sure that you check all the packing material. Some small PC pieces, such as connectors and knobs, come in boxes or wrapping that's easy to mistake for packing material.

CAUTION

Don't put away the software manuals, such as the one that comes with every Windows-based PC sold today, before you finish setting up the PC. Although you might not need the actual instructions, the manuals often include a special registration number you'll need to type into the PC before you can use the software. This is just one of the minor annoyances within the industry. It has something to do with copy protection, but if you give away the software after you install it, wouldn't you also give away that registration number? The software companies are not completely unreasonable, however. They know that most people don't give away licensed programs (it's against the law and can be a felony), but that people who use programs a lot want to be properly registered (which means buying the software) so they can receive updates, bug fixes, and discounts on future versions.

5

The Cabling

If any documentation tells you to connect a certain cable first, follow the documentation. Usually the only hard-core rules are that you should plug the power cord in *last* after everything else looks ready to go, and your laser printer requires enough current to warrant its own half of your outlet (the other half should handle your power strip).

The back of your system unit probably contains connections that look like Figure 5.1. Before you connect the cables, grab the smallest flathead screwdriver you can find. Many PC cable connections have screws that help keep the PC and cables connected properly and snugly.

Figure 5.1.

Peripherals connect to the back of your system unit.

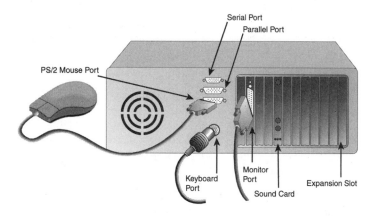

Table 5.1 describes each of the plug-in locations in the back of your system unit. Use the table to plug all your cables into the proper locations. A PC *port* is a place into which you plug connectors to peripheral devices such as the printer and external modem. Some of the newer PCs have these places nicely labeled, but many vendors seem to think you want the challenge of figuring out what goes where. Fortunately, some PCs color-code their cable connectors to colors on each system unit connection to eliminate ambiguity. Most of the cables can only go in one connection, but if your PC happens to have multiple ports, such as two serial ports, you'll need to be more careful.

CAUTION

Plug in your peripheral cables, but not the peripherals themselves. In other words, plug one end of each cable into the back of the PC, one for each device you want to use, but don't connect your printer or external modem to the other end of their cables just yet. Some devices, such as your mouse and keyboard, require that you plug in the device along with the cable because the device does not detach from its end of the cable. After you

connect all the cables, you then can better place the remaining peripherals and plug them in when you know which cables will need to go where.
Besides, a monitor often gets in the way when you're trying to plug in
additional equipment.

Table 5.1. Use this table to make the proper connections.

Connection	Description
Serial port	The serial port holds your external modem's cable or mouse. Look at your mouse and, if the plug is round, use the serial port for an external modem if you have one. If the mouse does not fit here and you have an internal modem, you will not need the serial port for now. If you have both a serial mouse (if the mouse cable plugs in here and no adapter for a round connection came with the mouse) and an external modem, you must decide which device, the mouse or modem, is the most critical because you will not be able to plug in both unless you have two serial ports. If that's the case, consider adding a second serial port (they are inexpensive) or replacing your serial mouse with a *bus* mouse that fits in the round PS/2 port.
	If you have two serial ports, plug the mouse into the first one. Which is the first one? You might have to guess, so hope they are marked as *Serial 1* and *Serial 2* (or with the alias names *Com1* and *Com2*). Some serial ports have 25 holes and others have only 9. The smaller serial ports look similar to the 15-hole video connection; if a cable won't plug in easily, check to make sure you're plugging the correct plug into the correct connector. Rarely will a connector be difficult to plug in. If a plug won't easily go, don't force it. Double- and triple-check every pin and hole to make sure that the plug truly goes there. Before trying again, make sure you have the plug's correct side turned up.
Parallel port	One end of your printer's cable fits here. If the printer's cable does contain the correct pins, you possibly have a serial printer. If one end of the printer cable fits in your serial port, you'll have yet another device possibly vying for your serial port. If you have two parallel ports, plug your printer into the first one (the one labeled *LPT1*). If you bought two printers, such as a laser printer for reports and an ink jet printer for fun, plug your primary printer into the first printer port.

5

Connection	Description
Keyboard	The keyboard port looks a lot like a mouse port. Your PC, if it contains a non-serial mouse port (called a *bus* or *PS/2 port*), will contain a marking that lets you know which round port is for the keyboard and which is for the mouse.
Mouse	If you have a PS/2 mouse cable, plug your mouse into the mouse port. Otherwise, plug the mouse into the first serial port.
Expansion slots	Often you'll plug your monitor's cable into a video card located in one of the expansion slots. If one or more of the expansion slots contains a shiny covering over the slot, that slot is probably free for later expansion if you want to drop another board (such as a PC/TV board) into the PC. In addition, if one of the expansion slots contains an internal modem, you'll see a *Phone* and a *Line* plug for your telephone and wall line, respectively. An extra phone cord that you'll need will be in the unpacked cabling or modem manual. When you plug your wall jack's phone line into the *Line* connection and your phone into the *Phone* connection, you'll be able to use your phone as you always have, but your PC will be able to call out and answer as well if you use the PC as an answering or dial-out PC for online services and faxing. Keep that phone away from disks! The magnets in the phone can erase disk information.
Sound card	The sound card, like the video card and internal modem, will reside in one of your PC's expansion slots. You'll find at least three connection holes in the sound card that use the 1/8" stereo jacks. Plug your microphone into the *Mic* jack, your speakers into the *Speaker* jack (PC speakers usually contain a y-connection, so both plug into a single jack). The *Line In* jack is for running another sound source (such as a stereo) through your PC's sound card.
Power cord	The power cord connects the PC to the electrical power. Do not plug your PC into the wall until you've connected all the devices and plugged those devices into their power outlets, as described in the next section.

If you brought home a PC with uninstalled expansion cards, jump to Hour 15, "Why and When to Upgrade," for instructions.

Finish the Connections

Now that you've cabled everything, finish plugging the other ends of the cables into their respective devices, such as the printer and external modem. If you use a trackball instead of a mouse, you might have a left-hand or right-hand cable plug-in option on the side of the trackball.

After you've plugged in the peripherals, plug their power cords into the power strip. Often, printers and monitors have a separate power cord (one end is not permanently attached to the device), so you'll have to plug both ends of the power cord into the device and then into their proper electrical location (laser printers in the wall and the monitor in the power strip). Of course, if you use a power strip, you'll plug items into the strip before plugging the strip into the wall.

JUST A MINUTE

You'll find out that many devices, such as external modems and many ink jet printers, use power supply bricks that plug directly into the outlet. Rarely can you fit two or more of these plugs next to each other into the same power strip. Don't the peripheral makers ever use their own devices in the real world? Try to juggle the plugs until you get them all plugged in at once. You might have to find a second outlet close to your PC, but a general rule of thumb is that you'll never have one close enough.

The printer often has its own complicated setup. Each printer differs, so you'll unfortunately need to read the manual. Most of the time the manufacturer will give you a cardboard layout with fast track instructions that let you set up the printer without wading through the manual. Sadly, you can damage a printer's internal parts very easily if you aren't careful to do exactly what the setup instructions tell you to do.

Loading toner or an ink jet cartridge can be tricky, so expect to take your time. If the paper-loading instructions show lots of pictures, you'll be better off. This book cannot help much more than this because almost every printer model has its own unique setup problems—have patience.

TIME SAVER

Before loading your printer's paper holder with paper, fan the corner of the paper once or twice. (Don't fan the paper enough to bend the edges, though.) Fanning will help the printer's paper retriever grasp individual sheets during printing.

5

CAUTION

Always keep disks and tapes off the top of your monitor. If the giant magnet inside doesn't erase the disks, the heat will melt them!

How Do Things Look?

Make a quick check of all the peripherals and cables. Any unplugged cables? Is your keyboard in a comfortable place? You're almost ready for the next test. After you complete the summary that comes next, turn to Hour 6, "Starting Your PC," and turn on your PC.

Summary

This hour shows you how to get your PC out of its box and onto your desk. The first time you set up a PC, the cables and boxes get very confusing. The industry is taking too long to realize that labeling and color-coding all the cables and connectors benefits the buyer! Some PC manufacturers label the connections well but many still do not, so you must be careful where and when to plug things in.

If you read every word of every manual before you set up your PC, you'll be more confused than helped. Most system units and monitors come with quick-start cards that, along with this lesson, will get you going in no time.

The next hour walks you through a typical PC's startup. Turning on the PC is simple, but troubleshooting problems and knowing how to proceed are acts that can turn into messes.

Q&A

Q What if I don't have much room for my new PC?

A Room for air circulation is critical because heat builds up quickly in some PCs and in almost every monitor. As long as your PC has space for air circulation, and as long as you've kept the air vents clear, your primary concern should be your own comfort as you work at the PC.

Q What does *ergonomic* mean?

A Ergonomics is the study of people (the scientists call them *humans*!) interacting with machines. If you read that a chair or keyboard is *ergonomically correct*, it means that some people like that particular chair's or keyboard's style more than others. Not to belittle ergonomics, because many people have benefited from the manufacturing of ergonomically correct hardware and furniture, you must know that manufacturers often seem to use that term just a little too loosely.

5

Q How do I obtain a cable I seem to be missing?

A Before going back to the store, check all the packing. The manufacturers put cables in some of the strangest-looking packs that seem just like trash when you unpack the PC. Remember that printers don't often come with cables, so if you're missing a printer cable, your salesperson forgot to sell you one. If you're missing another kind of cable, you can call the mail-order dealer or return to the store and convince them that the cable's not in the box where it should be.

Almost all PC vendors sell a complete line of cables. If you don't want to mess with talking the salesperson out of a cable, you can often buy exactly what you need for just a few bucks.

Hour 6

Starting Your PC

You've plugged in everything and you're ready to tour your PC. Great! The fun now begins.

This lesson teaches you how to turn your computer on and off. PCs are finicky devices sometimes and, unlike lamps, they require more effort than a simple on-and-off switch. Today's PCs are fairly reliable. If something's wrong when you first turn on your PC, you probably have something plugged in wrong. If everything checks out physically and the PC still doesn't work, you might have a bad system. This lesson helps you troubleshoot problems and get going.

The highlights of this hour include

- [ ] What common myth blames computers for people problems
- [ ] How to turn your PC on and off
- [ ] How to set your PC's time and date
- [ ] Which Windows tasks all newcomers need to master
- [ ] How to manage program windows
- [ ] When to shut down your PC
- [ ] How to format diskettes

Computer Errors

Computers don't make mistakes. Read that again. One of the all-time biggest, top-10 lies in the world is "the computer made a mistake." Given the circuitry, a computer simply doesn't make mistakes. At least, computers don't make the kind of mistakes for which people often blame them. When a computer has a problem, you (and everybody else) know about it. The hard drive *crashes* (if you've ever heard one break down, you'd know why they use the term *crash*), the printer garbles paper, the modem lights refuse to come on, or sparks fly out of the monitor (that probably only happens when someone gets *really* angry with the PC and strikes the monitor's on/off switch just a little too hard with that ax). In other words, when a computer has a problem it usually has a big problem.

That's good news. Nobody wants a broken computer, but when a computer has trouble you *want* to know about it.

Consider the incorrect bank balances and telephone-bill discrepancies that are often blamed on a computer. Because of a computer's internal digital circuitry, the computer just *will not* deduct a few dollars from an account here and there once in a while. A computer *will not* mail someone whose last name begins with an *S* a $10,000,000 phone bill just for the heck of it. Those problems can occur, but it's because the people who entered the data or who programmed the computer made a mistake; the computer was just following orders even though those orders might have been wrong.

Remember this accurate review of computer errors as you learn to use your PC. No offense is intended here, but if the PC seems to be making a mistake, it's almost always your fault or the fault of the program currently running. Not that fault is an issue, but if you remember that you're *probably* doing something wrong, you then are more likely to analyze what you're doing and try a different path. It's the people who say, "My computer won't give me the correct answer!" who never seem to have working computers.

Powering On

In the olden days (about 5 years ago), PC users had to turn on all the peripherals before the system unit. When the user wanted to quit computing, the system unit would have to go off first. History buffs will appreciate the saying that helped everybody remember the correct power-up sequence: "The boss always comes to work last and goes home first."

Without this order, the system unit might not get in synch with a peripheral device in time because the system unit might have looked for the device before you turned on the device. In addition, fewer people used surge protectors, so the printer's power surge might drain the system unit enough to shut it down or erase whatever was in memory at the time.

Fortunately, you don't have to remember such power-up sequences and platitudes these days because the power is fairly steady among PC components, and most people's surge protectors handle peripheral power-up tasks without a problem. In a few cases, some computers don't recognize peripheral devices if you turn them on after you turn on the system unit. You'll be the first to know if this happens to you. If so, use a power strip to turn on everything at once or make a habit of turning on the peripherals (you don't need to turn on the printer until you are ready to use it) first.

TIME SAVER

A good reason exists to turn on your monitor before the system unit, but it has nothing to do with power surges. The system unit prints all kinds of strange messages during the system's startup stages (a PC can take as long as three minutes to settle down and get ready for you after you turn it on). If a problem occurs, you'll probably see the cause or get a good clue from the messages that appear on the monitor.

Turn on your monitor, system unit, external devices such as an external modem or tape drive, and printer. Although you might not plan to use all these devices right away, you should test them the first time you power up. In addition, Windows will look for these devices and set up as many devices as possible automatically if you have them turned on the first time you start the PC.

When you first turn on the system unit, you'll see text on your screen like that shown in Figure 6.1. This is all technical jargon that appears, and you can almost always ignore it completely. Noises will occur while the PC revs things up and, unless something begins to grind louder than a transistor radio at medium volume, you can ignore the sounds. The noises are part of the PC's normal self-test.

If you hear a single beep during the startup process, that's generally good. The original IBM-PC beeped once if the PC's self-test worked flawlessly and beeped more than once if a self-test failed. PC manufacturers followed that single-beep standard for years afterward.

Here's the problem: Some young bright-eyed marketing guru in one of the modern PC companies got the idea that he would change things so that a single beep meant an *error* occurred during the self-test and multiple beeps meant that things were dandy! A handful of other companies followed so that nobody exactly knows what a single beep means anymore. If you hear a single beep (as you'll *probably* hear) and the PC seems to power-up just fine, you're okay, and a single beep means the self-test worked on your PC. If you see a message telling you to press the F1 key (the first function key across the top of your keyboard), you have a problem.

6

Figure 6.1.

System startup messages are extremely cryptic.

Eventually, if no self-test errors occurred, you'll see one of the following kinds of screens:

☐ A Windows 95 screen that looks something like the one in Figure 6.2. Many of the called-out items should appear on your screen; this lesson describes what those items are all about.

☐ A *menu* (a list of choices available to you) asking what you want to do next.

☐ An error that reads like this:

```
Invalid system disk
Replace the disk, and then press any key
```

The error means that you or someone else has accidentally left a disk in the A drive. Push the eject button to eject the disk and then press any key on the keyboard to restart the PC. If no disk appears in drive A, you have a more major problem because your hard disk either has no operating system or the disk has a problem; you'll need to contact your dealer.

CAUTION

Your Windows 95 screen may not look *anything* like Figure 6.2's screen, but that's okay. Often, new PCs contain a Windows background image (called the Windows *wallpaper*) that displays the PC brand's logo or another wallpaper background image than the one this figure shows.

If Windows appears, skip to the Windows overview section, "Windows Fast Track," later in this hour.

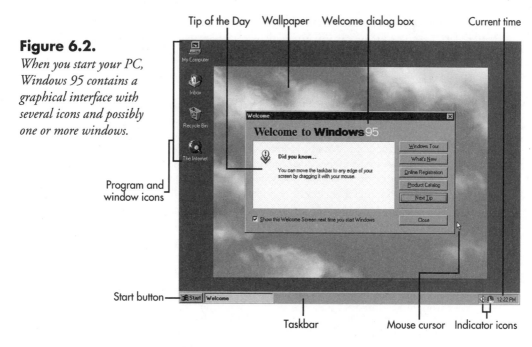

Tip of the Day   Wallpaper   Welcome dialog box   Current time

Figure 6.2.

When you start your PC, Windows 95 contains a graphical interface with several icons and possibly one or more windows.

Program and
window icons

Start button

Taskbar   Mouse cursor   Indicator icons

Window's Initial Setup

Often, today's PC manufacturers do not install Windows, but they install the setup's trigger so that Windows and the bundled programs begin installing from compacted files when you turn on the PC for the first time. The manufacturer can store compressed setup files onto your new hard disk faster than installing all the software. The bottom line for you is that you might have to wait for Windows and the other bundled software to install before you can do any work on your PC.

You'll rarely have to interact with the setup. The setup is designed to begin upon the first power-up sequence and will not repeat itself again. The setup will detect and install all included hardware and will usually detect any extra hardware you purchased with your PC, especially if that hardware is Plug-and-Play compatible (see Hour 5, "Setting Up Your New PC").

Toward the end of the setup, you'll be asked a few simple questions. If you don't know the answers, the questions often contain default answers that you can accept without changing anything. The default answers suffice in most cases. (If you discover later that the default values were not the best choices, you can override that selection at that time.) Press Enter when you are presented with a question or window to accept the default value. If the setup requests your name and organization, type your name in the Name area (called a *field*); then press Tab (to move to the Organization field) and type your company name or just press Enter to leave the Organization field blank. If setup ever requests a password, leave it blank for now.

Often a password-enter window asks that you type your password twice to ensure that you entered it correctly, but you can leave it blank twice, which tells Windows that you don't want to use a password right now.

JUST A MINUTE

The setup might want to print a test page to make sure the printer is installed properly. When the setup routine gets to the printer test, make sure your printer has paper, is turned on, and has its *OnLine* (or Ready) light glowing. When a printer is online, it can receive information to print, but when it's offline, the printer ignores the PC so you can change paper forms or do something else with the printer without worry that data will begin printing while you're in the middle of a change.

Watch for a time-and-day window that often appears (see Figure 6.3). Your PC has a battery-backed-up clock and calendar, and you'll need to set the date and time as well as select the proper time zone in which you live. If you really don't understand Windows or how to use a mouse because you've never touched a PC before in your life, the following guidelines can get you through the time-and-date setup:

1. If you don't want to mess with the day and time, or if the day and time look correct already, press the Enter key on the keyboard to get rid of the time-and-date window.

2. To change the date, press the Alt key and, while still holding Alt, press the D key. (The rest of this book will refer to this kind of Alt- and Ctrl-based keystroke as Alt+D, or Ctrl+D if the Ctrl key is required in place of Alt.) Press the down- or up-arrow key to move forward or backward in the month listed until the current month appears. After you master the mouse, you'll be able to adjust the day and time with it.

3. Press the Tab key to highlight the year. Press the up or down arrows to scroll through the years until you select the current year.

4. Press Tab and then the left- or right-arrow keys to select the current day.

5. Keep alternating with the Tab key and up/down arrow combinations four more times until you've set the time.

6. When all the values are correct (you can repeat the process if you made a mistake by returning to step 2), press Ctrl+Tab to display Figure 6.4's Daylight Savings Time window. Cool, right?

7. Press the up- or down-arrow keys until you've selected your time zone.

8. Press Enter after you've set the time zone to let Windows know that the date and time are correct and that you're ready to continue the setup. The setup will continue.

6

Figure 6.3.
Set your PC's date and time when you set up the PC.

Figure 6.4.
Select the proper Daylight Savings Time setting so your PC can automatically adjust your clock twice a year if needed.

JUST A MINUTE

It's common for setup routines to restart your PC one or more times during the setup.

TIME SAVER

Double-click the clock on your taskbar at the bottom of the screen to display the time-and-date window any time you want to change the settings.

Windows Fast Track

You can't get an introduction to Windows in just a few pages. Nevertheless, you seem to have a *can-do attitude* so we'll give it a try. If this discussion piques your interest, you might want to check out a Sams publication titled *Teach Yourself Windows 95 in 24 Hours*.

Using the Mouse

The mouse is as important as your keyboard when you work within Windows. Table 6.1 explains the mouse operations you'll use within Windows. As you move the mouse, the mouse cursor moves on the screen to show where you're pointing. (The mouse cursor will change from its default white pointing-arrow shape depending on what your PC is doing.)

Table 6.1. Master these mouse operations.

Operation	Description
Move	Move your mouse around your desk to see the mouse cursor move on the screen.
Click	Click the left mouse button to select screen objects or to move the text cursor.
Double-click	Click the left mouse button twice in succession (you'll get the hang of it) to select certain actions.
Drag	Click and hold down the mouse button over a screen object and move the mouse to move the object across the screen.
Drop	Release the held mouse button to stop moving a dragged object.
Right-click	Click the right mouse button. Often a right-click produces a small pop-up menu from which you can select commands that apply to a given situation.

JUST A MINUTE

A second cursor, called a *text cursor* (or *caret*), appears when a program needs text from you. As you type on the keyboard, the text cursor moves ahead, showing where your *next* typed character will appear. You can often move the text cursor to a different place by using your arrow keys, Tab, or Shift+Tab, or by clicking in another text-entry screen area with your mouse.

The Welcome to Windows Window

If you see Figure 6.2's window when you start your PC, you'll notice that the window contains a Tip of the Day that displays a different tip every time you start Windows. To get rid of today's tip and clear the tip window from the Windows desktop area, click the Close button. If a window has a Close button, that button will close the window and stop whatever program is running in that window.

When you first begin learning Windows the tips are great, but they can start to get in your way after you learn Windows and no longer need the tips displaying every time you start the program. If you click the checkmark to the left of the caption that reads Show this Welcome

6

Screen next time you start Windows, the checkmark goes away; thereafter, the window won't reappear when you start Windows.

A Whirlwind Windows Tour

The Start button on the taskbar is where you typically begin your work in Windows. When you click Start, a menu pops up out of the Start button called the *Start menu*. Most newer keyboards have a key with the Windows logo on it that you can press to display the Start menu. When a Windows menu appears, you can select a choice from the menu by pressing the up- and down-arrow keys to move the selection highlight from choice to choice or by clicking with your mouse.

TIME SAVER

Drag the taskbar to another edge of your screen (including the top edge) if you want the taskbar to appear elsewhere.

If a Start menu item displays a small arrow at the right of its option, as Programs does, that option produces yet another menu of options. The Programs option gives you access to all the programs on your PC. If you select one of these program group options, you'll view yet another menu. As Figure 6.5 shows, these *cascading menus*, as they're sometimes called, can consume a lot of screen space! Fortunately, when you finally select a program (as opposed to yet another cascaded menu group), the program begins, the Start menu goes away, and the next time you view the Windows desktop, the screen will be free from clutter except for the standard icons and any program windows you have started.

Figure 6.5.

If you have a lot of programs, you'll have a lot of Start menu program choices.

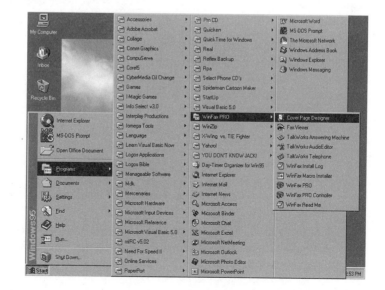

JUST A MINUTE

> As you master Windows, you'll be able to create your own program groups and add menu items to the Start menu.

As you use Windows over time, icons will begin to appear on your desktop in addition to those already there such as the My Computer and Recycle Bin icons. These icons often represent programs; you can quickly start these programs by double-clicking their icon. The icons, although they can clutter your Windows desktop, give you quicker access to the program than wading through the cascading Start menu. As you learn more about Windows, you'll find ways to set up such program icons so that you can start your more useful programs quickly.

Practice now by starting a handy program that comes with Windows. Follow these steps to run the Windows Paint program:

1. Click the Start button.
2. Select Programs. The Programs menu group appears.
3. Select Accessories.
4. Select Paint. You'll know that Paint is a program and not another menu group because the menu choice does not use a folder icon and does not display an arrow out to the right of the name. Figure 6.6 shows the window that appears.

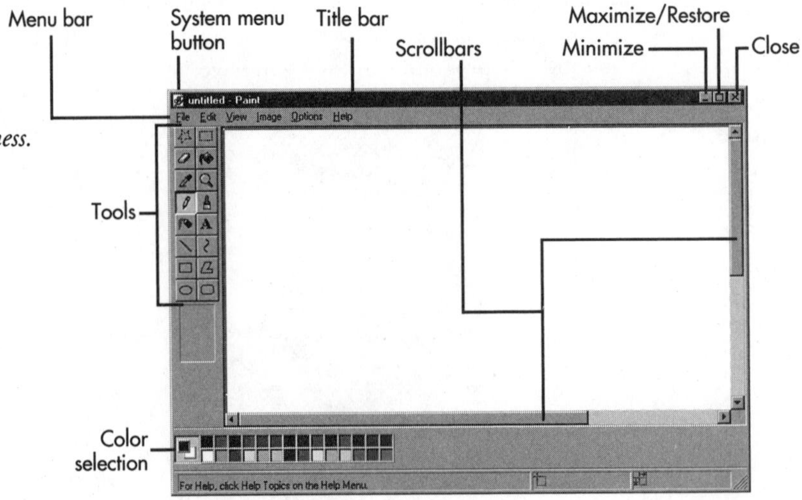
Menu bar
System menu button
Title bar
Maximize/Restore
Scrollbars
Minimize
Close
Tools
Color selection
untitled - Paint
File Edit View Image Options Help
For Help, click Help Topics on the Help Menu.

Figure 6.6.
Paint without the mess.

Paint lets you draw pictures by using tools for lines, boxes, free-form shapes, and color selection. Click on the pencil tool in the Tools area and then drag your mouse around the screen to watch the lines appear. Click on a color and draw again. Click on the circle tool and drag your mouse around to see circles appear.

Almost all Windows programs contain a menu bar like the one across the top of Paint. To select an option from a menu bar, click on that option. For example, if you click on the File option, a list of file-related commands drop down from which you can select with a mouse click or with the up- and down-arrow keys. For example, if you want to save your drawing, select File and then Save (noted hereafter as File | Save) and type a filename in the File Save window (called a *dialog box*) that appears. If you later start Paint and want to make changes to a saved drawing, select File | Open and locate the file in the dialog box that you want to edit.

The Esc key always lets you back out of a menu you've selected.

TIME SAVER

Your hands don't have to leave the keyboard to select from a menu. The underlined letter in the menu option gives you the clue. If you press Alt+F (F is the underlined letter in the File option), the menu drops down as if you'd clicked the File option itself.

Paint is fun to work with, and you can learn a lot about Windows from the Paint window. Click the System menu button (in the window's upper-left corner) to see a list of choices. Almost all windows contain a System menu. From that menu you can close the program or move and resize the program window. As always, Esc gets rid of the System menu.

Click Paint's Minimize button (refer to Figure 6.6 for its location), and Paint seems to go away. If, however, you look at the taskbar, you'll see the Paint entry (along with your drawing's filename or untitled if you've yet to save the drawing area). The taskbar always holds a button for the Start menu as well as for every running program you open. If you ran a second program, such as the Calculator program (via Start | Programs | Accessories | Calculator), both Paint and Calculator would have a button on the taskbar. When you run multiple programs at the same time, you can switch back and forth between them, activating their windows as needed, by clicking the taskbar button to select that program window just as you'd change a television channel to watch a different program. (Alt+Tab also switches between running programs.)

Paint's Maximize window enlarges the program window to your entire screen. You can also maximize a program's window by double-clicking on its title bar. If the program is already maximized (as some are when you first run them), the Maximize button turns into a Restore button that you can click to shrink the window to a smaller area.

JUST A MINUTE

Most windows contain a System menu and the window-resizing and Close buttons. The great thing about Windows is that after you learn one program, you know a lot about other programs' interfaces.

6

If Paint is maximized now, click the Restore button to shrink the window. Drag the title bar around the screen, and Paint's window goes with it. Move the mouse to any of Paint's window corners, and the mouse cursor changes into a double-pointing arrow. You can resize the window with your mouse when you point and drag a corner or edge in or out. Drag the corner into the center of the screen to see Paint's window get smaller. Drag the corner (or an edge) outward to see the window grow larger.

Click the Close window button to exit the program. Most Windows programs are good about letting you know you haven't saved your work if you forget to save. For now, click No if Paint asks if you want to save your drawing's changes, and you will be returned to the Windows desktop.

In most Windows programs you can often perform the same action by using different means. For example, you can quit almost every running Windows program in one of three ways:

☐ Click the Close window button.

☐ Click the System menu and select Close.

☐ Select File | Exit from the menu bar.

All the window-resizing and moving operations are available from most programs. Some programs might contain multiple windows; the window-control features you now know will come in handy as you rearrange and manage the windows you want to view.

Help Is There

Windows offers help if you get stuck. Almost every Windows program contains a Help menu option you can click to get help on the program. The help dialog box that appears, such as the one in Figure 6.7, offers a library of resources (clicking on any of the book icons next to a topic opens that "book" and lists its contents, from which you can select the information you need). You can often get help by pressing F1 from any program because most programs reserve the F1 key for the help-generation command.

Figure 6.7.

*Request program help if
you need assistance.*

6

The Start menu also contains a Help option that you can select to get help on Windows itself. Use this help option if you want to know more about using the taskbar, starting programs, organizing folders, or managing your Windows desktop.

JUST A MINUTE

Help interfaces are getting more powerful all the time. Help windows loaded from the Internet, along with video- and audio-based help windows, are making inroads into many help window screens that now appear in newer programs.

One of the hallmark features of most help systems is the *hotspot* feature. A hotspot is a place on the help window that you can click on to get additional help on different topics. For example, many help windows put new terms in green, underlined text; move the mouse cursor over the underlined text and the mouse cursor will change to a pointing-hand shape, letting you know that you've found a hotspot. Click your mouse, and a small dialog box will pop up offering the definition of the term. Some hotspots take you to a different help window altogether; you can click on the help window's Back menu option to return from a hotspot path you might take as a detour.

Common Windows in Windows

The Windows desktop provides several standard icons you can double-click to open special windows and start system programs. Double-click on the My Computer icon and Figure 6.8's window appears, showing an icon for every storage device on your PC as well as a Printers folder that contains your printer information (the printer information appears in a folder in case you have multiple printers) and a special Control Panel icon that gives you access to all your system setup information.

Figure 6.8.

The My Computer window displays all your PC's storage devices as icons.

The My Computer window is not actually a program but a window that opens to give you access to system programs. Any time you open a window, the taskbar adds a new button for that window. Therefore, you can click any button on the taskbar to switch from a program you're running to that button's window.

Whereas the My Computer window gives you access to your hardware's setup, the *Explorer* program window gives you access to your files. Hour 3's lesson ("Software, Disks, and Files") introduced you to your PC's file system; Explorer is the tool that gives you powerful access to file management. (You can double-click a disk drive icon in your My Computer window to get access to your files and folders in a different way.

One of the fastest ways to start Explorer is to right-click the Start button and select Explorer. Figure 6.9 shows a typical Explorer window. Explorer's left-hand side shows your drive and folders, and the right-hand side shows more detail. For example, if you click a folder in the left-hand window, that folder's contents display in the right window so that you can see the files and folders located in your selected folder.

Figure 6.9.

Manage your files and folders from the Explorer window.

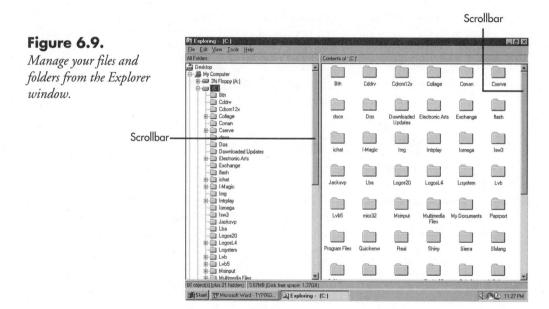

Explorer's left-hand section shows your PC's tree-structured folders in an organized fashion. As you open folders that contain subfolders (folders with a plus sign next to its icon contain folders as well as possibly files), the tree structure shows more detail. The indention helps show which folders belong to other folders, and also which folders are in the root folder of the disk drive.

Although you should familiarize yourself more with your PC before you do much with folders and files, shortly you'll be ready to use Explorer to move files and folders, delete and rename them, and copy one or more of them to a disk in your disk drive.

6

Not everything can fit on one screen as you use Windows. If Windows cannot display everything needed, you'll see *scrollbars* such as those shown in Figure 6.9. By dragging the bar up and down its column, you will move the screen's contents up and down, not unlike a video camera panning around a scene. You can click the arrow at either end of a scrollbar to move the screen's contents up or down one line at a time.

If you were to locate and double-click the Windows folder, several folders and files located within the Windows folder would appear in the right side's section. The icons next to each filename indicate the type of the file listed. For example, a notepad icon indicates the file is a text file. A flying *W* icon indicates the file is a Word document. Therefore, whether or not your Explorer is set up to display filename extensions (the Tools | Options menu choice lets you turn the display of extensions on and off), you'll still be able to glean an understanding of the file's use from its icon.

Ready for a Break?

This hour's lesson is almost up. Before you take a break or move to the next hour's lesson, you need to learn how to properly shut down your PC.

CAUTION Don't turn off your PC whenever you want to leave without properly shutting down Windows!

Before you turn off your PC, close all running program windows. Don't just minimize the windows, because another program with a minimized program window is still running—it's just hiding. After you close the programs, click the Start button and select Shut Down. Figure 6.10's window appears, asking if you want to completely shut down; restart the PC to its startup, freshly loaded Windows state; or restart in MS-DOS mode where you'll be taken out of Windows and returned to the textual MS-DOS operating system.

Figure 6.10.

The Shut Down Windows dialog box lets you select how to exit your Windows session.

6

If you select the first option (to shut down your PC), a message will appear after Windows takes care of some housekeeping that lets you know you can turn off the PC. Some of the newer PCs actually turn off on their own when you perform the shutdown operation.

If Things Ever Get Really Stuck...

If your PC completely hangs up and nothing seems to work, you might still have a chance to recover without turning off your PC. Press Ctrl+Alt+Del to perform a system *reboot* (a fancy term for reset). This is a difficult keystroke so that you do not accidentally press the combination during your regular work and lose all your data.

When you reboot, a window appears, showing a list of every program running. Although some will be system programs you don't recognize, if you see the program listed that you were last running and that hung things up, click that program's entry and then click the End Task button.

Sometimes Windows will close the offending program and return to Windows, and everything will be fine. If your system is still hung a minute or two after you press the End Task button, you'll have to press Ctrl+Alt+Del once again or press a reset button that sometimes appears on the front panel of your system unit to reset your computer to its startup state. Unfortunately, any data you've yet to save will be lost.

Summary

This hour got you going at the keyboard working through an introduction to Windows. Although this lesson's goal is to provide a *brief* tour, Windows makes it easy to learn a lot in a short time due to the graphical interface. Before graphical environments, users had to learn long lists of commands to make the PC perform its job. Now a quick click or two often does the trick.

The next hour takes you from the operating system to application programs. Part III of this book, "Software Drives the PC," explores many popular programs in use today. Before you get there, though, Hour 7, "Your PC's Software," explains how to install those programs and work with new software on your PC.

Q&A

Q How can I get used to this silly mouse?

A Play a game! No matter how much work you want to get done, take some time out and have some fun. Nothing teaches the mouse better than a game, especially the card game *Solitaire* that comes with Windows. Click the Windows Start button, and then select Programs | Games | Solitaire. The click, drag, and drop requirements in the game quickly make you a mouse pro.

After you master your mouse, double-click the time indicator at the right of the taskbar to see the clock setting window. Change the time and date settings solely with your mouse instead of with the keyboard as you did earlier in this lesson. Click the up- and down-arrow buttons throughout the window to adjust settings up and down and then click on a day in the calendar to select a new day. See how you can control almost every Windows program with only the mouse?

Q Will I hurt Windows if I look around?

A You won't hurt Windows' feelings, and you probably won't hurt any Windows file setup as long as you're careful. Certainly you should practice as much as you can. Start programs, look at the taskbar, change between two running programs, and adjust program window sizes for practice. Here's a good trick to know early: Learn to format disks for those times when you get an unformatted one or when you want to erase one completely.

Make sure you format a disk without critical data because formatting erases everything on it. Insert the disk in the drive (label up, silver end in first) and double-click the My Computer window to open the window. Right-click the disk drive icon and select Format from the pop-up menu that appears. Click OK and Windows formats the disk. When finished, you can eject the disk and format another one or close the formatting window. If you cannot find the My Computer window for all the other windows on your screen, right-click a blank spot on the taskbar and select Minimize All Windows from the pop-up menu. The windows will shrink down to the taskbar but will still be available for you to select them later.

6

Hour **7**

Your PC's Software

Now that you've become a PC hardware master, how about getting on the keyboard and really working! The best hardware is worthless without programs to drive that hardware. Over the life of your PC, you'll purchase and install numerous application programs to do the work you want done. Whether you use a PC for word processing, for accounting, for home finances, for games, or for reference, you need to understand how to install the software you obtain.

This lesson teaches you how to get purchased software onto your PC. Although de facto standards exist, not all software installs the same way. Therefore, you should know what to expect before you face the task required of all PC owners: software installation.

The highlights of this hour include

☐ How to insert and eject disks and CD-ROMs

☐ Why proper installation is critical

☐ How to use the Add/Remove Programs dialog box effectively

☐ Where to go when you need to add or remove a Windows option

☐ How to properly uninstall programs

☐ What to do when no adequate uninstall procedure exists

First Things First

Nearly every 6-year-old can insert disks and CD-ROMs into their drives. Of course, there's rarely a 6-year-old around when you need one! Therefore, if you've yet to work on a PC very much, you need to understand how to insert and eject disks and CD-ROMs into their drives without harming the *media* (the disks and CD-ROM), the drives, or yourself. (Seriously, you won't get hurt doing this!)

If you already know how to insert and eject disks and CDs, skip this section. Most of you probably will, but those of you totally new to a PC's operation will need this short lesson.

Figure 7.1 shows the proper way to insert a 3-1/2" disk (label side up). The silver cover over part of one end of the disk is the disk door that opens when you insert the disk into the drive. This silver door helps keep dust and smoke from the disk's internal platter and should be kept shut to protect the disk's internal platter from dust and fingerprints. Insert the disk all the way into the drive's slot until the drive's slot grabs the disk and you hear a click.

Figure 7.1.

Insert a disk like this.

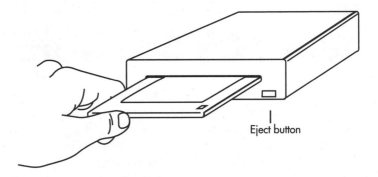

Eject button

In most disk drives, a button pops out toward you when you insert the disk all the way into the drive. When you want to eject the disk, push the eject button and the disk pops out toward you, disengaging itself from the drive.

CAUTION

Never eject a disk from a drive with the drive light still on—except in those rare instances when your PC hangs up during a disk operation and nothing happens except the disk's drive churning for a couple minutes or more.

Label your disks well so you know what's on them, but use a felt-tipped pen or write on the label before you stick the label onto the disk. You don't want to write with a ball-point pen

7

after you apply the label or you'll risk damaging the data. Most boxes of new disks come with ample labels.

Be Safe with Write-Protection

Although a magnet or physical abuse can damage a disk's data, you can help guard important data by sliding a disk's write-protect tab toward the edge of the disk, as Figure 7.2 demonstrates. A pen helps if your finger is too big to reach the small sliding write-protect tab.

When the write-protect tab is toward the disk's edge, no disk drive will write or change the disk's contents. You can issue the command for your PC to format the disk, but your PC will refuse to modify the disk (you'll get an error message). This is one of the few times your PC won't do exactly what you tell it to do! The drive is made to disengage the drive's write capabilities if the write-protect tab is set to its protected position.

If you finish with a protected disk or need to modify the data, slide the tab back toward the disk's center and you can once again write to or format the disk.

Figure 7.2.
Write-protection helps guard your disk's data.

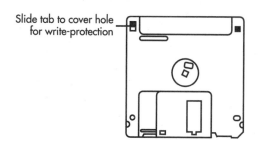

Slide tab to cover hole for write-protection

Sometimes a CD-ROM won't come out of its plastic protective case (called a *jewel case*) very easily. With your thumb, firmly press the center hub that holds the CD-ROM, and the CD-ROM will often come right out.

TIME SAVER

Some CD-ROMs come in a thin cardboard liner instead of a plastic jewel case. The jewel case better protects the CD-ROM. You can purchase jewel case 10-packs at any software store for those CD-ROMs without cases.

7

This section pertains to both CD-ROMs and audio CDs as well.

JUST A MINUTE

CD-ROMs don't insert exactly the same way as disks. Two kinds of CD-ROM mechanisms exist that let you insert CD-ROMs into the drives. Some older CD-ROM drives require that you place the CD-ROM in a *CD-ROM caddy*, a plastic box you insert into the CD-ROM drive. The CD-ROM caddy is *not* the same thing as the jewel case your CD-ROMs come in. A caddy comes with all caddy-based CD-ROM drives.

Follow these steps to insert a CD-ROM into a caddy-based drive:

1. Open the CD-ROM caddy. Often, two small tabs keep the plastic lid closed; by squeezing the two edges of the caddy, the plastic lid releases so that you can open the caddy.

2. Place your CD-ROM into the caddy with the label up.

3. Close the caddy door (see Figure 7.3).

4. Insert the CD-ROM caddy into the drive. Position it with the plastic case up and the silver caddy door (similar to a disk's door) pointing in toward the drive as you insert the caddy.

Figure 7.3.

Using a CD-ROM caddy.

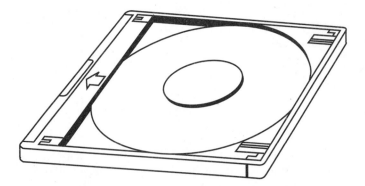

To eject a CD-ROM's caddy from the drive, you must press the eject button. When you finish with the CD-ROM, open the caddy (squeezing the two ends again to release the lid) and remove the CD-ROM so you can put it back in its jewel case.

If you have a PC built in the last two years, chances are that your drive does not require a caddy. You'll simply press a button to open the CD-ROM door, place the CD-ROM inside the CD-ROM door that opens (centered as well as possible with the label's side up), and press the button once again to close the door. Often you can push the CD-ROM's platter inward

7

to close the door, but use the button because your CD-ROM mechanism will last longer. To remove the CD-ROM when you're through with it, press the button to open the door and put the CD-ROM back in its protective jewel case.

CAUTION

Don't write on the label side of a CD-ROM with anything other than a very soft felt marker! A ball-point pen or pencil will scratch the thin silver coating and ruin the data side of the CD-ROM, rendering it useless except as a rear-view mirror's dangling light prism or coffee coaster.

Now that you know how to insert and eject disks and CD-ROMs, you're ready to install some software.

Why Install New Software?

By itself, Windows doesn't do work for you. Your application programs do your work. You use application programs to write documents, create graphics, explore the Internet, manage database files, and play games. Somehow you have to get application programs onto your PC.

Today's programs come on CD-ROMs (and, less commonly, on disks), and you must run those programs through an *installation routine* so that Windows properly recognizes the programs. Although every application program requires a unique, one-of-a-kind installation routine, you'll install most of today's programs the same way.

The Add/Remove Programs Icon

Before Windows, you could add a program to your computer simply by copying a file from the disk you purchased to your hard disk. To remove the program, you only had to delete the file. Things got messier starting with Windows, however, because Windows requires a lot from application programs. Those programs are no longer simple to add or remove, so you must familiarize yourself with the proper techniques.

CAUTION

If you don't follow the proper program-installation techniques, your application probably will not run correctly. Even worse, with the Windows integrated set of files, a program you add to your PC incorrectly might make other programs fail.

7

The Windows Control Panel contains an entry you'll frequently visit to manage the programs on your PC. You can display the Control Panel by selecting Settings | Control Panel from the

Start menu. The Control Panel contains several program icons you can select to modify the way Windows looks and acts. The installation icon is labeled Add/Remove Programs. When you open the icon, Figure 7.4's tabbed dialog box appears.

Figure 7.4.

You manage your installed programs from the Add/Remove Programs Properties dialog box.

The dialog box's top half contains an Install button you can click to install new software. Surprisingly, you'll rarely, if ever, use this button when installing Windows programs because most programs install somewhat automatically, as explained later in this hour. The lower half contains a list of application programs on your PC. The list is not exhaustive because not every program on your PC appears in it; it contains only those programs you can *uninstall* (or *deinstall*) from your system. If you uninstall using the Add/Remove Programs Properties dialog box, you can be assured that the application will completely go away. If you created data files, the uninstallation program should leave those on your disk.

Icons and Programs

Most icons on your Windows Start menu and desktop represent programs and windows that you open. The icons are often shortcuts to your applications. You can delete the icon without actually deleting the program if the icon represents a shortcut and not the program file itself.

If you delete a program's icon from your desktop by clicking on the icon and pressing the Delete key, the icon will go away but you will not properly remove the program from Windows. In most cases you will remove nothing about the program except the shortcut file that points to the actual program.

Sometimes an icon is not a shortcut pointer but represents the file itself, so if you delete the icon in that case, the file goes away as well. Nevertheless, Windows

7

programs most often span multiple files on your system. Some reside in the Windows folder and others in the application's folder; therefore, removing one of these files does not erase all the application from your disk. In some cases, those extra files can cause problems, and they always consume disk space you'd probably like to recapture.

Therefore, always perform a proper uninstallation when you want to remove a Windows program. This hour's final section discusses uninstallation procedures.

The Windows Setup Page

Click on the dialog box's Windows Setup tab to display Figure 7.5's dialog box. Unlike applications, you'll never remove Windows because you would be removing the operating system that controls your PC. (You wouldn't sit on the same tree branch you're sawing off, would you?) When you update to a new Windows version, the new version will remove Windows, but you have plenty of time to worry about that later. For now, the Windows Setup page lets you change Windows options.

Figure 7.5.

Change Windows settings from the Windows Setup dialog box.

Sometimes you'll rerun an application program's installation routine to change installation settings just as you change Windows settings from the Windows Setup page. Program installations are sometimes the only place where you can modify the program's installed options. When you need to change such programs, you will have to run the program's install procedure once again (perhaps by clicking Install on the Install/Uninstall page), but it won't really install a second time. Instead, the program will prompt you for changes you want to make to the installation.

7

TIME SAVER

If a program stops working properly, you might have to reinstall it completely. Although you can rerun the installation again in some cases, you are probably better off uninstalling the program first to remove all traces of it and then running the installation from scratch once again. Be sure to back up your data files before you do that so that you'll have them intact when you reinstall the program. Some uninstall programs remove all files—including data files associated with an application.

When you make a change to a Windows setting, that setting might not show itself until you restart Windows.

CAUTION

Make sure you know what you're doing before you make a change to Windows! The Windows setup is a fairly advanced procedure. If you read somewhere about a Windows accessory program that should be on your system but is not, such as a program called *System Monitor*, you'll need to change your Windows setup (as explained in the next section) to add that Windows accessory.

Modifying Your Windows Setup

The next few steps show you how to change Windows installation settings. Although the various Properties menu options you find throughout Windows let you change settings that affect Windows's performance, look, and operation, the Add/Remove Programs Properties dialog box's Windows Setup page lets you add or remove parts of Windows properly.

CAUTION

This task requires your Windows CD-ROM, so place it in your CD-ROM drive. If the Windows banner automatically appears, close the window. If your system did not come with a Windows CD-ROM, the Windows files will probably be on your hard disk, and the setup program will get its files there.

To change your Windows installation settings, perform these steps:

1. Open the Control Panel's Add/Remove Programs icon by double-clicking the icon.
2. Click the tab at the top of the dialog box labeled Windows Setup. The Components scrolling list box shows which groups of Windows options are currently installed. An empty checkmark option means that none of those options is installed

7

to run. A grayed-out checkmark means that some of the programs in the group are installed. A checkmark means that the entire group is installed. If you did not install Windows, or if you installed Windows by using all the default options, you might not be completely familiar with all the groups that appear.

The checked options indicate that every program in that group is installed. For example, rarely will all the Windows Accessories group be installed. You'll see a grayed-out checkmark there.

3. Click the title for Accessories (if you click the checkmark itself, you'll change the setting) and then click the Details button. You'll see a scrollable list of Accessories programs (these are the programs that appear when you select the Start menu's Programs|Accessories option) like the one shown in Figure 7.6.

Figure 7.6.

In this dialog box, you can see the Accessories options that are installed.

4. Scroll down to the entry titled System Monitor. Rarely will Windows users have this option checked. If you do, uncheck it to remove it from your Windows. (You can repeat this task later to put it back.) If your System Monitor is not installed, check it.

JUST A MINUTE

When you check or uncheck options, Windows will not completely reinstall; rather, Windows adds or removes the programs necessary to make the changes you request on the Windows Setup page. Whether you install or remove the System Monitor, you'll see the same procedure occur when you begin the update process in the next step.

5. Click OK to close the Details window.

6. At the Windows Setup page, click OK once again to start the Windows setup modification. A dialog box appears, telling you the status of the update. The update can take a while if you were to add or remove several Windows components.

7. Click the Close window button to close the Control Panel. (The upper-right corner of every window shows a small button with an X on it that closes the window (and any program running in the window). The next time you restart Windows, you'll see System Monitor on your Start menu's Programs|Accessories|System Tools menu.

System Monitor is called a *utility program* because it works in the background letting you analyze the performance of Windows itself. If your PC ever begins to act sluggish, run the System Monitor to see which Windows resources you need.

Installing Applications

Almost always, when you purchase a new application program to install on your PC, you'll insert its CD-ROM in the drive, close the drive door, and see an automatic message appear, such as the one in Figure 7.7.

Figure 7.7.

Windows like this indicate that an application program is about to install.

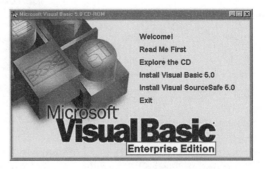

In most cases, such an application checks your PC to see whether the program is already installed. If it is not, the program gives you a prompt like the one in Figure 7.6. The software authors know that you would probably not be inserting the CD-ROM in the drive if you did not want to install the program.

JUST A MINUTE

If the program is already installed, the program begins executing (without the install prompt) after you close the CD-ROM drive door.

JUST A MINUTE

If you insert the CD-ROM and nothing happens, your CD-ROM's *AutoPlay* feature might be turned off so that Windows does not recognize that you've inserted a new CD-ROM. See Hour 9, "Multimedia on Your PC," for AutoPlay setup information.

7

If the CD-ROM does not start, or if you have AutoPlay turned off and want to leave it off, you can open the Start menu's Run menu and type `d:\Setup` to begin the installation. (Replace the `d:` with your CD-ROM's drive name.)

Just a Minute

> For disk installations, you will have to insert the first installation disk into the disk drive and type `a:\Setup` from the Start menu's Run command.

If you get an error message, issue Start | Run once again to make sure you've entered the drive, backslash, and Setup command properly. If you have, your program might require a different command. Replace *Setup* with *Install* to see what happens. If the Run command still fails, you must check the program owner's manual to locate the correct command.

Each application's setup is different; therefore, unless every reader had identical software to install, this book could not describe every scenario that occurs past the original installation window. Nevertheless, the following list provides guidelines that almost every installation follows:

- [ ] You can often read installation notes (often called a *Readme* file) by clicking the installation window's appropriate selection.

- [ ] Sometimes, multiple installation options are available. Check the manual, if one comes with the program, for the installation that suits you if you cannot determine the best options from the opening window. If an option says *Typical* or *Standard*, that option works best for most situations.

- [ ] After you start the installation, a *wizard* (windows that guide you, step-by-step through a process) usually guides you step-by-step through the installation.

- [ ] You can often accept all installation default answers if you're unsure whether or not to install an option during the wizard's performance. The wizard asks questions such as which disk drive and folder to which you want to install.

- [ ] If you don't have adequate disk space, the installation program will tell you. You'll have to remove other files, get a bigger disk space, reduce the installation options, or do without the program if you don't have the space for it.

- [ ] At the installation's end, you will probably have to restart Windows for all the installation options to go into effect. If asked if you want to restart Windows, you can answer No, but don't run the installed program until you do restart Windows.

Uninstallation Procedures

Most application programs written for Windows include a standard uninstallation routine that removes the application from Windows and from your PC. Remember that an

7

application program is often made of several files. The program's installation routine stores those files in several locations. Therefore, without an uninstallation routine, removing the application is a tedious task.

Before displaying the Control Panel's Add/Remove Programs window to uninstall a program, check the menu group in which the program resides. Sometimes, in a program's menu group, the installation routine sets up the uninstallation routine that you can run from that group. For example, if you installed a game called Side-to-Side, you might start the game by selecting from a series of menus that might look like this: Programs | Side Game | Play Side-to-Side. Look on the same menu and see if there's an uninstall option that you would select, such as Programs | Side Game | Uninstall Side-to-Side. When you begin the uninstallation process, a wizard begins and prompts you through the program's removal.

Without a menu option for the uninstall routine, you should look once again to the Control Panel's Add/Remove Programs dialog box. Open the dialog box and scroll through the list of items in the window's lower part to see if the program you want to remove appears in the list. If it does, select that entry and click the Add/Remove button to begin the uninstall wizard.

If no entry appears, you are running out of options! Insert the program's CD-ROM once again and see if the opening window contains an uninstall option. If it does not, look through the Readme file to see if you can get help. Also look in the program owner's manual. Lacking any uninstall routine at all, you can try one more place if you have Internet access: the Web. See if you can find the address for the company's Web page somewhere in the Readme or owner's manual. Lacking one, try going to this Web address: www.companyname.com and see if something comes up. (If you have no idea how to get on the Web, you'll learn how in Hour 21, "Enter the Internet.")

A Last Resort

If your search for an uninstall procedure comes up empty, you are forced to do one of two things:

- [ ] Leave the program on your system if you have ample disk space
- [ ] Manually remove as much of the program as you can

That last option can get messy. You'll need to wait until you master Windows fully before you begin to tackle such a task.

TIME SAVER

Several software companies offer uninstallation utility programs you can purchase that attempt to remove all traces of unwanted programs from your disk. If you purchase such a program, the program should be able to

7

remove most programs known about before the uninstall product was
released. As new programs appear on the market, these software
companies update their uninstallation utility programs, so upgrade the
utility to ensure that you've got the latest when you need it. (Often you can
download updates from the company's Web site.)

Summary

This hour starts easy and ends up guru-level! You first learned how to insert and eject disks
and CD-ROMs in your drives. New software that you purchase will come on disks or (more
likely) a CD-ROM. Obviously you'll need to insert the CD-ROM or disk before you can
install the software onto your PC.

As you learned in this hour, software installation and uninstallation can get tricky. Much of
the time there's no getting around the fact that installation is not always simple. Newcomers
have a tough time because one of the first tasks they need to perform after they purchase a
new PC is install software, yet software installation sometimes requires some advanced skills!
You have to get through the installation to use the software. Fortunately, more and more
software companies are making installations as hands-off as possible, so software installation
should get easier as companies make smarter install routines.

The next hour lets you work on the PC with software that's already there.

Q&A

**Q Why don't I ever use the Add/Remove Programs dialog box's Install button to
install programs?**

A Nobody seems to have a good answer for that! It seems as though software companies don't want to access this already-supplied installation resource. If they did, all
program installations would basically require the same steps—and, one would
think, users would be happier. Nevertheless, the companies seem to prefer that the
installation routine begin automatically when users insert the CD-ROM.

The drawback to this approach is that many times such an installation will not
work as expected. If this happens, either the AutoPlay feature is turned off or the
user bought the program on disks. (No disk drive supports AutoPlay.)

7

Q Should I turn on AutoPlay so my CDs install automatically?

A As you learned in this hour, even those users with AutoPlay turned on don't always see a proper installation. If your AutoPlay is turned off, keep in mind that several Windows users prefer to turn off AutoPlay. These users can insert a CD-ROM at any time without having to wait for a startup or installation window to appear. When they want to see the window or start the program that requires the CD-ROM, they can do so from the Start menu.

PART

III

Software Drives the PC

Hour

Hour 8

Creating with Your PC

Ready to do some work on your PC? If so, this hour takes you on a whirlwind tour through some of the most popular applications in use today. You'll learn a little about a lot! This lesson quickly demonstrates software that you'll use over the life of your PC.

At the end of this hour you'll better understand the software you see when you peruse the aisles at the PC store. An hour's session gives you only a glimpse, so perhaps it's best to get started without further ado.

The highlights of this hour include

- ☐ Why a word processor makes writing easier
- ☐ What formatting capabilities a word processor contains
- ☐ Why a word processor will not eliminate proofreading or editing
- ☐ How an electronic spreadsheet program works with numbers as easily as a word processor works with text
- ☐ Why to use a presentation program
- ☐ How a database offers information when you need it

Word Crafting

The most common PC program in use today is a word processor. In just a few years, the word processor replaced electric typewriters in virtually every office in the world. Word processors let you write and edit as much as you like, and every printed copy is an original.

Perhaps the most important thing to remember about word processors is that they handle line spacing for you depending on the margins currently in use. You can keep typing at the end of a line; the word processor moves down to the next line when needed. You press Enter only when you want to end a paragraph or complete a line of text that stands alone.

Figure 8.1 shows Microsoft Word, the most popular word processor currently in use, in action. As you can see, with a word processor, you can make documents look good. By selecting from the menus and tools at the top of the screen you can change *fonts* (the style of characters), *styles* (underlines, boldfacing, and italics), spacing, columns, tab stops, margins, headings, footers, automatic page numbers, and too many more features to mention. In addition, the word processor can check your spelling, correct your grammar, and provide a synonym when you request one.

Figure 8.1.

Write with word-processed style.

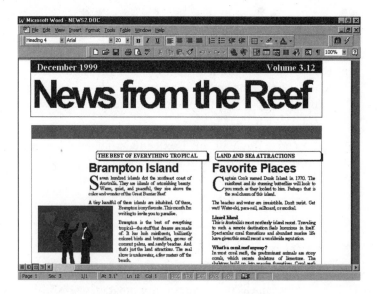

Word processors make writing much easier. Your rough drafts become your final drafts through editing. Unlike using white-out solutions or manual cut-and-paste operations, your final document shows nothing but the finished work. You edit as you compose.

8

CAUTION

Although word processors help you write, they will not make you a better writer. Bad writing doesn't get better just because it *looks* better!

A word processor comes in handy when you want to organize your writing. With a *page preview* feature, you can see on your screen the final printed output before you actually print. Figure 8.2 shows such a preview. If you want to adjust margins or change the font size, you'll know what to do by looking at the preview screen instead of wasting costly paper.

Figure 8.2.

You can preview your document before you print it.

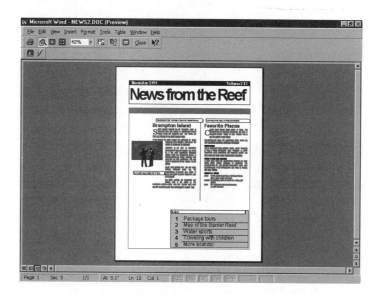

Page preview does more than save paper. You can rearrange pages and lay out your entire manuscript by previewing multiple pages at once, as shown in Figure 8.3. You can drag pages to and from locations to change your publication's order.

JUST A MINUTE

The small previews are called *thumbnail sketches*. The thumbnail sketches let you work with your document's big picture so that you can adjust page order and see the overall pattern of pages and where page breaks will occur.

Figure 8.3.

View all your publication's thumbnail sketches.

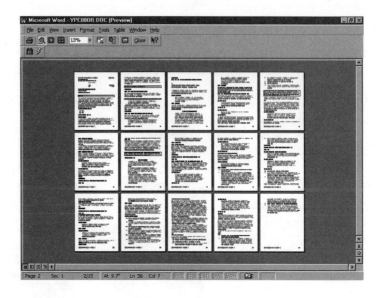

Word processors such as Microsoft Word 97 check your spelling and grammar as you create your document. Some users prefer to save the spelling and grammar check until they write the entire document, and you can set up Word to check things later if you prefer. Word processors such as Word do not just tell you that you've made a mistake; they also offer suggested corrections from which you can select.

You'll work a lot with the spelling and grammar dictionaries that your word processor uses. As you write, you'll customize the dictionaries so that the word processor responds to your writing style. If you write technical documents with words that don't appear in the spelling dictionary, you can add the new words so the word processor will not bother you with that correction again.

CAUTION

A spelling checker does not ensure that your document is spelled perfectly! Consider the following sentence:

Eye went too the zoo two sea the hairs.

No spelling checker will say a misspelling occurred in this sentence! The grammar checker will probably find something wrong, yet today's grammar checkers are powerful but imperfect. You still have to proofread your documents. The built-in tools help you locate problems faster, but they do not eliminate them or even locate all problems every time.

8

8

One of the neatest features that you can find in today's software is the *AutoComplete* feature. Most of Microsoft's newest products contain AutoComplete, and other products are now supporting the feature as well. When you begin typing a word, a command, a sentence, or even an Internet location where you've been before, you only need to type the first few letters and the software finishes the name for you. This kind of *artificial intelligence* feature is improving the speed with which PC users can compose. If the PC guesses correctly and completes your word, phrase, or sentence, you can press Enter to accept the completion. If the PC guesses incorrectly and does not complete your typing with the proper text, just keep typing and the replacement goes away.

Perhaps the biggest advantage that today's word processors provide is their *WYSIWYG* abilities. WYSIWYG, pronounced *wiz-zee-wig*, stands for *What-you-see-is-what-you-get*. Your document appears on the screen formatted close to the way it looks when you print the document. Although you must use a page preview mode to see an entire page (or multiple pages) at once, when you can adjust margins, type styles, embed pictures, and underline as you create, you'll achieve the finished product more quickly and get home from work earlier.

TIME SAVER

Windows comes with a simple word processor with which you can practice: *WordPad*. WordPad supports many introductory word processor features such as special type styles, margins, and tabs, and also allows you to combine text and pictures.

Spreadsheets: Word Processors for Numbers

You'll find word processors on almost every PC. Almost as many *electronic spreadsheets* (often called *electronic worksheets*) are sold as word processors. Spreadsheets do for numbers what word processors do for text: They let you create and customize financial information so you can present that information professionally.

Figure 8.4 shows a sample electronic spreadsheet screen from a popular program called *Microsoft Excel*. As you can see, Excel lets you combine text and numbers to produce the spreadsheet. The text and numbers appear in *cells*. The cells are labeled with letters across the top of the columns and numbers down the side of the rows. The intersection of each column and row forms the cell's address. For example, in Figure 8.4, the cell with the address H8 is selected and contains a total interest earned out of $7,700. The corresponding row number and column name buttons depress to show the selected cell.

Figure 8.4.

*Lay out text and
numbers with an
electronic spreadsheet.*

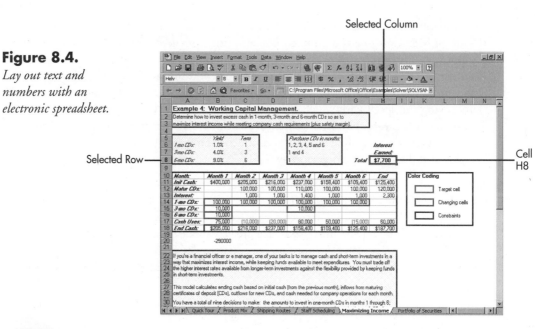

Selected Column

Selected Row

Cell
H8

JUST A MINUTE

As you can see, each spreadsheet cell has its own unique address.

Getting around the spreadsheet screen is simple. You'll traverse the spreadsheet with your mouse (click a cell to move the text cursor there) or use your keyboard's arrow and Tab keys to move from cell to cell. To enter values into a cell, just highlight the cell and type the value.

You can rearrange the spreadsheet data by moving or copying cells from one place to another. In addition, you can adjust the width and height of a cell. A cell can contain text, numbers, dates, percentages, dollar amounts, and formulas.

A spreadsheet recalculates all its formulas every time you change the spreadsheet. For example, if you created a spreadsheet to compute net payroll, you could use that same spreadsheet for all your employees. You only need to change each employee's pay rate and number of hours worked. The bottom line—that is, the pay amount cell—displays the proper amount depending on which employee's rate information you enter.

When you want to enter a formula, you'll enter both cell addresses as well as numbers and *mathematical operators*. A mathematical operator can be a +, a -, an * for multiplication, a / for division, parentheses, or a combination of several operators.

8

As a simple example, consider how you might use a spreadsheet to calculate an employee's pay if you know the employee's hours worked and pay rate. You could place both figures in spreadsheet cells and then enter a formula to produce the resulting pay. Suppose that you type the employee's number of hours worked into cell G3 and the pay rate per hour into cell G4. The following formula computes the total pay:

```
=(G3 * G4)
```

JUST A MINUTE

The equal sign tells Excel that the cell's contents are a formula. When a formula appears in a cell, Excel does not display the formula; instead, Excel displays the formula's *answer*.

Every time you change the amount in G3 or the amount in G4, the product of the two cells that appears in cell G6 changes also. Figure 8.5 shows a simple spreadsheet to illustrate this application.

Figure 8.5.

Your formulas change every time you change any cell's value included in that formula.

Cell G6 shows total pay ——

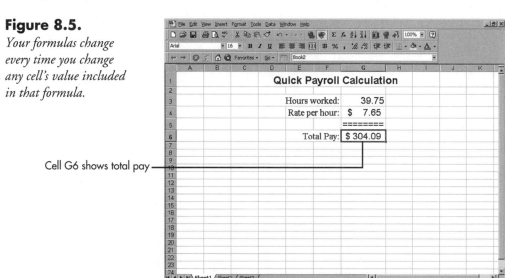

For this simple calculation, a spreadsheet might seem like overkill. A calculator might be simpler to use than an interactive spreadsheet when you want the result of a single calculation. Nevertheless, the payroll's simple nature clearly shows you how spreadsheets automatically update their formulas when any cell value changes.

Consider what happens when you take a simple spreadsheet such as the one in Figure 8.5 and increase the number of formulas and cells to hundreds of calculations. Some companies' balance sheets contain hundreds and possibly thousands of calculations. What if you were rushing to a meeting to present such a complex balance sheet and you learned at the last minute that the gross sales number, the figure on which almost every line in the balance sheet is based, is incorrect. Without a spreadsheet program, you would have to recalculate the *entire* balance sheet. With a program such as Excel, you correct only the single number, and *every* cell with a formula recomputes to show the corrected result. Your balance sheet is always up-to-date and ready for printing.

Spreadsheets aren't just for business. Obviously, the numerical spreadsheet's processing and formatting capabilities help businesses and the financial community, but spreadsheets are flexible for other areas as well. Any time you need to organize information in a row-and-column format, a spreadsheet might be able to help you. Spreadsheet cells can now hold any data, including Internet Web site addresses, graphics, scheduling times for project resources, and videos.

A popular saying goes something like this: "A picture is worth a thousand words." Figure 8.6 shows Excel's graphics. A spreadsheet can represent, using a series of different kinds of graphs, numbers and comparisons so that you can analyze numerical data visually. A bar chart shows obvious comparisons, whereas the data you base that bar chart on might be composed of thousands of numbers. Comparisons are difficult to analyze when you wade through so much numerical information, but anyone can see the widths of bars on a chart.

Figure 8.6.

Graphs such as this one show comparisons better than lists of numbers.

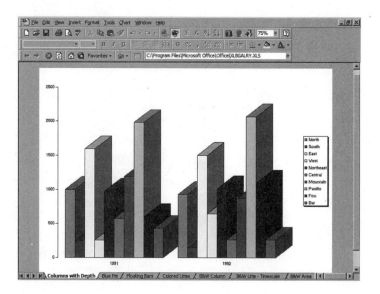

In addition to a spreadsheet's numerical and graphic representations, a spreadsheet can organize and search through data, offer special formatting of its cells so you can publish the spreadsheet in an annual report, and provide many of the quick AutoComplete features described in the previous section. For example, if you enter the days Monday and Tuesday in two cells next to each other, Excel will finish the days of the week for you as far as you extend the range. You can begin entering a series of numbers (by 1s, 10s, or ordinal numbers such as *1st* and *2nd*), and Excel will complete the series whether you want a series of four or 400 values. Spreadsheets can automatically compute cross totals and sums as well as analyze what-if scenarios to determine the best parameters for a forecast.

Spreadsheets Changed Business

Although this section only has time to scratch the spreadsheet surface, you've gotten a glimpse into the importance of spreadsheets in business today. Spread-sheets have changed the way businesses do their business!

Although more word processors are sold than spreadsheets, spreadsheet programs now comprise the top third spot in software category sales due to their benefits in the financial and business world. (Internet software is the second most common software category in use today.)

Despite the high sales of word processors, most PC analysts credit spreadsheets for the true growth and use of PCs today. Without the huge impact spreadsheets had in businesses in the early 1980s, businesses probably would not have purchased so many PCs, and PCs probably would not be as prevalent today.

Presenting Your Creations

Virtually any public speaker, teacher, or pastor either uses a PC now for developing, presenting, and teaching material or is considering doing so soon. Over the past few years, *presentation programs* have become a staple program on which presenters rely to present information clearly to audiences.

The information you present with a presentation program might include text, graphics, numbers, sound, and video. You will use your word processor, spreadsheet, and other programs to develop the data for your presentation. The presentation program then lets you put that data together in a package for presentation to an audience.

Hardware is catching up with PCs. Several companies are now providing inexpensive projection systems that, by plugging the system into a PC's video output jack, allow you to show your PC screen to an audience.

Following are just some of a presentation program's capabilities:

- ☐ Lets you arrange information into slide-like screens.
- ☐ Provides colorful backgrounds for your information.
- ☐ Spell-checks and analyzes grammar so your presentations are correct.
- ☐ Provides output for 35mm slides that you can make through special slide-printing machines or slide services that convert the output to slides.
- ☐ Prints details or summaries of the slides you are presenting for audience handouts.
- ☐ Allows for buttons and hot spots you can click with your mouse, during the presentation itself, that can send the presentation to a Web address or play a video in response to the click.
- ☐ Prints speaker's notes that differ in detail from the slide information that, may again, differ in detail from the notes you print to hand out to your audience. All three of these *views* might come from the same source of presentation data. You only need to manage one set of data (your presentation), but you let the presentation know which data is for which output.
- ☐ Provides overhead transparency output if you have no projection hardware available.
- ☐ Inserts video and lets you time sound to make your presentations come alive.
- ☐ Controls the presentation. Not only can the presentation program create a professional presentation, but the program also controls the presentation, letting you present the presentation slide screens just as you might a slide show. Time an automatic presentation to a recorded soundtrack. If you want, add fading and special effects to the presentation slides as you go through the presentation.

You'll gather your presentation data from several sources. Most presentations include text, numerical data, and pictures. Some word processors, such as Word, let you select certain portions of a document and send those portions directly to a presentation program where you then can quickly add backgrounds and order the slides to produce a presentation quickly. If you want to create a presentation from scratch, you can start with a blank presentation and create it entirely from within your presentation program.

Figure 8.7 shows a presentation being generated from Microsoft PowerPoint. The screen contains several slides from a presentation. From the screen, you could arrange the slides in

8

the order you want, change the background of one or all of the slides with a simple mouse selection, and turn the presentation slides into a live presentation by selecting a single menu option.

Figure 8.7.

Build your presentation from your data sources.

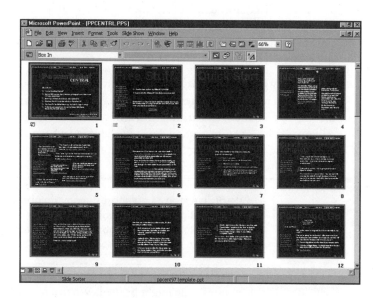

Combine and Act

Perhaps the most important use of PCs is not one use but a multiple use made possible through the PC's ease of sharing information between its programs. Many word processors, spreadsheets, and graphics programs are sold today in a *suite* of software packages. You can use the programs individually or together and share the data between them. For example, suppose that you have to prepare an annual report for the annual meeting of your neighborhood's investment club. If you have a PC, a word processor, a spreadsheet, and a presentation program, you won't have to duplicate effort.

Use the synergy available through *data sharing*: Create your financial information in the spreadsheet. Write up the analysis with your word processor. Import the spreadsheets and corresponding spreadsheet graphs into your word processed documents. Send highlights of that document to your presentation program, where you can format the background of the presentation slides with fancy graphics. Your job is finished! Print the report, present your speech, and your audience members will think you've put weeks of effort into that professional presentation that might have taken just a few hours!

Organizing Your Data

Another software category you're sure to run into is the *database* category. A database is an organized collection of data. A database might be as simple as a card catalog of books, a parts inventory, or perhaps a company-wide distribution center management system for vendor, customer, and employee information that interacts with a general ledger accounting system and mail-order service.

The primary goal of a database is to hold as much data as you need to hold for an particular purpose and to retrieve whatever data you need, whenever you need it, in a format presented the way you require. The database task is not always simple because some databases contain millions of pieces of information; knowing how and when to retrieve requested information is a daunting task.

JUST A MINUTE

To streamline today's databases, many databases present their data as a form. The designers of a database will create one or more forms to hold information stored in the database. You then can use the forms to add data to and to retrieve data from the database.

Consider how an employee file might be used. When a new employee goes to work, he fills out a form that lists his name, address, and other contact information. At a later point, when the employee is up for a promotion, the manager might request the employee's information (the form) be sent up from the Personnel Department for review. The blank form became the usable form after it was filed with the employee's information.

A database program uses this same form concept to manage its information. The database designer might design the database form. Instead of a paper form, the form will appear on the screen when a new employee comes to work. The Personnel Department fills in the onscreen form. Later, the manager can bring the form up on his networked company PC to review the information in consideration of a raise. The form, when blank, provides the vehicle to get the data into the database; after it's completed, the form is used to display data from the database.

Figure 8.8 shows a typical database collection of forms in use. As with most programs today, a database is not limited to text and numbers. You can store graphics, sounds, and videos in the forms.

Figure 8.8.

Forms provide the data vehicle for your database programs.

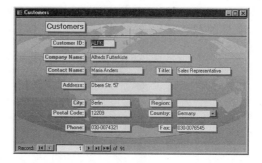

CAUTION

Although the form approach is one of the most popular means of entering and reviewing database information, a database is not limited to forms only. A database can print lists of information in a tabular format for reports. In addition, most of today's databases allow for searching and selecting of specific slices of the data. For example, if you needed to send a mailing to every employee who lives outside the company's city limits, you could request a report of those employees. To make life even easier, you could request that the database print mailing labels, in ZIP code order, for those employees who live outside the company's city limits.

The forms show a single database *record* at a time. A record is a single entity from a database, such as a part from an inventory, a person from a customer database, or a book from a library's online card catalog. As you can see in Figure 8.9, you can view your database in a tabular format that looks something like a spreadsheet's cells. The tabular format lets you look at multiple records at a time, whereas you can only view one record at a time in a form view.

When you or a database designer develops the database you will use, the database will be able to answer *queries* that you give it to request data. A query is simply a question, worded in a tight format required by the database, that requests matching information from the database. For example, a query might produce a list of all employees who have worked for more than 10 years. A query might produce a list of parts on backorder. A query might, in ZIP code order, produce a list of your top 20% of customers. A query simply tells the database exactly the information you need.

Despite today's database ease of use, databases do require quite a bit of knowledge to develop properly. In addition, today's database programs are so powerful that they often are complex to manage. Although beginners can produce fancy documents with a word processor, create useful spreadsheets, and build an effective presentation, a database will require some study to use effectively. If, however, you need the tools that a database offers and you study the background needed to create an effective database, the time-savings reward you get from a database over a paper-based information system (in a file cabinet) will pay dividends.

Figure 8.9.

View your database data in a tabular format when you want to view multiple records at once.

Customer ID	Company Name	Contact Name	Contact Title	
ALFKI	Alfreds Futterkiste	Maria Anders	Sales Representative	Obere Str. 57
ANATR	Ana Trujillo Emparedados y helados	Ana Trujillo	Owner	Avda. de la Const
ANTON	Antonio Moreno Taquería	Antonio Moreno	Owner	Mataderos 2312
AROUT	Around the Horn	Thomas Hardy	Sales Representative	120 Hanover Sq.
BERGS	Berglunds snabbköp	Christina Berglund	Order Administrator	Berguvsvägen B
BLAUS	Blauer See Delikatessen	Hanna Moos	Sales Representative	Forsterstr. 57
BLONP	Blondel père et fils	Frédérique Citeaux	Marketing Manager	24, place Kléber
BOLID	Bólido Comidas preparadas	Martín Sommer	Owner	C/ Araquil, 67
BONAP	Bon app'	Laurence Lebihan	Owner	12, rue des Bouc
BOTTM	Bottom-Dollar Markets	Elizabeth Lincoln	Accounting Manager	23 Tsawassen Bl
BSBEV	B's Beverages	Victoria Ashworth	Sales Representative	Fauntleroy Circus
CACTU	Cactus Comidas para llevar	Patricio Simpson	Sales Agent	Cerrito 333
CENTC	Centro comercial Moctezuma	Francisco Chang	Marketing Manager	Sierras de Grana
CHOPS	Chop-suey Chinese	Yang Wang	Owner	Hauptstr. 29
COMMI	Comércio Mineiro	Pedro Afonso	Sales Associate	Av. dos Lusíadas
CONSH	Consolidated Holdings	Elizabeth Brown	Sales Representative	Berkeley Gardens
DRACD	Drachenblut Delikatessen	Sven Ottlieb	Order Administrator	Walserweg 21
DUMON	Du monde entier	Janine Labrune	Owner	67, rue des Cinqu
EASTC	Eastern Connection	Ann Devon	Sales Agent	35 King George
ERNSH	Ernst Handel	Roland Mendel	Sales Manager	Kirchgasse 6
FAMIA	Familia Arquibaldo	Aria Cruz	Marketing Assistant	Rua Orós, 92
FISSA	FISSA Fabrica Inter. Salchichas S.A.	Diego Roel	Accounting Manager	C/ Moralzarzal, B
FOLIG	Folies gourmandes	Martine Rancé	Assistant Sales Agent	184, chaussée de
FOLKO	Folk och fä HB	Maria Larsson	Owner	Åkergatan 24
FRANK	Frankenversand	Peter Franken	Marketing Manager	Berliner Platz 43
FRANR	France restauration	Carine Schmitt	Marketing Manager	54, rue Royale

Record: 1 of 91

Unique five-character code based on customer name.

Summary

This hour presented the four major application programs in use today: word processors, spreadsheets, presentation programs, and databases. Sure, you're not an expert at any software program described in this hour just yet. Nevertheless, the mystery of programs such as spreadsheets and presentation programs should now be reduced greatly. Although these programs are powerful, they are simple to use and understand.

The next hour explains how you can spice up your PC fun by working with multimedia. Data isn't just text and numbers anymore, as you learned in this hour. Hour 9's lesson, "Multimedia on Your PC," shows you ways to access graphics, sound, and video from your PC.

Q&A

Q Where do I find the WordPad program mentioned in this hour?

A Display the Start menu's Programs | Accessories menu and select WordPad. The WordPad screen will load and you can begin typing text. Read through the online help (available from the Help menu option) to learn more about the program.

Q Do I need a software suite, such as Microsoft Office, to combine data from multiple programs?

A Generally, if you use Windows programs, you can share data between them. Not all programs offer the seamless data integration that software suites offer, but the data is generally transferable between programs. Windows supports the use of the *Clipboard*, a special area of memory that temporarily holds data. For example, in your checkbook program you can copy a check's information to the Windows Clipboard and then *paste* that information from the Clipboard memory into a word processor when you want to write your bank and request information on the check.

Hour 9

Multimedia on Your PC

There's no doubt that multimedia makes using a PC fun. Today's data comes in a huge variety of formats; in the past, computers worked only with numerical and textual data, but even today's least expensive PCs can reproduce color graphics, sound, and full-motion video.

This hour shows you ways to explore your PC's multimedia capabilities. You'll learn ways to create pictures, play music, and watch full-motion video. Several standards for each kind of multimedia exist, but you, the user, rarely have to worry about the standards. When you have a music file to play, your PC will, in virtually every case, be able to play the music without your needing to worry about data formats.

The highlights of this hour include

- ☐ What kind of color pictures you can create and display on a PC
- ☐ How to draw your own color graphics
- ☐ Where to find new color drawing and photo files to use in your applications
- ☐ What you need to turn your PC into a copier and fax machine
- ☐ How to create, play, and edit sounds on your PC

☐ How to assign sounds to various Windows events

☐ Which full-motion video files you can view

☐ What hardware you need to import full-motion video directly to your PC

Color Pictures

As long as you have a color video adapter card and a color monitor, as most PCs have today, you can reproduce color. Windows itself appears in color when it first appears. The days of the *monochrome* (one-color) monitors are past.

On your PC, a color picture is really just a collection of colored dots. The dots, as in a Seurat painting, are so small you do not notice them as being individual dots. Instead, they are close enough on your screen that you see them as a color picture. By the way, those dots are called pixels in techie-speak. The term *pixel* is a combination of the words *picture* and *element*.

All pictures on your screen are composed of the little color pixels, whether they are simple drawings or photo-like pictures.

JUST A MINUTE

Drawing Your Own

Windows includes the *Paint* program, with which you can draw color pictures. (Paint used to be called Paintbrush, and some people still refer to Paint as such.) Even if you're artistic, you probably won't be able to create extremely high-quality drawings with Paint, but Paint is nice for quick color line drawings you may need for a presentation—and it keeps your kids busy for hours.

Start Paint by selecting the Start menu's Programs | Accessories | Paint option. Paint appears, as shown in Figure 9.1. The large center area is your drawing area where your creation will appear. You will use the tools that appear around the drawing area to create or edit drawings.

Here are the basic steps for using Paint:

1. Select a tool to draw with.

2. Select a color to draw with. You can select both a foreground and a background color.

3. Drag your mouse while holding down the button to direct the tool and create the drawing.

Just as an artist uses lots of different drawing and painting tools, so does Paint. Figure 9.2 shows Paint's toolbox and lists all the tools you can use.

9

Menu bar   Drawing area   Scrollbars

Figure 9.1.

Paint contains all the tools you need to create Renaissance reproductions.

Toolbox

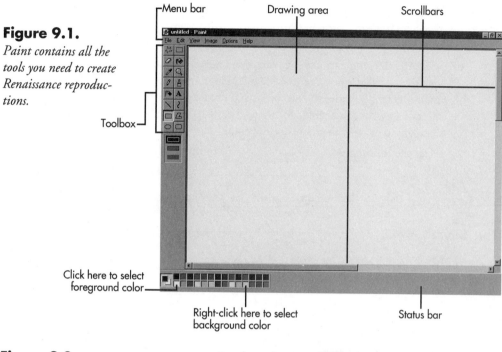

Click here to select
foreground color

Right-click here to select
background color

Status bar

Figure 9.2.

Paint contains several drawing and painting tools.

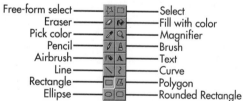

Free-form select ———————— Select
Eraser ———————————— Fill with color
Pick color ————————— Magnifier
Pencil —————————————— Brush
Airbrush ——————————— Text
Line ———————————————— Curve
Rectangle ————————— Polygon
Ellipse ——————————— Rounded Rectangle

The following steps explain how to use some of Paint's more popular tools. Try the steps, play around with Paint, and send this author royalties on any creations that you sell. Here you go:

1. Click on the Pencil tool and drag your mouse around the drawing area. The pencil draws every time you drag your mouse.

2. Click on a color and draw some more. You're now working with a colored pencil.

3. Click on the Paintbrush tool, select a color, and drag your mouse around the window. The Paintbrush tool puts more color (more paint) onto the screen as you drag the mouse.

4. Notice the shapes beneath the toolbox that appeared when you clicked on the paintbrush. Click on a different shape to change the way the paintbrush draws.

5. Here's a fun one: Select the Airbrush tool and drag your mouse around the screen. The color appears as if you were spraying paint from a can. Change the color. The longer you spray over an area, the darker the area becomes.

6. Select the Rectangle tool. Click and drag your mouse to draw a rectangle. Right-click over a color, click over the filled rectangle shape beneath the toolbox (the second rectangle under the toolbox), and draw another rectangle. Your right-click selected a new internal color for the rectangle. Click a new color and draw another rectangle to draw with a new outline color.

7. Select the Ellipse tool. Click and drag your mouse to draw an ellipse.

TIME SAVER

Hold Shift when drawing with the Rectangle tool to draw a perfect square. Combine Shift with the Ellipse tool to draw a perfect circle.

8. Click the Fill with Color tool. Select a new color. Click within one of the rectangles or circles you just drew. Paint completely fills the enclosed rectangle or circle with the color.

9. Select the Eraser tool and drag over something you've drawn to erase part of your drawing.

10. You can save your drawing by selecting File|Save and entering a filename. Quit Paint, if you want to, by selecting File|Exit.

Paint supports several additional drawing tools and menu commands that manipulate your drawings. You'll have fun experimenting with Paint's tools. You can even add text to a drawing by selecting the text tool and typing characters. Figure 9.3 shows an image of a PC user who just received one too many errors.

Paint is simple, but fairly powerful given its ease of use. One of Paint's biggest advantages is its price: free with Windows. Nevertheless, if you routinely create color pictures you may want to purchase a more powerful drawing program such as CorelDRAW! or Visio. Most suite packages, such as Microsoft Office, support drawings and offer some drawing tools as well.

External Drawings and Photos

You don't have to be artistic to work with color pictures. Your PC lets you load drawings and pictures into memory from several different sources. Paint and the other drawing programs can help you create some interesting color drawings, but no drawing program alone will let you create computer pictures with photo-like quality. For photo-quality pictures, you must get the pictures from another source.

Figure 9.3.

Paint lets you create all kinds of images.

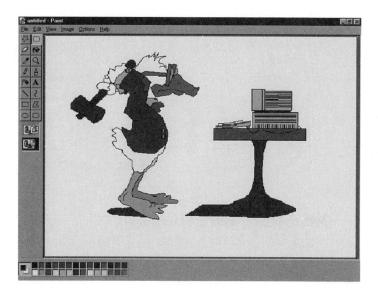

Scanning Pictures

A *scanner* is a peripheral device that takes a picture of any paper-based source and creates a disk file from that source. Three primary kinds of scanners exist:

- ☐ Flatbed scanners: Scanners that lie flat, not unlike a copier, that scan paper or open books that you place on the scanning surface.

- ☐ Roller scanners: Scanners that operate like old wringer-washers and scan sheets of paper, pictures, scraps of paper, and even business cards.

- ☐ Hand-held scanners: Small (4-inch) scanners that you drag across the document you want to scan. Often, two or more passes are necessary to scan a complete page.

Figure 9.4 shows these three kinds of scanners. The interesting thing about PC scanners is that they not only quickly get photos and drawings into your computer where you can save the graphics files, but they also scan text such as magazine articles. You can use the scanner's *OCR (Optical Character Recognition) software* to convert the text to text files you can edit with your word processor.

TIME SAVER

When you have a scanner, you don't need a copier or fax machine to copy or fax from paper sources. You can just scan the item to fax or copy and then print the item onto your printer or send the item, via your modem, to another fax machine.

Figure 9.4.

Three primary kinds of scanners exist: flatbed, roller, and handheld.

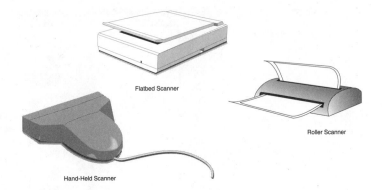

Flatbed Scanner

Roller Scanner

Hand-Held Scanner

Other Hardware Support

Look at any PC or camera store today and you'll find several digital cameras that compete for your purchase dollars. A digital camera can bypass film and store images directly onto a disk or load them directly into your PC.

JUST A MINUTE

Most photo-developing studios have the hardware to develop regular pictures and slides from your digital cameras. Although today's digital cameras don't produce the same quality of photos as a regular camera, their output works well for PC pictures. Manufacturers are improving their quality all the time.

Not only can you load still images into your PC with a digital camera, but if you insert a video-capture board into your PC, you can store video onto your disk that you can view with the motion-video tools described later in this hour.

Clip Art Files

Many software programs supply *clip art files*, files with collections of drawings and photos you can use in your own publications and Web pages (assuming the clip art is not copyrighted; most clip art is available royalty-free for you to use).

Microsoft Office, Corel Suite, and several other packages contain large collections of clip art. You can go to a software store and purchase CD-ROMs that contain nothing but royalty-free clip art that you can import into your publications.

9

Don't Forget Online Files

The Internet and online services such as Prodigy contain thousands and thousands of clip art pieces you can download and use. Be careful that the clip art that you use is free from copyright restrictions; much is, but some is not. Locating the files is fairly simple with today's Internet-searching tools and the searching tools that online services provide. Often you can narrow down a search to clip art files that fall within specific categories, such as holidays, business, and art specific to children.

Working with Pictures

After your picture has been created, scanned, imported, or loaded from a digital camera, what more can you do with it? The answer is, a lot of things! You can use the picture in a word-processed document, you can add the picture to an Internet Web page that you create, or you might want to use the image in a presentation you are giving.

CAUTION

Although several graphic formats are available, the most popular have these filename extensions: `.BMP`, `.WMF`, `.PCX`, `.JPG` (or JPEG), `.TIF` (or TIFF), and `.GIF`. You must make sure that the image's file format, determined by its extension, matches one of the formats that can be read by the program that will use that image. For example, Paint can load only `.BMP` and `.PCX` images, but it is not as full-featured as most graphics-based programs. Most programs can read an assortment of graphic images.

Almost all programs that work with graphic images combined with other elements such as text (for example, a word-processed document or a presentation) let you move and resize the image the same way. Figure 9.5 shows an image embedded in a Microsoft Word document. When you import a graphic image into most programs, you'll see the eight *resizing handles* that you see in Figure 9.5. Drag the handles in or out to shrink or enlarge the picture. By clicking within the center of the image and dragging your mouse, you can move the image around the document to a different location. Although not every program displays a Picture toolbar as Word does, often a toolbar or menu will be available from which you can change the picture's properties and crop the picture so that only a selected portion of the image appears.

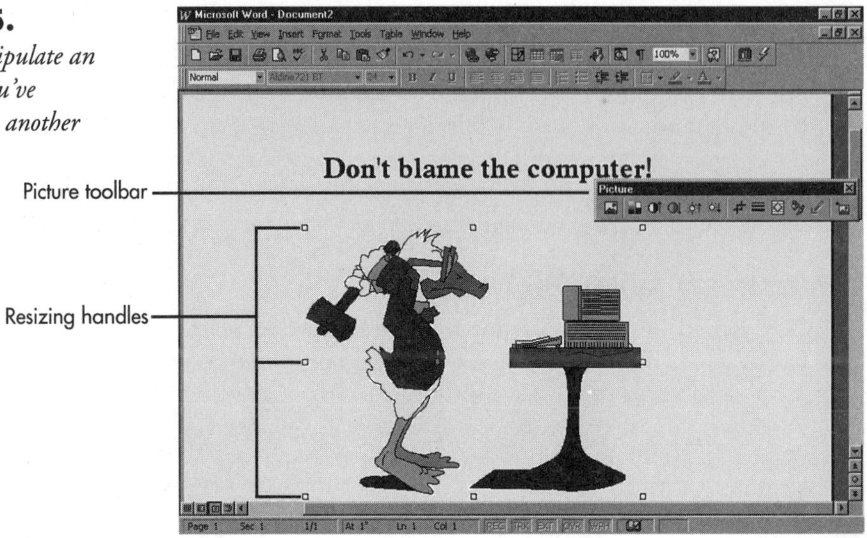

Figure 9.5.

You can manipulate an image that you've imported into another program.

Picture toolbar ──

Resizing handles ──

All About Sound

Early PCs could beep—and that's about it. Today's PCs support sound. Sound might reside in sound files, on an audio compact disc (CD), or on a CD-ROM along with a program such as a game. The sound might be a digital recording (as often appears in a *wave* file with the filename extension .WAV) or a reproduction of musical instruments (as often appears in *MIDI* files with the filename extension .MID). Sounds might be music, race-car sounds, or anything else.

Hearing the PC's Sounds

The speakers that come with most PCs are often not of the highest quality. Actually, the speakers that come with most PCs are downright cheap, cheap, *cheap*! If you want good sound, consider purchasing new speakers.

Most sound cards have a *Line Out* plug from which you can run a cable from the sound card to your stereo system's auxiliary input. If you go this route, your PC sound will be as good as your stereo's sound. Even if you don't run a cable to your stereo, most PC stores and mail-order catalogs sell inexpensive speakers that are vastly better than the ones that come with your PC.

One of the newer trends is to add a *sub-woofer*, a speaker that boosts your PC's low-end bass sounds. If you want to hear the thud when your teenager beats up a game's bad guy, get a sub-woofer for those low sounds.

Audio CDs

Your CD-ROM drive supports both computer CD-ROMs and audio CDs. Insert an audio CD and, after a brief pause, the music begins. Windows automatically starts the *CD Player* program when you insert an audio CD, as shown in Figure 9.6. (If you hear the CD but don't see the CD Player, click the CD Player's button on the taskbar to see the CD Player program.) CD Player contains all the usual Play, Reverse, Pause, Stop, and Eject buttons you'll find on regular CD players. Some manufacturers supply their own CD Player program that contains different interfaces from the one Window provides.

Figure 9.6.

The CD Player program can keep track of a CD's music.

Here's the magic of CD Player: Select Disc | Edit Play List to enter the CD's artist, title, and songs (you can get this information from the CD's back cover). After you enter this information, if you *ever* play that CD again, Windows recognizes the CD and automatically loads the information!

JUST A MINUTE

Some of the newer audio CDs are called *extended CDs*. When you play extended CDs, the CD contains all the CD Player information so you don't have to type in the data.

Volume Control

When you play a CD or work with any multimedia element, a speaker icon appears at the right of your taskbar. If you double-click on the speaker icon, the volume control window, shown in Figure 9.7, appears. You can adjust the various sound volumes by dragging the volume control up or down with your mouse. Most of the time you'll adjust the master volume control (the left control), but individual controls, such as the microphone and CD volume controls, let you adjust those individual settings.

File-Based Sound

Windows contains several accessory programs that can play sound files. Generally, you'll use one of these two programs to play sound files:

☐ Media Player, which plays virtually all sound file formats

Figure 9.7.

Control your system volume from the Volume Control dialog box.

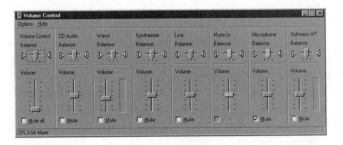

☐ Sound Recorder, which plays and lets you record wave sound files (the sounds that you can attach to Windows events from the Control Panel's Sounds icon, as you'll read about in the next section)

Both of these programs appear on the Start menu's Programs|Accessories|Multimedia menu. They contain the usual Play, Reverse, and Pause buttons that the CD Player contains.

TIME SAVER

> Don't forget that sound in files is data just as video, graphics, and text are data. You can insert a sound file in the middle of a word-processed document or an e-mail message. A speaker icon will appear. When you or your e-mail's recipient double-clicks on the sound icon, the sound plays. Be careful, though, because sound can consume quite a bit of file space and can make e-mail time-consuming to send and receive.

Media Player is not just for sound. The Media Player program also lets you control the playing of an audio CD as well as video files stored on your PC.

Use the Sound Recorder to record sound files that you want to send to others or embed in documents. Sound Recorder even shows the sound patterns (see Figure 9.8) as you play sounds. This program also contains menu commands that let you insert new sound files inside existing sounds (letting you digitally edit the sound files) and record a sound backward and at various speeds.

Windows Sounds

You can assign sounds to various Windows events. An *event* is anything you commonly do in Windows, such as opening and closing windows as well as sending e-mail and emptying the Recycle Bin. Open the Sounds dialog box by opening the Start menu's Settings|Control Panel|Sounds window.

Scroll through the list of events. A speaker icon appears next to an event to which a sound is currently assigned. You can listen to the current sound by clicking the Play button. To add a sound to an event not currently assigned a sound, select the event, click the Browse button, and locate a file whose filename matches the kind of sound you want to assign.

9

Figure 9.8.
*Sound Recorder graphically
shows the sound currently
playing.*

Windows includes a few sets of predefined sound schemes, such as jungle sounds, that assign
a group of related sounds (such as a snake's *hissss*) to common Windows events.

Full-Motion Video

Several kinds of video files exist for PCs. The most common have the filename extension .AVI
or .MPG. Both Media Player and the ActiveMovie Control program can play video files.

JUST A MINUTE

> The ActiveMovie Control program is a better implementation of a video
> player and can more accurately reproduce smooth video playback. Not
> all PCs contain the ActiveMovie Control program, however. Both
> ActiveMovie Control and the Media Player appear on the Start menu's
> Programs | Accessories | Multimedia menu if they are installed.

Your Windows installation CD-ROM contains several video files you can play. In addition,
the Windows | Help folder lists several you can play. To play one of the Help folder's videos,
start ActiveMovie Control or Media Player and locate the Windows | Help folder. The files
there are all AVI files that demonstrate various Windows tasks. Select the Taskswch.AVI file
to play that file. You'll see a moving video that demonstrates how to switch between Windows
tasks, such as the one in Figure 9.9.

Figure 9.9.
*Watch this full-motion
video that demonstrates a
Windows operation.*

Today's games and tutorials often contain videos that help you use your PC's resources more
effectively. The Internet Web pages that you view often contain videos as well. As the Internet
gains speed, you will see live video, just as on television, become more common.

Speaking of television, you can insert a special television expansion board into your PC and watch broadcast television inside one window while you work on a spreadsheet in another window.

One of the most interesting hardware devices becoming more standard today is the *DVD player* (for *Digital Video Disc*). DVDs hold as much information as several CD-ROMs, but also play regular CD-ROMs. A full-length movie fits easily on a DVD, so you'll be taking your home theater with you if you travel in the future with a DVD-based laptop. The DVD, combined with the speed of modern PCs, means that you'll begin to see larger applications that run off the larger DVD storage devices that more fully integrate multimedia even more than today's software titles can do.

Summary

This hour has explained the many ways you can access multimedia on your PC. From color graphics to sound to full-motion video, your PC becomes both a data-access device and an entertainment system. Even if you don't play PC games, take a look at some of the game titles demonstrated in PC stores. You'll be amazed at the technology inside a common household PC.

Hour 10, "Learning on Your PC," explains how you can use your PC to learn from and search for reference information (your PC is at its best when it gathers and presents information). The lesson describes how you can use your PC to learn a new foreign language and to access interactive encyclopedias.

Q&A

Q Where can I find video files?

A You won't find as many video files as you will sound and graphic clip art files. Video files consume a lot of disk space and take a long time to download if you get them from the Internet or from an online service.

You can produce your own video files, as explained in this hour's material, as long as you insert a video-capture board into your PC. Again, video consumes a tremendous amount of disk space. A five-minute video can consume a gigabyte or more of disk space.

As disks get larger and software becomes more powerful, you'll be editing your home videos directly on your PC. Proper video editing is virtually impossible to do today because rarely does a PC system have enough free disk space to help with holding large amounts of video that you want to piece together to form a new video. As disks approach the 100GB capacities, you'll see such video-editing software and hardware become more popular.

9

Q Why does my PC not start playing audio CDs when I insert them?

A If your PC does not automatically play CDs when you insert them, your Windows *AutoPlay* feature is turned off. AutoPlay is the name of the system option that starts playing audio CDs when you insert them and starts programs or their installations when you insert CD-ROMs into your CD drive.

If your AutoPlay is turned off, keep in mind that several Windows users prefer to have AutoPlay turned off. Those users can insert a CD-ROM at any time without having to wait for a startup screen or an installation window to appear. When they want to see the window or start the program that requires the CD-ROM, they can do so by selecting the CD from the My Computer window. (If you want to temporarily insert a CD without the AutoPlay feature starting, press and hold Shift as you close the CD-ROM drive door until your CD-ROM drive light goes out.)

Here are some quick instructions to turn on AutoPlay:

1. Display the Start menu.
2. Select Settings|Control Panel.
3. Double-click on the System icon.
4. Click on the Device Manager tab.
5. Click on the plus sign next to your CD-ROM drive; the CD-ROM drive's description appears.
6. Select the description.
7. Click Properties.
8. Click on the Settings tab. Windows 95 displays a Settings dialog box.
9. Check the option labeled `Auto insert notification` to turn on AutoPlay. (If you subsequently uncheck this option, AutoPlay turns off.)
10. Click OK to close the Settings dialog box.
11. Click OK to close the System dialog box.
12. Close the Control Panel window. When you next insert a CD-ROM, Windows will start the installation, the program (if installed), or the music (if you insert an audio CD in the drive).

Hour 10

Learning on Your PC

In Hour 9, you learned about your PC's multimedia capabilities. Those multimedia capabilities make your PC a superior teaching and reference machine. Whereas a vast library search a few years ago might result in a few general books on your topic of interest, a few seconds on the PC (with possible help from the Internet) can bring extremely specific answers you need directly to your PC.

In this hour you will learn ways that people use PCs as reference and learning tools. If you want to learn a foreign language, you will be doing yourself an injustice if you don't check out the language software that abounds. If you have children who won't do math drills, put them in front of an interactive, animated, PC-based math tutor and watch them beg you for more time in math.

The highlights of this hour include

☐ How electronic encyclopedias differ from book-based encyclopedias

☐ Which reference books translate well to the electronic CD-ROM medium

☐ What kinds of PC-based reference materials help you in the home

☐ How online reference works have changed the way researchers gather information

☐ How reference and educational titles improve your child's learning

A Reference Giant

To learn about a famous actor, you can open an encyclopedia and read an article on the actor's life. If, however, you open an interactive, multimedia-based, software encyclopedia, you will read about the person, watch a video or two, hear the actor's voice, and scroll though several color photos you can print or save for later.

Figure 10.1 shows a multimedia-based encyclopedia program called *Encarta*. Probably no other software better demonstrates the PC's reference and teaching power than the software encyclopedias on the market today. If you or someone in your family is going to school or doing in-depth research across several subjects, run, don't walk, to your nearest software store and purchase one of the CD-ROM–based encyclopedias.

Figure 10.1.

Stop, look, and listen to the encyclopedia's entry.

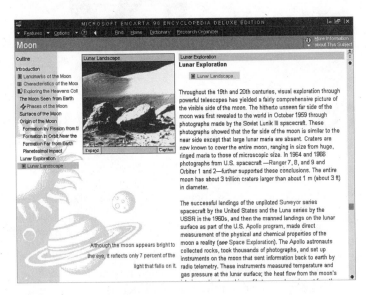

 JUST A MINUTE

Most software-based encyclopedia program vendors offer annual subscriptions with which you can update your encyclopedia's information with the latest version each year. Not only do you receive updated information, but new software tools often appear in the updates as well that let you enjoy the encyclopedia in more ways.

Perhaps the biggest reason for the success of the CD-ROM encyclopedia is the searching capability that such a program offers. Locating specific information on CD-ROM is often quicker and almost always more accurate than looking for a topic in a written encyclopedia. The encyclopedia search engines often support *Boolean expressions*, which means you can

10

combine words and phrases to locate only articles that contain every item for which you're looking. As you use your CD-ROM–based encyclopedia more and more, you'll learn new ways to narrow your searches and locate specific information faster.

Of course, encyclopedias are not the sole source of information. All the reference materials for the PC are too numerous to mention, but to round out your introduction to PCs, you should learn a little more about the kind of reference software you can find.

Almost all word processors offer a thesaurus for locating synonyms, but you can find add-on CD-ROMs that also integrate the following kinds of services into your word processing:

- [ ] **Dictionaries**: Instantly look up a word in the online dictionary to find a meaning. If you *really* want an electronic dictionary, check out the CD-ROM–based Oxford English Dictionary (the collection spans several CD-ROMs) and trace the lineage of every word ever coined in the English language.

- [ ] **Quotations**: Locate a quote when you search by a person's name or search for quotes on a given topic. Writing a lecture on the weather? Find a couple humorous quotes to drive home your point.

- [ ] **Almanac**: Search for statistics, records, top-ten lists, sports winners and losers, country populations, and more when you search the electronic almanacs available for your PC.

- [ ] **ZIP code directory**: Lets you locate ZIP codes, often by typing the address.

- [ ] **Atlas**: Shows geographic and demographic information about the world and lets you view varying levels of detail.

- [ ] **Maps**: Enter an address and look at a map showing that exact address, or enter two addresses and the software can tell you the shortest route between the two locations. (See Figure 10.2.)

10

Figure 10.2.

Drive right to your destination with mapping software.

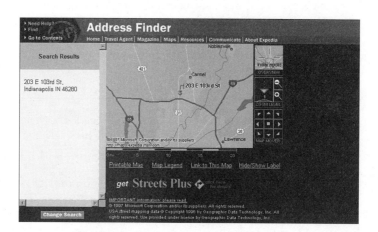

Software titles such as *Microsoft Bookshelf* supply several of these and other reference works on a single CD-ROM. You will not have to purchase a separate CD-ROM for each reference you want to use.

As your software library expands, you'll learn new uses for your PC when you see the variety of reference materials out there. The next section takes a look at several additional reference titles available to give you a feel for the kind of stuff vying for your purchase dollars. As more people use reference software, the software vendors are getting more competitive. For example, not only does mapping software exist (as shown in Figure 10.2) to locate a destination, but many of the mapping programs support the use of *GPS* (*Global Positioning Satellite*) navigation hardware. With the GPS antenna attached to your laptop, the software, using the positional capabilities of satellites in orbit, can pinpoint your exact latitude, longitude, country, state, city, and exact address as you move!

Personal travel software is getting extremely smart. Some products now recognize certain voice commands so that you can inquire, hands-free, about your position or for directions to a specific address as you drive with your laptop open next to you in the seat. Unlike most passengers, the laptop won't comment on your driving habits either!

Additional References

The PC's searching capabilities make reference software a natural use for computers. Virtually all kinds of data now reside on the PC in some form. Of course, timeliness is critical, and if you want the latest reference information, such as this year's electronic European Restaurant Guide, you'll have to update your CD-ROM to this year's edition. At first this constant update might seem to be an expensive burden, but if you consider that a reference book is out of date the moment the publisher prints it, you'll realize that one never has the latest information.

As you'll learn in the next section, the Internet supplies a constant flood of information, much of which will be timely and updated.

Because CD-ROM–based reference information provides so much more multimedia and searching capabilities than a corresponding book can provide, though, the updates are not a great problem. In addition, corresponding printed material, such as a complete set of encyclopedia books, is much more costly than the CD-ROM version and consumes much more shelf space; rarely do people update their printed encyclopedias because of the cost and inconvenience.

Are Books Obsolete Today?

Look at the sales figures of any major book chain, or walk into any bookstore, and you'll see that the demise of printed material is greatly exaggerated! No matter how fast a CD-ROM–based search engine zips requested information to you, no software on the PC can come close to matching the enjoyment and enlightenment people get flipping through a book.

How often have you looked up something in a book only to learn something totally unrelated as you are going to the section you need? Of course, you'll have the same experience when you search through a CD-ROM–based reference work, but the experience will be different. Books don't consume electricity, they work when you get them dusty, they don't break down, and many consider the book's personal nature unbeatable by any machine.

When people were sold PCs a few years ago, they were told that one could keep checkbooks and recipes on the PC (see Hour 1, "Get Started Now," for a discussion on these kinds of promises that the PC might or might not fulfill). Finally, years after the PC's first appearance, electronic cookbooks are changing the way people file their recipes.

As Figure 10.3 shows, an electronic cookbook is more than just a recipe filing cabinet. Today's multimedia-based cooking software gives the recipe, shows the finished product, and often includes a step-by-step video of the recipe. If you want to make the recipe for a specific number of people, enter the figure and the software instantly recalculates all the recipe's requirements! You can print shopping lists, plan weekly meals, order random meals that meet your exact caloric content, and plan meals based on cost.

JUST A MINUTE

Your old recipes don't go to waste when you get a computerized cookbook. Most cooking programs let you enter your own recipes into the recipe database.

Home reference titles abound on the software shelves. You'll find home gardening planners and support programs, room-design software, remodeling software that shows you with video how to install wallboard, flower-arranging tutorials, wiring and plumbing tutorials, improvement planners, window covering designers, and automotive repair titles. Your CD-ROM shelf can house a complete collection of home improvement and maintenance reference titles that, interactively, explore and instruct you about the projects you face as a homeowner.

Figure 10.3.

Want something good to eat? Ask your PC.

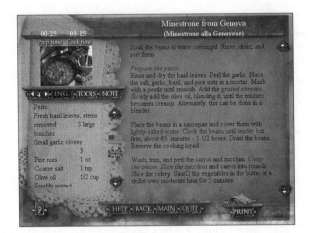

Browse your library's reference shelves and you'll get a glimpse into the software available on PCs. Statistical information is available from a variety of public and governmental sources. Doing a word comparison of ancient Greek and Hebrew texts against one of today's Bible translations? You'll find several collections of Bibles with Greek and Hebrew concordances that provide a deeper word study than you could ever achieve without the electronic aid. Learning to fly? Flying simulation programs prepare novices as well as advanced pilots without risk. In-depth study of virtually any discipline is enhanced by the electronic information now available to any home PC user.

Speaking of libraries, most libraries now provide online access. If you have Internet access, you can view current information about your local library branch to make sure that a certain book is checked in before you make the drive to check it out.

Although computers will never replace the human element in teaching, they can enhance the learning and enjoyment of any subject. Consider for a moment the study of a foreign language. Today's multimedia language-teaching tools not only teach you pronunciation, grammar, translation, and spelling of a new language, but they also let you repeat foreign words and phrases aloud and have the computer judge how closely your diction matches that of the recorded speaker's.

How-to guides are now making their way into the electronic medium with a fierceness. The PC lends itself extremely well to electronic-based reference, more so than many books are able to do by themselves. For example, David Macauley's *The Way Things Work* book is not only a fun read but also an interactive teaching tool, as Figure 10.4 illustrates.

10

Figure 10.4.

Don't just read, but interact *with such titles as* The Way Things Work.

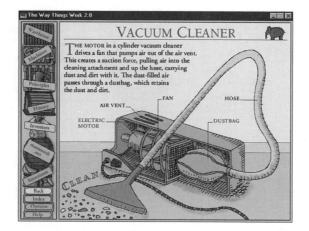

Online References

This 24-hour tutorial doesn't explore the Internet in depth until the final four hours, but one cannot discuss reference software without describing the online reference services available from the Internet. Many of these reference services don't charge for their information (above and beyond your normal monthly Internet fee).

The government's presence on the Internet is, as in life, abundant. All U.S. senators and representatives offer some kind of contact information, as does the White House. In the United States, your representative government can hear your views without excuse. Most of the government's services are now available from the Internet, including vast information about housing, judicial, and law enforcement agencies.

If you travel a lot, the online travel services are invaluable. You can book a flight, compare foreign hotel prices, learn museum hours, rent a car, and converse with others who love travel as well. As the Internet gains more speed, you'll see more tourist-destination videos that transcend books or sequential video tape and give you a 3D virtual reality walkthrough of the sites you want to visit in person.

Not only can you find dedicated general travel sites such as Figure 10.5's *Expedia* site, but all the major airline, hotel, and rental car agencies also provide their own Internet locations you can visit for specials and reservations. You can often sign up for free e-mail from the travel sites to get advance notice of special bargain fares available for the countries and cities you want to visit.

If you are a member of a frequent flier club, you can check your current mileage credits. Some airlines take as long as 45 days to send you written confirmation of a frequent-flier mileage credit, but the online sites reflect your credits as of the previous business day or two in most cases.

Figure 10.5.

Book a trip with an online travel service.

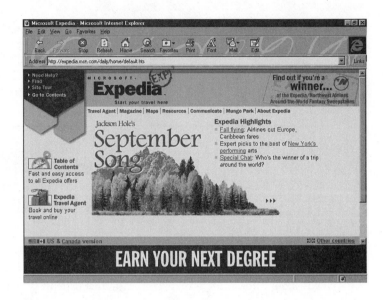

Higher-level award members, or so-called *gold* and *platinum* members of frequent flier clubs, can often process free upgrades on certain airline Internet sites.

Universities from all over the world now have Internet locations. Not only can you find entrance requirements and course schedules, but several colleges now offer online degree programs you can receive from your own home. Some of these courses combine videos broadcast over the Internet and over regular cable outlets, and as well as printed and online testing services to determine your skill levels in the courses you complete. Often schools show off their collections, such as the online map room from Italy's University of Bologna, the greatest collection of ancient maps on the Internet in existence.

The serious investor will almost certainly already use the PC for the recording and analysis of financial information, but the online investment community can find an unlimited number of resources for instant retrieval. Real-time stock quotes (most sites provide 15- or 20-minute delayed quotes, but if you invest with an investment service that has an online site, you can often get real-time quotes) keep your investment timing equal to those on Wall Street. (See Figure 10.6.)

Needless to say, the Internet is too vast to begin discussing in one section, and even the final part of this book covers only an overview of the fundamentals. Nevertheless, the Internet's reference resources are growing every day and are now already huge. So much information

10

exists on the Internet, for all to see, that governments are beginning to fear that foreign governments will intercept and piece together information that could be damaging if not kept more in check.

Figure 10.6.

Manage your own finances, buy and sell stock, and track your portfolios online.

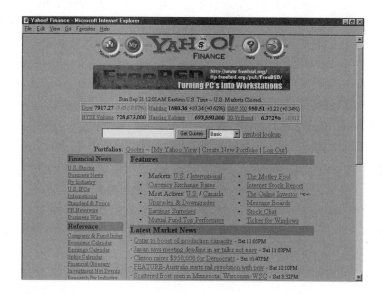

10

JUST A MINUTE

This quick section has discussed several online locations, but how can you find such information? Fortunately, as you'll learn in this 24-hour tutorial's final hours, the Internet includes massive searching tools that pinpoint the information you want. Although this book could give you exact Internet addresses, those addresses change frequently. The search tools will send you to the latest locations for the information you need.

Add Shopping Sites to your Reference Library!

Although one does not (and should not) count shopping as a subject underneath the *reference* title, the Internet's shopping sites *do* give you somewhat of a reference when you want to search for product details on something you're considering purchasing. Nearly everything's available online, from clothes, food, and movies to software, hardware, music, and books—just about anything you can go to a store and purchase.

In addition, if you cannot find the exact information you need, you can shop for books, magazines, and newspapers, both current and back issues, that will support the kind of information you need for your study. The online bookstores, for example, rival the super book chains in price because of the Internet's low overhead as opposed to the plant and equipment needed for retail outlets.

Children's Education

Although the previous sections demonstrate some of the ways that people of all ages can learn with PC-based references, perhaps children more than anyone can benefit from today's learning and reference software. Children almost always adapt to PC technology more quickly than do adults. To children, the PC is an electronic gadget to be played with, not feared.

Perhaps the first skill set that a child can master at the PC is typing. Software exists for children (and adults), such as the *Kid's Typing* title shown in Figure 10.7, so that children can have fun and not even realize they are learning something as "boring" as the tedious typing classes many adults went through in their high school days.

Figure 10.7.

The quicker kids can type, the faster they can master the PC.

Most of the children's educational software that exists helps children learn skills such as math and reading, hopefully in a fun game-like style. Try to review the software or read related magazine reviews before you spend much on the purchase because some products are really good and some are really bad.

10

CAUTION

Parents find that children who do math or reading drills at school rarely want to repeat those drills at home, even on the PC. The challenge of good educational software for those basic subjects is to keep the kids wanting to stay at the keyboard so that the repetition sinks in. Sadly, some software tutorials simply don't do the job as well as others. Home-schooled children use the drill-based software perhaps more successfully than children educated out of the home, perhaps because drills aren't administered twice. Be sure to analyze your child's school curriculum so you can purchase software that complements and does not compete with the education at school.

10

Some children's educational software titles have proved to be more than a drill-based rote skill-builder. Educational software works only when the children use it. Some educational software not only teaches, but also draws in the children. Such titles have become so successful that the company has released several editions.

The *Magic School Bus*, shown in Figure 10.8, is a yellow school bus that takes children through science journeys by using a familiar interface throughout all the titles available. After your child masters the first title, he jumps right into the remaining titles and enjoys the same characters, interface, and scientific exploration.

Figure 10.8.
The Magic School Bus *software titles teach children several facets of science, such as ocean exploration.*

Another title that turned into multiple television series, including cartoons and a game show, is the *Where Is Carmen Sandiego?* software series. More than just a cartoon, the *Where Is*

Carmen Sandiego? series comes with a world almanac and maps. Your child's goal is to track the notorious Carmen and her henchmen by using geographical and demographic information gleaned from the almanac by using the clues provided along the way. Figure 10.9 shows one of the hunt screens for Carmen. While your child solves the "crime," he learns about geography, countries, capitals, and cultures. The *Carmen* series includes several titles that span historical time (*Where in Time Is Carmen Sandiego?*) and that reside in specific countries (*Where in the USA Is Carmen Sandiego?*).

TIME SAVER

The makers of *Carmen* are smart. Your children probably watch *Carmen* on television now and have no idea that the program began as a software education title that teaches geography. When you load the *Carmen* program for the first time, your child will be thrilled because the software is a natural interactive extension of the shows.

Figure 10.9.
Your child will use geographical skills gleaned from the World Almanac *to help track Carmen.*

When your child gets older, he should be about as PC-literate as four adults. When college entrance time comes, get the interactive SAT, ACT, GRE, GMAT, and LSAT testing and drill software that prepares your student for the best scores possible.

Summary

This hour has shown you how your PC becomes a multimedia reference tool, both for you as well as your children. Encyclopedias come alive, as do other reference works, so that you can read, hear, and watch for the answers that your research requires. Looking for answers is the forte of your PC's strength; reference-searching tools return answers quickly.

10

The Internet not only brings vast amounts of reference information to your PC; that information, if properly updated, is as current as possible. As the Internet gets faster and the Internet's information grows even further, the Internet will be able to bring tomorrow's library to your doorstep.

Hour 11, "Games on Your PC," moves from work to play as you learn all about PC games.

Q&A

Q I live close to a good library, so should I mess with reference software?

A Perhaps you should, depending on how often you research, how in-depth your research is, which software titles are available that can directly benefit your research, and how timely your reference works must be.

Your library is rapidly becoming electronic—perhaps not by replacing books, but by accenting books dramatically with electronic works. Therefore, even your library regards the PC as a valuable reference source. In addition, many libraries are now going online to the Internet to keep current with the latest information that lags in the print media.

If your library keeps up with the resources you need, you don't need to update your software reference library, but surely you have several books at home that your library also has. Software reference works are often less expensive and more timely and make for quicker searching than printed material, so if you need reference materials often, your home software library will complement your library's references down the street.

Q Why didn't we have fun software when we were learning as children?

A You might not have, depending on your age, but you do *now*. Need to brush up on your algebra skills before your child asks a question you can't answer? Buy algebra software for yourself and, in the privacy of your own home with the blinds closed while your child's at school, use your PC to fill in the holes with the skills you might never have learned.

10

Hour 11

Games on Your PC

PC games are important for many reasons. The PC industry tells you that games are important because of the tremendous sales figures games produce. That's true. Teachers tell you that games are important because they make computers fun and encourage children to adapt to computers faster than they otherwise would do. That's also true. PC technicians tell you games are important because games are often the first kinds of application to take advantage of the newest hardware on the market. That's true because today's multimedia-based games require the fastest and most efficient computer systems to run as smoothly as possible.

This hour explains some of the game phenomenon that resounds throughout the industry today. Walk into any PC store and you won't find the word processors and spreadsheets on the front shelves, but the latest games. After this hour you'll have a better appreciation for PC games, and you'll also be tempted to start playing some before you move to Hour 12!

The highlights of this hour include

- ☐ What games you get free with Windows
- ☐ How to build a new game library quickly

☐ Why game writers are revisiting the past for today's games

☐ How sports games provide realistic details

☐ Which gaming peripheral devices you might want

☐ How board games translate to the PC

☐ How you can play online games against others from around the world

Starting Simple

A game does not have to include the latest in multimedia capabilities to be fun. Windows comes with a few games that are simple, yet addicting. From the Start menu, select Programs | Accessories | Games | Solitaire to start the familiar card game shown (in progress) in Figure 11.1.

Figure 11.1.

Solitaire is always there when you need a short break.

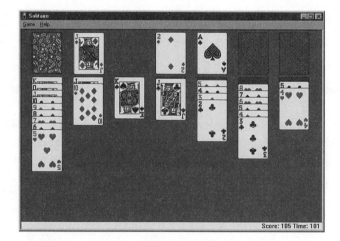

JUST A MINUTE

On some Windows menus, Solitaire is located on the Programs | Games menu; in that case, you won't select from the Accessories menu.

TIME SAVER

Not only is Solitaire a fun game, but no other program has been written before or since that makes you a mouse expert as well as Solitaire does. After a few games, you'll be completely comfortable clicking, double-clicking, and dragging your mouse.

Windows includes several other games such as Minesweeper, Hearts (which you can play against others over a network), and FreeCell (a different kind of Solitaire card game). If you don't find these games on your menu, you might have to choose Settings | Add/Remove Programs from the Start menu and select the Windows Setup tab in the box that appears to add the games that did not previously install when you installed Windows.

Game Collections

Several software vendors that write PC games often group several games in CD-ROM collections that you can purchase at a low package price. Often, many of these games are older and no longer sell well on their own, but you can obtain a large collection of various games, many of which contain far more graphics and multimedia challenges than the basic Windows games described in the previous section.

TIME SAVER

> Often, PCs come with several of these game collections to attract buyers. If you recently purchased a PC, search your Start menu and the CD-ROMs that came with your system and you'll probably find several games among the other software that came with your PC.

Another way to stock up a game assortment quickly if you're currently low on titles is to look in the sale bins at software stores and discount office-supply houses. Bins of slightly older PC games abound, and many titles run less than $10 each for a CD-ROM–based game that might have cost $50 just a year or two ago.

If you have company coming and you want to add a few games to your computer to keep the kids busy, consider browsing the game collections and sale bins that are so common in today's PC stores. After you gather up an assortment, peruse the new game titles because you might want a new title to give your game collection a combination that the kids will love.

JUST A MINUTE

> Many of today's PC stores offer demonstration machines on which you can try games before you actually purchase them. You'll select games from a menu on these dedicated PCs that will run only the programs on the menu. Often the stores offer a wide variety of modern games as well as games and educational software from the past.

CAUTION

Check the game's hardware requirements before you take the game to the register to purchase it. You'll want to make sure you have enough RAM and CPU speed to handle the game adequately. All games list their requirements on the edge or back of the box. In addition, check to make sure that you have the correct operating environment. If, for example, a game requires Windows 95, you cannot run it under Windows 3.1.

Oldies but Goodies

If you're into or past your thirties, you may remember the arcade craze of the early 1980s that was made possible when the microprocessor was invented. Pinball machines took a side seat to the colorful, noisy, computer-based arcade games. Figure 11.2 shows one such game you may remember.

Figure 11.2.

Did you ever play Missile Command in the arcades?

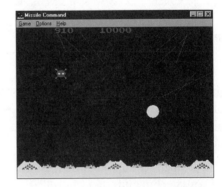

These arcade games were so much more realistic and had such better graphics than the home-based arcade game devices that came out around that time period. As Figure 11.3 shows, the home-based games, led by Atari, often used block graphics that did not lend themselves to realism as well as the arcade games.

Despite the more primitive graphics, the home-based games were often fun to play and offered challenges that sometimes rivaled the challenges in the arcades. Well, software vendors must have been watching all the movies lately that are remakes of old television shows, because they've realized that people enjoy nostalgia. Despite the primitive home-based game play, and although the arcades of the 1980s did not provide the same realism as today's multimedia PC games, software vendors are rereleasing those older games for the PC! Relive your college days and revisit those noon hours when you'd sneak out of work to play

11

Dig Dug. Both Figures 11.2 and 11.3 are screen shots from PC games that you'll find on the software shelves today! If you miss the old days, you can live them all over again.

Figure 11.3.
Home-based game graphics used to be limited.

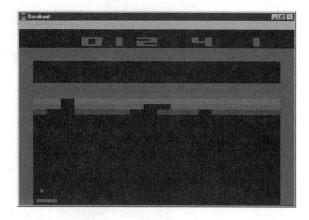

JUST A MINUTE

These PC nostalgia games are quite respectful of their original counter-parts. They play the same and respond the same way, true to the original games. The vendors have put a lot of effort into completely implementing these old games on today's hardware. Enjoy!

11

Take It to the Limits

No single book can cover all the PC games out there. Not only are they too numerous, but new ones come out at least weekly. Nevertheless, you can get a good feel for the nature and quality of games by learning about a few that represent the current gaming industry.

Future Arcade Action Is Here

The arcade-style games—the action games that require flying, shooting, or fighting—blanket the PC gaming industry. Today's games don't just let you turn a plane or control a gun; they literally put you in the pilot's seat of yesterday's planes or tomorrow's space ships. Figure 11.4 shows a Star Wars game called *X-Wing vs. Tie-Fighter* that leaves other shoot-'em-up games in the space dust. Your body will be turning with every twist of your ship as you dodge the evil empire and fight the dark side.

Figure 11.4.

You're the pilot, aiming your guns in X-Wing.

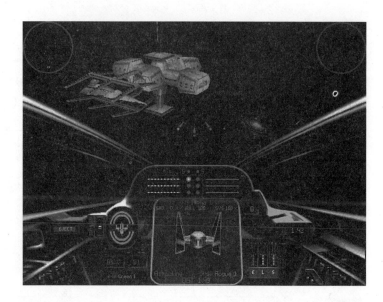

Controlling Games Properly

Most games let you play with just a keyboard, or a keyboard and mouse combination, but if you really want to hone your gaming skills, you'll invest in better game-controlling hardware.

A joystick is a must and, generally, the more expensive the stick, the better it performs. Several of the newer joysticks such as the Thrustmaster contain not only a joystick, but several firing buttons and programmable buttons on the base as well as other controls such as a thrust controller. With such a stick you can control all the major game controls without going to the keyboard. Microsoft has set a trend with the *Microsoft Sidewinder* joystick, which adds a jolting feedback when you bank a sharp turn to give you the total feel of a game.

If you like the racing games, such as *Need for Speed II* (shown in Figure 11.5), you'll want to purchase a PC steering wheel and pedal set. You'll hit those hairpin turns that would otherwise put you in the repair pit. If you've used a dedicated game machine recently, you've used a game controller that includes several buttons and controls on a small, handheld box. The game makers have made those handheld controllers for PCs as well, and you can get away from the keyboard more easily with such controllers for nonracing and nonflying games. Figure 11.6 shows a joystick, a game controller, and a steering wheel and pedal set like the ones you can buy to master your games. You'll plug all these game controllers into your PC's game port.

11

Figure 11.5.

Racing games require split-second accuracy, which you can get with a steering wheel controller.

Figure 11.6.

Do you want to beat your game competition? Get the right hardware to gain a gaming edge.

The arcade games don't just cover the war/space/fighter gauntlet. The game makers have put their designers' thinking caps in high gear and come up with some amazing backdrops for games. *Interstate '76* places you in a beefed-up, gas-guzzling, machine-gun-equipped, super-fast car out in the Arizona dessert, chasing and being chased by some baddies who don't seem to know there's a gas shortage keeping most people under 55 (the year of the game's setting is 1976). Who would have thought such a game would get off the drawing boards? Not only has Interstate '76 become a reality, but sequels are now being penned, and the game consistently hits the top-ten game sales.

If that doesn't take the cake, get a load (literally) of *Redneck Rampage*. If the moonshine holds out and the chickens stay out of your way, you and a buddy shoot your way through the corn fields of Arkansas (you didn't even know Arkansas had corn fields!), ripping your overalls but having fun and leaving a whole lot of rib bones and empties in your trail. Now, which Wall Street investment firm would have sent clients to purchase *that* game company's stock a month before the software hit number one in sales?

JUST A MINUTE

I hope this chapter will, at the very least, intrigue you enough to make you walk down the game aisles of your PC store just to see what this industry is going to do next!

Sports Without the Sweat

Today's PC-based sports provide everything but the popcorn smell. Baseball, football, soccer, skiing, championship racing, and Olympic trials are just some of the games competing for the sports enthusiast's game dollars. These sports games are not just simulations that you watch play out; you control every aspect of the game, at varying levels depending on your skills. You'll call the plays, control the pitch, line up the field goal, replace failing players, call time-outs, and even react to changing weather conditions. When you line up a pitch you'll have to check for base-stealers, when you kick a field goal you'll need to compensate for wind direction, and when you kick a goal you'd better guard against an own goal (that's soccer lingo for kicking into your own goal) by making sure you kick the ball into your *opponent's goal*.

TIME SAVER

Most companies update their sports games annually to include the current year's players and stats so that you can control your favorite teams.

Sports games don't need to have the high-pitched excitement of an arcade game to be exciting. Figure 11.7 shows a Microsoft Golf simulation with a realism that will amaze you.

11

When you swing the club, you hear the swoosh and watch the ball (and its shadow) travel over the green (and plop into the water if you slice the drive). The birds even chirp on sunny days.

Figure 11.7.

Wear the proper clothing when you play a few holes on Microsoft Golf's courses.

JUST A MINUTE

By the way, Microsoft Golf and the other golfing games let you play on accurately reproduced famous courses around the world. Want to play nine holes at Pebble Beach and then try one of Scotland's par-3s? No problem.

Blood and Gore

Very few approach the blood-and-gore PC games with mixed emotions; generally, people really like them or really abhor them. No matter which camp you fall into, you should look at one or two games to see perhaps the most incredible technology on PCs today.

Games such as *Doom* and *Quake* permanently raised the gaming standard several levels. These games put you in the middle of a dungeon-like 3D world, armed to the hilt with guns (not just guns but machine guns, sawed-off shotguns, nail guns, fire-throwing guns, and others that can really get nasty when you fire them), axes, blades, bombs, chains, and other self-defense artifacts that you'll need to battle the beyond-bad beings that approach you, the least of which will be heavily armed Nazis and vicious giant dogs whose only goal in life and afterward is to see you die agonizingly.

Figure 11.8 shows a shot from Quake. The figure can do little justice to the game, but you can get an idea of the setting. You watch and participate in the game through the eyes of the hero; if you get too close to one of your victims before you blow him away, you'll need a washcloth fast.

Figure 11.8.

Don't tread through Quake with closed eyes because they are after you!

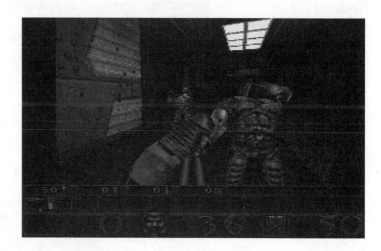

JUST A MINUTE

Games such as Quake provide amazing smoothness as you travel about and fight the creatures you encounter. Although your electronic spreadsheet might take a few moments to produce a color graph from your sales figures, you'll instantly glide from room to room, viewing the new areas from every angle smoothly, and fighting creatures and watching the result of your accurate shooting while listening to the gory sounds.

Strategy and Role-Playing

If the arcade, sports, and gore games don't thrill you, don't give up on game software just yet. Tons of strategy and role-playing games abound on the shelves. You'll be able to re-create King Arthur's castle, and create and manage cities and worlds from scratch. Many of the role-playing games that came out years ago, originally in boxes, now appear as interactive PC games. The computer takes care of all the bookkeeping about which players used to have to worry.

Strategy games such as graphic challenges and graphic puzzles offer hours of play for people who want the mental (as opposed to the wrist) challenges. Even crossword puzzles have made their way onto the PC.

One of the most amazing game stories in the past few years is the rebirth of PC-based trivia games. Although non-PC trivia game sales have faltered over the past few years, and the trivia

11

fever that hit the world a few years ago has faded, a game called *You Don't Know Jack* has brought back trivia with a vengeance.

You Don't Know Jack tests your trivia knowledge and lets you play against one or two other players. This game, however, doesn't just test your knowledge; it makes ample fun of you all along the way! *You Don't Know Jack* uses a self-deprecating game-show format with an announcer who zaps you with zingers as you play. The show flies along, sending you from question to question, but the questions come at you in different formats with a catchy introductory jingle. As Figure 11.9 shows, *You Don't Know Jack*'s appeal comes from its simple interface and its humorous question slant, which are married perfectly with the wiseguy announcer's antics.

Figure 11.9.
You'll never have more fun being ridiculed for your intelligence (or lack thereof) than with You Don't Know Jack.

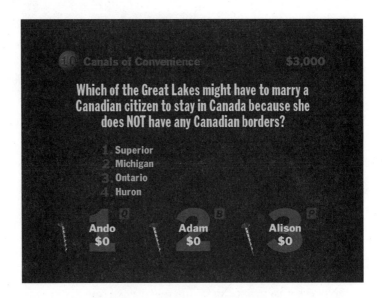

You Won't Get Bored with PC Board Games

If you enjoy or used to enjoy board games, you should know that most reside on the PC now. The PC plays the record-keeping role so that you (and the other players, if you elect not to play against the PC) can concentrate on the game. The games all have graphically animated interfaces. When you blow up a battleship you'll hear the blast, see the smoke, and watch the pieces fall. When you invade enemy territory with *Risk*, the PC's feedback of the battle that ensues can make you regret ever joining the ranks.

As Figure 11.10 shows, the PC version of *Monopoly* brings the board game's action alive. In addition to activating board games and introducing the classic games to a new computerized generation, you can play against other interested players all over the world if you have online access. Many of the board games, including *Monopoly*, support Internet play so that, at any hour of the day or night, you can link up with other *Monopoly* players (who have the same software) using the game's automatic searching capabilities for players, and then trade properties all over the world.

Figure 11.10.
Your PC counts your money and puts you in the poorhouse with Monopoly.

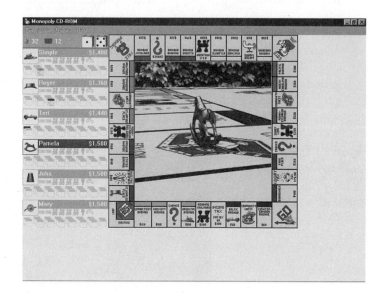

Online Gaming

Online gaming is getting to be a favorite pastime. So many arcade games pit you against the PC, but a human opponent is so much more fun to beat. The worldwide access to the Internet and commercial online services offer a unique hook-up medium with which game players from all over the world can play against each other.

Not every game is set up for Internet play, of course, but most of the more recent games are. Arguably, one of the games that matured the online gaming community and paved the way for online games is *Air Warrior*, now in its second version, which puts you in the cockpit of a World War I biplane fighter in the middle of real, history-based battlefields. Other planes and wars are there too. Figure 11.11 shows a World War II plane battling the Axis forces.

How do you find other players? When you purchase a game that you can play online, the game should offer several clues. Sometimes, only an Internet connection is required, but more often than not, online gamers benefit more from an online service. In fact, if you don't currently use an online service such as America Online, you might want to check them out to see which online games they offer if you do enjoy games. If your favorite game is available online, you'll enjoy battling against the human factor far more than against the computer in most cases.

11

Figure 11.11.

Air Warrior *puts together thousands of players and pits them against each other to reenact famous fighter battles from previous wars.*

Hour 22, "Using Online Services," explains more about using and signing up for online services.

JUST A MINUTE

Some online services charge an hourly rate, on top of the usual monthly charge, for their online gaming sections due to the high demand such sections place on the service's resources.

CAUTION

Most of the online services offer popular games, such as *Quake* and *Air Warrior* but they also offer other games. You can play *Blackjack* against the house with a set of fellow players from around the world, for example. Many of these games, such as the *Blackjack* game in CompuServe's gaming area, are available for download so that you don't even have to purchase software to play the game.

To show that nothing's new under the sun, one of the most popular online gaming areas in use today is Microsoft Network's *Backgammon* game area. When you sit down at a table with another player, the *Backgammon* board appears; you play as if you were actually looking down at the board, as Figure 11.12 shows. When you roll the dice you'll hear the bones click on the board, and a warning sound alerts you when your opponent doubles on you.

Figure 11.12.

Play a leisurely game of Backgammon *on your lunch break against someone from the other side of the world.*

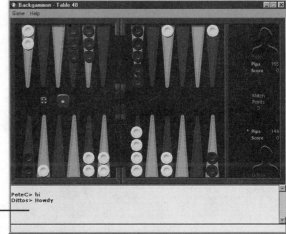

You can chat with the other player by typing here

TIME SAVER

Many online games offer language independence—that is, if an American plays against someone in Italy, the American's instructions appear in English while the Italian's instructions appear in *Italiano*. Although most games don't translate the actual typed chat conversations between players, the games do respond with commands and status messages in the player's native toungue.

Summary

PC games are vital, not just for the money they generate every month for the computer industry, but also for their demands on PC resources. Games help encourage PC makers to make faster PCs with better hardware and more accurate and smoother graphics. If games did not routinely test a PC's performance to the limits, PC makers would have less incentive to develop the quick machines to keep up with the gaming software market.

This hour has introduced you to the world of PC games. If you don't play them, your child will. If you like more laid-back board games, don't give up your PC for entertainment just yet because, as you read here, board games come alive on the PC, especially those you play against others around the world.

Hour 12, "Organizing Your PC," gets back down to basics by explaining ways you can streamline your PC. Life's not all play and no work, so you will want to organize your PC so that your system provides the information you require when you require it.

Q&A

Q What's the best game with which to start?

A So many games exist that this question has no answer except from you when you browse the gaming software aisles. Perhaps you should consider starting with two games: a remake of a board game you might now (or you used to) enjoy, such as *Scrabble* or *Monopoly*. You'll see right away that the PC's interactive nature makes the games more fun than you ever before realized.

If funds are a problem, consider a collection of several games on CD-ROM, as offered in most gaming aisles. The games aren't always the newest on the market, but they offer an inexpensive assortment of games with which you can start. If you purchased your PC with software already loaded, your PC probably already contains the Windows games as well as several more, so check your manuals and CD-ROMs that came with your PC.

If you already subscribe to one of the major online services such as Prodigy or The Microsoft Network, visit one of the service's gaming sites to see what's out there. You can download most of the games. If you want to play a game whose software is sold in stores, such as *Air Warrior*, the gaming service often lets you download, for the normal connection fee that you pay each month, a limited version of the game just to see if you like the game enough to purchase the full product.

11

PART

IV

Digging Deeper

Hour

Hour 12

Organizing Your PC

Congratulations! You've reached the halfway point of your 24-hour tutorial. By now you know how to select the right PC, set up the PC when you get it home or to the office, install software, navigate Windows, and work with software. You're already ready for the next step: taking your PC to a more advanced level.

This hour describes ways to use your PC more effectively. Instead of concentrating on one area, this hour offers numerous tips and shortcuts that help you manage your PC's software, Windows environment, and operation. Now that you've used Windows and your PC for a while, you probably want more depth; this hour gives you that depth.

The highlights of this hour include

- ☐ How to control the Start menu
- ☐ Where you can move the Start menu and taskbar
- ☐ Where to find your PC's clock and calendar
- ☐ When to change your desktop wallpaper
- ☐ Which options you can select when printing

Controlling the Start Menu

One of the cornerstones of Windows is the Start menu. Perhaps not too surprising is that you can do a lot to improve your Windows environment by learning more about your Start menu's capabilities; as you'll see, the Start menu is not just for starting programs.

The Documents Menu

As you've learned, the Start menu is your key to the PC. You access programs from the Start menu. From those programs, such as a word processor, you create or load your data document. This two-step process, starting a program and loading a data file, is so common that Windows offers a shortcut.

Every time you access a data file with a Windows program, the program updates the Start menu's Documents option. When you select Documents, as Figure 12.1 shows, a list of recently opened data documents appear. These documents might be a spreadsheet you recently created, a letter you wrote, a Paint image you changed, or a presentation you updated.

Figure 12.1.

The Start menu's Documents option keeps track of your recent data documents.

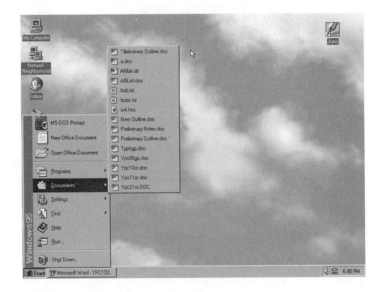

CAUTION

Some programs do not update the Start menu's Documents option properly, and not all your recent data files appear on the Start menu if you've recently used one of those programs.

12

The Documents menu option is more than just an accounting of your recent data files. More often than not, PC users work on the same data multiple times. If you create a report for your company's management, you and your departmental team members might want to make changes to that report over a period of a week or more. Therefore, PC users often load the same document several times before the document is finished.

Instead of first starting the document's program and *then* loading the document, Windows lets you work smarter. If you recently worked on the file that you want to update again, select the Start menu's Documents option and select the file from the menu list. Windows determines which program you used to edit the file and automatically starts the program for you.

JUST A MINUTE

Windows is *data-driven*. Nowhere is that more obvious than the Start menu's Documents option. Why should you worry about the program when it's the *data* that interests you? Suppose you want to edit a worksheet first and then edit a letter that you wrote. As you select the items from the Documents menu, Windows starts the spreadsheet program if it's not already started and your word processor if it's not already started. After the programs load, Windows loads the data for you as well. You get to concentrate on your data while Windows worries about the program that manages that data.

TIME SAVER

You can clear the Documents menu at any time by selecting the Start menu's Settings option, selecting Taskbar, and clicking the Start Menu Programs tab. Figure 12.2 shows the resulting dialog box. When you click the Clear button, Windows erases everything in the Documents menu. (The files still stay on your disk, but their entries in the Documents menu go away.)

12

Windows is so smart that if you recently used the Internet, even Internet locations you've recently visited often show up on the Documents menu. When you select any Internet document (called a *Web page* or *HTML document*) from the Documents menu, Windows starts your Internet connection and takes you to the page that you selected.

Changing Your Taskbar

The Taskbar Properties dialog box that you see when you choose the Start menu's Settings | Taskbar option also contains a tab called Taskbar Options (see Figure 12.3). You can adjust several settings from this tab:

Figure 12.2.
Clear the Documents menu from the Start Menu Programs tab.

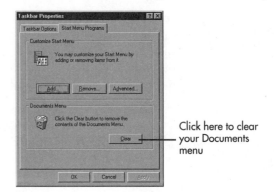

Click here to clear your Documents menu

☐ **Always on top**: When selected, this ensures that your taskbar appears on top of any windows you open on the screen. If you don't select the Always on top option, a large open window could hide your taskbar.

☐ **Auto hide**: When checked, the taskbar appears on your screen only as long as you are selecting from the Start menu and only when you move your mouse cursor to the bottom of your screen.

☐ **Show small icons in Start menu**: When checked, this changes the size of your Start menu and taskbar icons so you can see more of the Start menu at one time.

☐ **Show Clock**: When selected, this shows the time of day at the right of your taskbar.

Figure 12.3.
You can modify the behavior and appearance of the taskbar.

12

TIME SAVER

If you lose your taskbar, either because a window covered it up or because you hid it, press Ctrl+Esc to display the Start menu and taskbar once again. If you have a keyboard with Windows keys (the flying Windows logo appears on a key at each side of your spacebar), the Windows key will perform the same Ctrl+Esc operation and display the Start menu and your taskbar.

The benefit to hiding your taskbar with the Auto hide option is that the taskbar will not consume screen real estate and take space away from other programs. If you often work with several open programs at one time, the smaller icons will let more program buttons show at one time when you do display your taskbar.

Moving Your Taskbar

If you want your taskbar on a different edge of your screen, move it. By clicking your mouse over an empty taskbar region and dragging to either side or the top of your screen, you can place the taskbar elsewhere. The Start menu appears, as well as the clock and all the other icons that normally appear there.

If you work with rather wide data windows, such as spreadsheets, you'll probably like your taskbar kept at the bottom of your screen or, perhaps, at the top with the Start menu falling down from above. If, however, you work with graphics very much, you'll probably prefer your taskbar on one side of your screen to get as much of the vertical picture's portion as possible.

TIME SAVER

If you want to widen your taskbar because you run a lot of programs at the same time, drag the edge of the taskbar closest to the center of your screen in or out to widen or narrow the taskbar's height. Each increment that you widen the taskbar makes another row of icons available for you. The more rows you have, the more room that Windows can devote to each button and, therefore, the better you can read the descriptions of each program running. Don't make your taskbar too wide, though, or you'll take too much room away from your program viewing area.

12

Time and Date

If you've displayed the clock on your taskbar, you can rest your mouse cursor over the time of day, and after a brief pause the date appears over the time. Therefore, as long as you display the taskbar clock, the date and time are always just a mouse move away. Even when you've turned on Auto hide and can see your taskbar only if you point to the bottom of the screen, the date appears if you rest your cursor over the time.

If your PC's time or date is not correct, use the taskbar to make things right. Double-click the clock to display the Date/Time Properties dialog box, as shown in Figure 12.4.

Figure 12.4.

Keep your PC's date and time of day set properly.

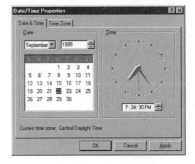

If you move to a different time zone, be sure to display the Date/Time Properties dialog box and click the Time Zone tab to set the new time zone. Your PC will automatically adjust the time, if needed by your time zone, twice a year.

> An internal clock, backed up with a battery inside your PC, keeps track of the date and time of day.

JUST A MINUTE

Searching for Files

If you know a file exists on your PC, but you don't remember the filename and the Documents menu does not display the file, make Windows tell you where the file is! The Start menu's Find command searches your computer, as well as networked PCs (if any are attached) and the Internet (if needed), for one or more files you want to find.

Depending on your version of Windows, your Start menu's Find menu might display a different set of search options, but you'll probably see some of the following items:

- ☐ **Files or folders**: Searches a specific disk drive or within a folder on a specific disk for a file or folder.

- ☐ **Computer**: Searches your entire computer system, including all disks, CD-ROMs, and networked drives for files and folders.

- ☐ **People**: Searches your Windows Address Book (used by several applications) for a person if you've entered the information into the Windows Address Book (found on the Accessories menu).

12

☐ **On the Internet**: Searches the Internet using one of the Internet *search engine* programs you'll learn about in Hour 21, "Enter the Internet."

Suppose you wrote a letter last year to KPC, a 24-hour PC radio network, but you cannot locate the file. Select Start | Find | Files or Folders to display the dialog box shown in Figure 12.5. Type the filename in the Named text box and click the Find Now button to start the search.

Figure 12.5.

Make Windows search for files and folders.

Click here to search through all folders within the current folder

Enter your file or folder name here

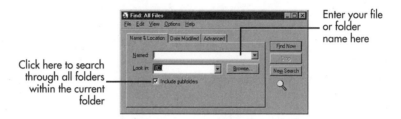

You don't have to know the exact file or folder name to locate specific files and folders. You can use *wildcard characters* to perform a more general search. Windows supports two wildcard characters, * and ?.

The asterisk, *, represents zero, one, or more characters in a search. Therefore, if you type 1stQtr98.* as the filename to search for, Windows would then look for any and all files whose filenames begin with 1stQtr98 and that have any filename extension. Both of these files, if found on your disk, would be found as a result: 1stQtr98.DAT and 1stQtr98.txt. If you typed FAX*.*, Windows would locate all files (or folders) whose filenames begin with the letters FAX. Windows would consider these files a match: FAX, FAX98, FAXtoMom.Doc, and Faxes.98.

JUST A MINUTE

Windows matches exact uppercase and lowercase letters if you select Options | Case Sensitive, and it ignores uppercase and lowercase differences if you deselect Options | Case Sensitive.

The question-mark wildcard, ?, matches one and only one character. Suppose you begin all quarterly accounting data filenames with the year and you need to search for all old accounting files from the 1980s that are still on your disk. You could specify the following search: 8?*.DAT to locate all files that begin with an 8, followed by *at least one character* (due to the question mark), followed by anything else, and that end with the .DAT filename extension. Realize that every question mark you specify indicates one character position. Therefore, ??.* finds all files and folders whose filenames contain two and only two characters followed by any extension (or no extension, because the asterisk allows for a missing extension as well).

The Find dialog box gets even more powerful when you click on the Date Modified tab to display the tabbed dialog box shown in Figure 12.6. You could enter a specific date or a date range. If you know the day or week you created a file, you can search for all files with that date even if you don't know anything about the filename.

Figure 12.6.

Search for files that fall within a date range.

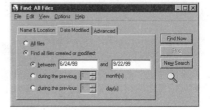

The Advanced tab displays a dialog box page that lets you search for files by any file type (such as a graphics file, a word-processed file, or whatever) or a size of file.

As you can see, the Find dialog box lets you create powerful searches, and after the search is over you can use those found files. For example, Figure 12.7 shows a list of several files found in a wildcard search. You can scroll through the list and locate the exact file you wanted to find. You'll be able to see the exact file location, and the date and time that you modified or created the file.

Figure 12.7.

Double-click a file to open it.

Double-click on any file here to open it ———

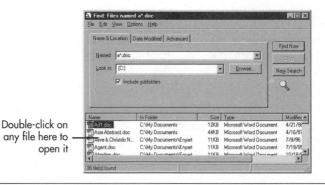

TIME SAVER

Click on any column's title in the dialog box's found list to sort the found list by that column. Click on the column a second time if you want the column sorted in *reverse* order (such as alphabetically from Z to A, or from the last date to the present).

Suppose you searched for a word-processed file and, in the found list, you see the file you want to edit. All you have to do is double-click on that filename, and Windows opens your word processor and automatically loads that file! If you were searching for a program file and found

12

the program, when you double-click the program's name, Windows starts the program. Therefore, the found list provides a launch pad for other activities you want to do once you find your file.

Adding Programs to the Start Menu

You can add your own programs to the Start menu for faster access to those programs. Instead of wading through a series of cascading Start menus and submenus, you can place your frequently accessed programs at the top of the Start menu so they appear as soon as you click the Start button.

The only requirement for adding programs to the top of your Start menu is that you must know the location and name of the program's executable file. One way to find such a program file is to search with the Start menu's Find command, but finding programs is not always as simple as finding it by name. Suppose you use your Microsoft Word word processor almost every time you use your PC, so you want to add Word to the top of the Start menu. If you use Find to look for *Word*, you'll be out of luck. The name of the executable program that begins running when you start Word is named `msword.exe`.

One of the best ways to locate a program is to open the My Computer window, double-click over the disk drive that you used to install the program, and then read through the folders and files and make a guess as to the program name. (You can also find programs this way by starting the Explorer program, which is discussed in Hour 6, "Starting Your PC.") When you locate the probable program name, double-click on it to see if the program starts; if it does, you've found the program.

From the program's filename listing inside My Computer or Explorer, drag the program name to the Start button. When you release your mouse button, Windows adds that program to your Start menu. Figure 12.8 shows Microsoft Word appearing at the top of a Start menu. Instead of wading through menus, you only need to click Start and select Microsoft Word to start your word processor.

Figure 12.8.

Add programs to the top of the Start menu for quick access.

Prettying Up the Desktop

Windows supplies several *wallpaper* files with which you can add flair to your desktop. (Your *desktop* is the background screen on which the icons, Start menu, and windows appear.) A wallpaper file is a graphics file with the filename extension .BMP. You can place any .BMP bitmap graphics file on your desktop.

Many of today's PCs come with wallpaper supplied by the manufacturer that displays an ad for your PC company. You can replace this wallpaper with a different picture if you want.

If you want to change your desktop's wallpaper, you can first minimize or close all open program windows to give you easier access to your desktop. One quick way to minimize all open windows, if you were to have several open at once, is to right-click over a blank area of your taskbar and select Minimize All Windows. Your clean desktop then appears. Right-click over your desktop to display a menu. Select Properties from this menu to display a dialog box similar to the one shown in Figure 12.9. (Depending on your version of Windows and your hardware settings, your Display Properties dialog box might differ somewhat.)

Figure 12.9.

Use the Display Properties dialog box to change your desktop's background picture.

The Pattern list box shows various graphic patterns you can add to your desktop, but the Wallpaper list box offers a more complete set of choices for papering your desktop. For example, if you select the Clouds wallpaper and then click OK, your desktop fills with a flowing sky of clouds behind the icons.

Some of the wallpaper patterns are small, but you can either tile your desktop with the selected pattern or center the pattern in the middle of your screen by selecting either Tile or Center.

12

CAUTION

Some screen resolutions are so great that the wallpaper does not fill the entire screen but appears as a square in the center of the desktop with a wide border that does not include the picture. Click the Display Properties box's Plus! tab, if the tab exists (if not, you cannot stretch the wallpaper without the Windows add-on program called Microsoft Plus!), and click the option labeled Stretch desktop wallpaper to fit the screen; this will expand the center wallpaper to your full screen.

JUST A MINUTE

Starting with Internet Explorer 4.0, you can activate your desktop and place Web material directly on the desktop. Therefore, you can watch a stock ticker or news headlines on your desktop as they comes across the Internet.

The Open Dialog Box

When you want to work with a document file, no matter what kind of file it is, you'll need to open that file. *Open* is the Windows term for loading a document file from the disk drive and using the file in a program. Perhaps the simplest example is a document file you open with a word processor in order to make changes to the document.

When using a program written for Windows, such as Microsoft Word, you select File | Open from the program's menu bar to inform the program that you want to load a document into memory and work on that document. Figure 12.10 shows the Open dialog box that is supported by several Windows programs when you open a document file.

Figure 12.10.

You'll select data to work with from the Open dialog box.

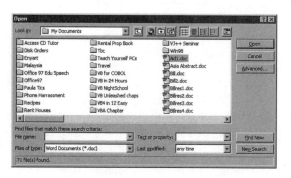

12

> Ctrl+O is the accelerator keystroke for the File | Open command in all Windows-compatible programs.

Whenever you need to specify a document to open, you must tell Windows the document's filename and the folder that contains that file on the disk (called the *pathname*). The Open dialog box always contains a text prompt where you can type the filename to open. A scrollable list appears in which you can select the proper folder where the document is located. The Look in list always appears as a drop-down list box and lets you select a specific disk, a network drive, or even an Internet location. Other selecting information, such as file types and properties, also appears in drop-down list boxes in many Open dialog boxes.

An Open dialog box will always have an Open command button and a Cancel command button. Clicking Open after specifying the filename and location information opens the file. Clicking Cancel closes the dialog box without opening the file. You can display the file and folder information in a list that shows the file's size and last date modified if you click the toolbar's Details button.

JUST A MINUTE

> A *drop-down list box* is a special Windows control that works like a scrolling list but consumes much less screen space. Figure 12.10 contains a File name drop-down list box as well as other list boxes you can use to help pinpoint the file you need to open. Unlike other kinds of list boxes such as the filename list, a drop-down list box normally consumes only a single line in a dialog box. When the user clicks the down arrow at the right of the drop-down list box, Windows displays the list of choices. When you select one of the choices, the drop-down list box closes again to give room back to the rest of the dialog box.

Common Dialog Boxes

Windows dialog boxes, such as the Open dialog box, are available for all programmers to use. Therefore, a programmer can write a unique file-opening dialog box, but if he uses one of the standard Windows Open dialog boxes (called a *common dialog box*), you and others who use the program will be more familiar with the interface.

One of the benefits that Windows offers PC users is the constant, familiar interface. No matter which Windows program you use, you'll already understand the menu and common dialog boxes (assuming the programmers who created the program used the common interface elements available to them instead of writing unique interface elements that confuse you). The faster you and others adapt to a program, the more likely it is that you'll use the program and update it in the future. Therefore, software companies have an interest in making software as easy to use and as standard as possible.

If you know the exact filename and location of the document you want to open, you can bypass the mouse clicks and type the full pathname in the File name text box prompt and click the OK button (or press Enter) to open that document. Given the powerful Open dialog box in Windows and considering the extremely long filenames that Windows supports, most users will enjoy the benefit of zeroing-in on the file using the mouse instead of typing complete path and document names such as these:

```
c:\winword\docs\balance.doc
a:\Note for James
```

The Open dialog box does more than provide a common interface for you to use. After you display the Open dialog box, you can point to any folder or document and click the right-mouse button to perform several other actions on the document. Here are the things you can do with documents:

- ☐ Select the document
- ☐ Play sound documents or open graphic documents
- ☐ Print the document
- ☐ Copy the file to a disk
- ☐ Cut or copy selected text to the Windows Clipboard
- ☐ Create a shortcut access to the file so you can later open the file without using the Open dialog box
- ☐ Delete the document
- ☐ Rename the document
- ☐ Change the document's system attributes

A right-click over a folder's name produces a menu that lets you perform these same actions as well as start the Windows Explorer program (described in Hour 6) or search the disk for other files and folders.

Placing Documents on the Desktop

Instead of adding programs to your Start menu, you can put programs on your desktop itself, with icons right alongside the My Computer and Recycle Bin icons. The items you place on

12

the desktop stay on the desktop until you remove them. Not only can you place programs on the desktop and execute those programs by double-clicking their icons, but if you place a data document on your desktop, Windows opens the appropriate parent program when you double-click the document's icon.

Although you shouldn't put too many documents out on the desktop, which would cause clutter, you may want to work with a document over a period of a few days. By putting the document on the desktop, it is always easily available to any application that's running. All you need to do is right-click over an empty area of your taskbar and select Minimize All Windows to minimize all open windows and give you access to the desktop icons.

To copy an item to your desktop, simply locate that item from Explorer or the My Computer window, hold down the Ctrl key, and drag the item to the desktop. When you release your mouse and Ctrl key, the item's icon will appear on the desktop. (Without the Ctrl keypress, Windows would *move* the item from its original location to the desktop folder in the Windows\Desktop folder. Ctrl tells Windows to create a shortcut (a pointer) to the item, so if you later delete the icon from your desktop (by selecting the icon and pressing Delete) you will not delete the actual file from its original location.

Printing Data

Although you've now mastered much of the hardware and software related to PCs, you'll still want to print data. Remember, in today's PCs, data might be a word-processed document, a color graph, a spreadsheet, a data listing, or a picture.

An Introduction to Spooled Printing

When you print documents, Windows automatically starts the *printer subsystem*. The printer subsystem controls all printing from within Windows. Windows *spools* output through the printer subsystem, as shown in Figure 12.11. When spooled, the printed output goes to a disk file, collected by the printer subsystem, before the printer subsystem sends the output to the printer itself.

Figure 12.11.

Windows spools output to the printer subsystem disk file.

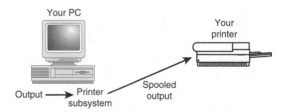

> Every document you print creates a unique *print job* that appears on the spooler.

By routing printed output to a spooled disk file instead of sending the output directly to the printer, you can intercept the printed output before that output goes to paper. You therefore have more control over how the output appears on the printer. You also can select which printer receives the output in case more than one printer is connected to your computer.

The Print Dialog Box

When you print from an application such as WordPad, you'll see the Print dialog box shown in Figure 12.12. The Print dialog box contains several options from which you can choose. Most of the time, the default option values are appropriate, so you'll simply press Enter to select the OK command button when printing.

Figure 12.12.

The Print dialog box controls the way a print job routes output.

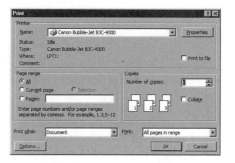

The Print dialog box contains a drop-down list box of every printer you've added to Windows. The Page range will be All if you want to print all pages. For example, if you are printing 20 pages from a word processor, the All option sends all 20 pages to the printer. If you select the Pages option, you can enter a starting page number and ending page number to print only a portion of the document. If you highlight part of the text before beginning the print process, you can click the Selection option button to print only the selected text.

The Copies section determines how many copies you want to print. The default is one copy, but you can request an additional number of copies. If you enter a number greater than 1, check the Collate option if you want the pages collated (you usually do).

For special print jobs, you can click the Properties button to display a printer Properties dialog box such as the one shown in Figure 12.13. Each printer model supports a different set of options, so each printer's Properties dialog box contains different options as well. In the Properties dialog box, you specify the type of paper in the printer's paper tray, the *orientation*

12

(the way the printed output appears on the paper), and the printer resolution (the higher the printer resolution, the better your output looks, but the longer the printer takes to print a single page), among other options your printer might support.

Figure 12.13.

A printer Properties dialog box controls your printer options.

Keep in mind that the output goes to the print spooler and *not* directly to the printer. The next section explains how you can manage the print spooler.

CAUTION

Some applications begin printing as soon as you click a Print toolbar button instead of displaying the Print dialog box before beginning to print. Be sure that you understand the way each of your applications handles printing. If you click such a toolbar button several times, you could inadvertently send many copies of output to your printer.

TIME SAVER

Some print jobs take a while to spool their output to the spool file and, subsequently, to the printer. The taskbar displays a printer icon to the left of the clock during the printing process. If you rest the cursor over the printer icon, Windows displays a description of how many jobs are in line to print. If you double-click on the printer icon, Windows displays the list of all print jobs (the next section describes the window that displays print jobs). If you right-click on the icon, Windows gives you the choice of displaying a window containing a list of all print jobs or the print jobs for specific printers that are queued up waiting for printed output.

Explorer and Open dialog boxes all display documents, as you've seen already. If you want to print a document, such as a bitmap graphic document file, a text document file, or a word processing document file, the right-click menu contains a Print command that automatically prints the selected document (or documents) that you right-clicked on. The right-click does *not* produce the Print dialog box described in this section; rather, Windows automatically prints one copy of the document on the default printer.

JUST A MINUTE

> Windows cannot print all types of documents. For example, executable programs (such as those ending with the `.EXE` or `.COM` extension) are not printable. When you right-click over these non-printable files, the right-click menu does not contain a Print command.

There's yet one more way to print documents that works well in some situations. If you have the My Computer window open or if you are using the Explorer, you can print any printable document by dragging that document to any printer icon inside the Printers window. Windows automatically begins spooling that document to the printer that you drag to.

Managing Print Jobs

When you print one or more documents, from whatever program you print, Windows formats the output into the format required by the Print dialog box's selected printer and then sends that output to a spool file. When the output completes, the printer subsystem begins to route the output to the actual printer, as long as your printer is connected and turned on.

Suppose that you want to print several documents in succession. Although today's printers are fairly fast, the computer's disk drives and memory are much faster than the relative speed of printers. Therefore, you can end up sending several documents to the printer before the first document even finishes printing on paper.

After printing one or more documents, you can open the Printer window and double-click on the printer icon that matches the printer to which you've routed all your output. A scrolling list of print jobs, such as the one shown in Figure 12.14, appears inside the window.

Figure 12.14.

You can see all the print jobs spooled up, waiting to print.

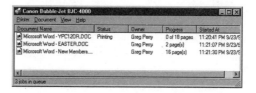

Each line in the window describes one print job. If you've printed three documents, all three documents appear inside the window. The window describes how far along the print job is.

The Progress column tells you how many pages of the current print job have completed. The remaining print jobs wait their turn in the list.

If you want to move one of the print jobs to the top or bottom of the *queue* (the list of print jobs), you can drag that print job to the top or bottom. Dragging a print job around in the list changes priority for that print job. For example, your boss might be waiting over your shoulder for a report. If you had several jobs waiting to print before your boss showed up, you could move the boss's print job to the top of the list so it will print next.

Right-clicking over a print job gives you the option of pausing a print job (putting it on hold until you resume the job) or canceling the print job altogether.

TIME SAVER

> If you select more than one print job by holding down the Ctrl key while you select print jobs, you can pause or cancel more than one print job at the same time.

Summary

This hour has multiplied your Windows skills by several factors. Most people, even those who have used Windows before, will have learned one or more shortcuts and time-saving tips from the material this hour. For example, you learned how to gain quicker access to your programs by placing them on the Start menu or on your desktop, and you now know you can improve your desktop's appearance by placing a wallpaper graphic on the desktop. After you've started a program, you can now manage the output that you produce from that program from within the print queue.

Hour 13, "Fine-Tuning Your PC," offers more tips, shortcuts, and safety precautions. You'll learn how to keep your system running at its best.

Q&A

Q Why use the Start menu's Documents option when I can open document files with File | Open from within my programs?

A The Documents option is much quicker. As long as a document's filename and icon appear on the Documents menu (and the name *will* appear if you've recently worked on that document and have not yet cleared the contents of the Documents option), you can click on that document's name, and Windows will start the program needed to view and edit it. Without the Documents option, you would have to start the program and then, in a second step, open the document you want to view and edit.

12

Q Why should I care how my output gets to the printer?

A There are times when you'll send several documents to the printer and then change your mind about printing one or more of them. As long as the documents haven't printed, you can keep the document from printing by utilizing the printer subsystem available within Windows.

All printer output goes through the print spooler instead of going directly to the printer. The spooler holds all print jobs and controls the order of the print jobs. When a job is on the spooler's list of documents, you can delete the documents or rearrange their printing priority. If you did not know how Windows spooled printed output, you would not be able to rearrange printer output.

12

Hour 13

Fine-Tuning Your PC

If you eat right and take care of yourself, your body has a better chance of running more smoothly with fewer downtimes. Likewise, you can keep your PC operating at a tip-top performance level by taking care of it properly. Windows includes several programs that make your PC run efficiently, as you'll learn in this hour.

You can change the way your screen displays data so that you can view more items at once on your screen. Your disk drive's performance determines how fast your programs and data load, so you'll want to keep your disk running as quickly as possible. In addition to speed, you can increase the free storage space on your disk without buying any hardware! By compressing the way your disk holds data, you'll be able to gain almost twice as much disk space.

The highlights of this hour include

- [ ] How screen colors affect the amount of information you can view
- [ ] How to adjust your screen's resolution so you can see more information at one time
- [ ] Why your hard disk slows down

☐ When to scan your disk's files and folders to ensure no errors exist

☐ What steps you can take to increase your free disk space

☐ How to manage your compressed disk drives

Improving Your Display

Often, new PCs are sold today with screen resolutions set to less than optimum performance. *Resolution* refers to the quality and amount of information you can view on your screen at any one time. Your screen's display, both text and graphics, is composed of colored pixel dots; the smaller and closer those dots are, the higher your screen's resolution is.

Most video cards and monitors support several resolution combinations. Generally, the manufacturer's settings are less than optimal. Therefore, you might want to increase your monitor's resolution. To do so, follow these steps:

1. Minimize your desktop's open windows by right-clicking on a blank area of your taskbar and selecting Minimize All Windows.

2. Right-click on your desktop.

3. Select Properties to open the Display Properties dialog box.

4. Click on the Settings tab to display the dialog box shown in Figure 13.1.

Figure 13.1.

Change your screen's resolution from the Settings property page.

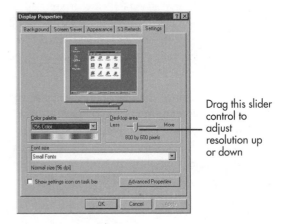

Drag this slider control to adjust resolution up or down

5. The more colors your screen displays at one time, the better your screen looks. You can increase the number of colors your screen displays by selecting from the Color palette drop-down list box. Click the down arrow to open the list box and select the number of colors you want to display. Almost all of today's monitors and video cards can display 256 colors, so if your palette is set for 16 colors, try a higher value.

13

You won't see a change immediately. Your screen details only take effect when you click the Apply or OK button. Even then, many of your screen settings require that you restart Windows before the settings will appear.

6. Drag the desktop area's slider control to the right to increase your screen's resolution. The resolution is measured in the number of horizontal pixels by the number of vertical pixels. An 800 (horizontal pixels) × 600 (vertical pixels) resolution shows a better picture than does a 640×480 resolution.

Figure 13.2 shows a message box that appears when you click Apply or OK to set the resolution to your selected value. Some video cards do not properly support Window's higher resolution settings. Therefore, after you change your screen's resolution, if the screen shows only garbage and not readable text or graphics, wait 15 seconds and Windows will restore your original resolution settings. If the resolution works, however, and you like the new resolution setting, click Yes within that 15-second time period and the new resolution will go into effect.

Figure 13.2.

If your resolution causes a display problem, Windows restores your previous resolution after 15 seconds.

The higher screen resolutions sometimes make your text and icons too small to read. For example, Figure 13.3 shows a high resolution that displays a lot of information on the screen at one time, but the information is so small and the text is so difficult to read that most users would be uncomfortable with this resolution. Therefore, you will have to try a few resolution settings before you'll find the best one for your working environment. Larger monitors don't have the same problems with small text as the smaller monitors have in higher resolutions.

7. Click the OK button to close the dialog box and put your new settings into operation. Again, Windows might request that you restart your PC (click Yes to restart or click No to delay the restart until you close other program windows) before your new settings go into effect.

13

Figure 13.3.

Some resolutions are too high for comfortable viewing.

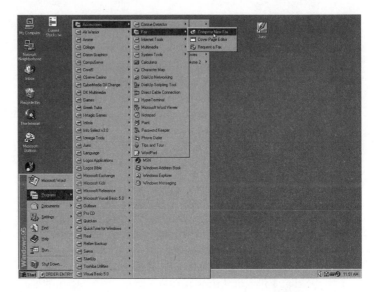

The larger your monitor, the more you can view at one time. Consider how helpful it may be to be able to view an entire page at one time within your word processor. If you cannot work with more than two windows on the screen comfortably, or if you need more viewing area for Internet pages or for word processing, consider upgrading your monitor to a larger viewing size and upgrading your video card to one that supports higher resolutions and colors. Hour 17, "Upgrading Your Disk and CD-ROM Storage," explains how to upgrade your monitor and video card.

Improving Disk Performance

Now that you know how to get more viewing space on your monitor, you should know how to get more storage space on your disk drive. By organizing your drive properly and regularly running utility programs that monitor and adjust your disk settings, you can keep your disk drives humming at their peak performance.

Defragmenting Your Disk

When you delete a file, Windows releases that space so that your disk drive has more free space available. Over time, the blank spots left by your deleted files begin to scatter over your disk drive. When you subsequently need free space to save a large file, your operating system must work extra hard to collect and link all those free areas together to store the large file. A disk with several free spots scattered over it is known as a *fragmented disk drive*. You can improve your disk's performance, often considerably, if you *defragment* the disk. When you defragment your disk drive, Windows moves all files together to eliminate fragments between them and stores your whole free space at the end of your disk drive. When you then need to store a file, Windows does not have difficulty finding a single large space big enough to handle the file.

13

Windows comes with a program called *Disk Defragmenter* you can use to defragment your hard disk. About every week or two of steady activity, if you defragment your disk drive, you'll keep your disk performance at its best. Follow these steps to defragment your disk:

1. Display the Start menu.

2. Select Programs | Accessories | System Tools | Disk Defragmenter. Windows displays the Select Drive window shown in Figure 13.4.

Figure 13.4.

The opening Disk Defragmenter window for analyzing your disk drives.

3. Select a drive from the center drop-down list box.

4. Click the OK command button to start the defragmentation process. Windows can multitask while defragmenting your disk space, so you can run other programs while Disk Defragmenter runs. At any point during the defragmentation, you can pause Disk Defragmenter or cancel the process. If the disk drive is not badly fragmented, Disk Defragmenter tells you so and asks if you want to run the Disk Defragmenter program on the drive anyway. You can cancel or go ahead with the defragmentation.

5. When it finishes, Disk Defragmenter lets you know that the fragmentation is complete. Click Yes to close the application.

TIME SAVER

Remember that Disk Defragmenter helps speed diskette drives as well as hard disk drives. In fact, if you run Disk Defragmenter on diskettes that you use regularly, you can greatly increase the speed of that diskette. You can also run Disk Defragmenter on high-capacity drives such as Zip drives. You cannot run Disk Defragmenter on tape backups, however. Tape does not contain fragments because of the way tapes sequentially store information without fragments.

13

Checking Your Disk's Reliability

Windows supplies a program named *ScanDisk* that checks your disk drive for problems and potential problems so that you can avoid future troubles. ScanDisk contains two levels of disk drive inspection: a *standard scan* and a *thorough scan*. The standard scan checks your disk files for errors; the thorough scan checks the files and performs a disk surface test to verify the integrity and safety of disk storage.

JUST A MINUTE

ScanDisk is just one of the applications inside the folder labeled System Tools that you can install when setting up Windows or when adding programs to Windows. Depending on your Windows installation, your System Tools menu might contain one or more of the icons shown in Figure 13.5.

Figure 13.5.

The System Tools menu contains several helpful utility applications.

TIME SAVER

Run ScanDisk regularly (perhaps once or twice a week). As with all Windows programs, you can multitask ScanDisk while running another program.

The following steps explain how to use the ScanDisk application. As you'll see, ScanDisk is simple to use and often takes only a few seconds to load and run:

1. Select Programs | Accessories | System Tools | ScanDisk from the Start menu. Windows displays the ScanDisk window shown in Figure 13.6.

Figure 13.6.

The opening ScanDisk window for analyzing your disk drives.

JUST A MINUTE

ScanDisk checks only disk drives, not CD-ROM drives.

13

2. The Standard option is initially checked by default. To perform a standard ScanDisk, press Enter to choose the Start command button now. ScanDisk begins its chore of checking your files. The ScanDisk window displays a moving graphics bar to show how much time remains in each ScanDisk step, as well as a description of each step in the process.

CAUTION

> If ScanDisk finds a problem and you've checked the option labeled Automatically fix errors, ScanDisk attempts to fix any problems it finds using default repair tools. (You can change the way ScanDisk repairs the disk by clicking the Advanced command button described toward the end of these steps.)

3. When ScanDisk finishes, you will see a ScanDisk results window, such as the one shown in Figure 13.7.

Figure 13.7.

ScanDisk reports its results to you upon completion of the disk scan.

The most important line in the results window is the number of bad sectors. Rarely will the number be anything but zero. If bad sectors appear, ScanDisk will attempt to repair them and report the results.

Press Enter to close the results window.

4. Click the Advanced command button. ScanDisk displays the ScanDisk Advanced Options dialog box shown in Figure 13.8. The default values are usually fine, but if you understand disk drive technology and file-storage details, you might want to change an option. Click the OK command button to close the dialog box.

5. Click the Thorough option and click the Start command button to perform a thorough ScanDisk check. The thorough scan performs a more intense disk check than the standard scan. You'll see the results dialog box when ScanDisk finishes.

You'll keep your disk running smoothly and correctly if you run ScanDisk once or twice weekly to make sure your disk is as free from defects as possible.

13

Figure 13.8.
The advanced ScanDisk options that you control.

Running DriveSpace

You can almost double the amount of disk space you have *without* purchasing new hardware! The *DriveSpace* program compresses your disk drive giving you more space. You only run DriveSpace once because after compressing the disk drive, the disk stays compressed. You also can reverse the DriveSpace compression if you want to, as long as you have enough space on the uncompressed disk drive to hold all your files.

JUST A MINUTE

DriveSpace doesn't defragment the disk. DriveSpace takes the extra step and actually compresses your disk storage to give you almost twice as much room as you had previously. Disk Defragmenter collects all your free space and puts it together in one more efficient spot; it does not give you any extra free space.

Accessing Compressed Data

Some people mistakenly believe that compressing the disk drive with a program such as DriveSpace slows down disk access. In the majority of cases, a compressed disk drive is as fast or faster than an uncompressed drive.

Mechanical devices are slower than electronic devices. Memory access is much faster than disk access. When Windows accesses a compressed disk drive, it only has to retrieve half as much physical data; Windows then quickly decompresses that data in fast memory. The overall result is faster disk access.

After you compress a disk drive, Windows and your computer act as if you've got more disk space. The free disk statistics will show the extra drive space, and all programs access the disk as if the disk were originally designed to have the extra space.

13

The following steps explain how to compress a disk drive using DriveSpace. The disk used here is a floppy disk. Once you've compressed a floppy disk drive, you will more fully understand the process and can then can compress your hard disk.

CAUTION

You cannot compress a CD-ROM. DriveSpace must be able to write to a device before compressing that device. CD-ROM drives are read-only.

JUST A MINUTE

When compressing a disk drive, DriveSpace adds a logical disk drive to your system called the *host drive*. DriveSpace names the new host drive *H*, or some other name that falls far down anyone's list of disk drives, so that you'll be able to determine which drive is a host drive and which drive is from your list of real disk drives. The host drive will not be compressed, and you will not work with the host drive. DriveSpace and Windows use the host drive to hold descriptive information about the compressed drive. About all you really need to know about the new host drive is that the host is not an actual drive on your system, and Windows uses the host drive to support the DriveSpace compression scheme. All open dialog boxes you see, as well as the My Computer window, will display the host drive now that you've compressed.

That said, follow these steps for using DriveSpace:

1. Select the Start menu's Programs|Accessories|System Tools|DriveSpace menu item. Windows displays the DriveSpace window shown in Figure 13.9.

Figure 13.9.

The opening DriveSpace window for compressing a disk drive.

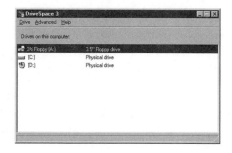

2. Insert a formatted disk in the disk drive. The disk can have data on it; it must, however, contain at least 512KB of free space so that DriveSpace can write some temporary files during the compression process. If the drive does not have enough free space, DriveSpace will tell you before starting the actual compression so that you can free some space.

CAUTION

If, while saving a file from an application during a regular work session, you receive an error message telling you that you are out of disk space, you must remove some files from the disk (using Explorer) before there will be room to save the file. If you then want to compress the disk, you will have to copy or move some of the disk's files to another disk drive to free enough space so that DriveSpace can compress the disk. It is always a good idea, when you think a disk is getting full, to check the amount of free space still available so that you can compress it before it no longer has enough free space for DriveSpace to work.

Obviously, DriveSpace cannot physically make a disk larger, but it does make the disk appear larger to Windows.

3. Select the floppy disk drive from the list of drives.

4. Select Drive | Compress. DriveSpace analyzes the disk and displays the Compress a Drive dialog box, such as the one shown in Figure 13.10.

Figure 13.10.

The before and after effect of the disk's compression.

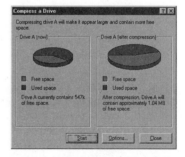

Depending on your disk's contents and original size, you can gain a little or a lot of extra space by the compression. DriveSpace will only compress the disk shown in Figure 13.10 by approximately 460KB, as you can see in the right-hand window labeled Drive A (after compression).

JUST A MINUTE

If you want to decompress a compressed drive, you would repeat these steps and choose Drive | Uncompress instead of Drive | Compress.

5. Click the Options command button. Windows displays the Compression Options dialog box shown in Figure 13.11. The Compression Options dialog box describes the host drive's name (you can select a different name if you want to) and free space

13

(usually there will be no free space). Click the OK command button to close the
Compression Options dialog box and return to the Compress a Drive dialog box.

Figure 13.11.

*The Compression
Options dialog box
explains how the
compression will operate.*

6. Click the Start command button to initiate the drive compression. Before compressing, DriveSpace gives you one last chance to cancel the compression. Also
   DriveSpace offers the option of backing up your files. Although there rarely will be
   a problem during the compression, it is possible that a power failure during the
   compression could interrupt the process and cause DriveSpace to corrupt the disk
   drive (so that the drive would need reformatting). By backing up the drive, you'll
   ensure that you can return to an uncompressed drive if needed.

JUST A MINUTE

> If you choose to back up before completing the drive's compression,
> DriveSpace will run the Microsoft Backup program described in the next
> hour.

After the compression begins, DriveSpace checks the diskette for errors and then
compresses the diskette. The compression can take a while. After finishing,
DriveSpace displays a completion dialog box. Close the dialog box.

TIME SAVER

> Start Explorer (right-click your Start button and select Explore), select the
> compressed disk, and read Explorer's status bar to see how much free
> space now resides on the drive.

13

CAUTION

> If you want to format a compressed disk, you must run DriveSpace and
> select Drive | Format. The Explorer Format command will not format
> compressed disks. The disk stays compressed during the formatting
> procedure.

Summary

This hour explains how to improve both your display and disk drive performance. Keeping your PC in top shape is vital if you want the most efficient performance.

Although your display speed does not noticeably change when you change screen resolutions, you'll be able to adjust the amount of information you see at one time by increasing the number of colors and resolution of your display. You may have to try a few different values before you find a resolution that works well for you. After you have changed resolutions, start the applications you run most frequently and make sure your screens display as much information as you want.

Disk Defragmenter is easy to run regularly because you can run other programs at the same time. Disk Defragmenter rearranges information and blank spots on your disk drive, putting all the data in contiguous disk space and all the empty holes into one large contiguous block. Once defragmented, your disk access will speed up.

After you have compressed a disk drive, Windows recognizes the compressed drive and stores up to 100% more data on that drive. There will actually be a second disk added to your drive letters, called the host disk, but you can ignore the host disk because DriveSpace uses it to store data tables used for accessing the compressed drive.

If you implement all this hour's tips, your system will run at its best, so you'll want to protect your investment. Hour 14, "Protecting Your PC," shows you how to protect both your hardware and your software.

Q&A

Q How often should I defragment and compress my hard disk?

A You should defragment every month or two. Depending on the amount of file access you do, you might need to defragment more or less often. If you notice your disk speed slowing down a bit, you'll often find that Disk Defragmenter speeds the access process somewhat.

Only compress your disk drive (or each floppy disk) *once*. After the compression, the drive stays compressed. Unless you uncompress the drive, Windows always recognizes the compressed drive.

Q Should I worry about the advanced ScanDisk options that I don't understand?

A Unfortunately, the advanced ScanDisk options are fairly advanced (that's why they're called *advanced* options!). The details of the options go beyond the scope of this book. Fortunately, you will rarely, if ever, need to modify any of the advanced

13

options. Unless you learn a lot about the disk and the way that Windows stores files on a disk, run ScanDisk using the default options, and you'll virtually always run the proper ScanDisk.

Q I don't know if my disk is fragmented, so should I still run Disk Defragmenter?

A Run Disk Defragmenter regardless of whether you know if your disk is fragmented. Disk Defragmenter will tell you that you don't need to continue if the disk has few or no free fragments to collect.

13

Hour **14**

Protecting Your PC

After you set up your PC, load programs, and store information on your PC, you'll want to protect your work. By following a series of preventive maintenance recommendations from this hour, you'll do the most you can to keep your PC safe. If, however, the worst happens and you lose your entire computer due to an electrical hit or a breakdown, you'll be able to restore your system if you follow the recommendations made here.

The highlights of this hour include

- [ ] What a disk crash means
- [ ] Why a startup disk can give you needed help in an emergency
- [ ] Why backups are important
- [ ] Where to store backup tapes and disks
- [ ] How to use the Microsoft Backup program
- [ ] What kinds of physical protection steps you can take to guard your hardware

Practice Safe Computing!

Your PC cost a lot of money, so you'll want to take the steps necessary to protect your investment. More than the hardware, however, is the software investment you make. Over time you will spend much more on software than on hardware, so you should regularly guard your software, both your programs and especially your data, so you can recover from a disaster.

Your PC is an electronic and mechanical device and, as such, is susceptible to breakdowns. Other than your printer, your disk drive contains the most moving parts in your PC, and your disk drive is the peripheral device most susceptible to harm. Sadly, unless you've prepared in advance for such a disaster, restoring a ruined disk drive can be difficult and even impossible. Sometimes you simply cannot restore a new disk drive with the same file setup as the disk that broke.

JUST A MINUTE

> A *disk crash* is the term computer users apply to disk failures. A disk crash does not always mean that the disk itself broke. Sometimes, when your disk stops working, the internal controller card might be the culprit. If you have multiple disks, one could crash, and if that disk is your *boot disk* (the disk on which Windows is stored), you will not be able to access your other drives in many instances.

Make a Startup Disk Now

If a hard disk crashes, you cannot easily determine the extent of the crash. Sometimes it's difficult to determine if the disk is broken or if the start-up *sectors* (pockets on the disk where data and programs reside) are erased or damaged. If you have multiple disk drives and your boot disk crashes, you still want to be able to copy the data on the other disks before you remove the boot disk and risk causing other problems.

One of the best things you can do *right now* is to make a *startup disk*. A startup disk contains enough information to start your PC if your primary boot disk crashes. The disk acts like a boot disk. You won't be able to start Windows from the boot disk, but you will be able to try to look at your disk drive using MS-DOS commands and possibly retrieve information from your hard disk that you might need.

TIME SAVER

> If your disk crashes, try to access your disk and additional drives with your startup disk *before* you take your PC into the repair shop for service. Unless you performed a backup right before the disk crashed (the next section explains how to back up your disk), you'll want to copy onto blank disks the data that you've entered since your previous backup. After you boot with the startup disk you can remove the disk and insert a blank, formatted disk to save your latest information.

14

To make a startup disk, follow these steps:

1. Select your Start menu's Settings|Control Panel dialog box and double-click the Add/Remove Programs icon.

2. Click the tab marked Startup Disk to display the property sheet shown in Figure 14.1.

Figure 14.1.

Make a startup disk so you can access your PC without booting from your hard disk.

3. Locate a blank disk. The disk does not have to be blank, but the startup disk routine erases everything on the disk, so make sure you don't need the disk's information.

4. Click the Create Disk button. After a brief pause, Windows displays the prompt shown in Figure 14.2.

5. Click the OK button to build the startup disk.

6. After a few moments, the startup disk routine will complete the startup disk and let you know that you can remove the disk.

TIME SAVER

After you boot with the startup disk and get to the A: prompt, type a:Scandisk to run the ScanDisk program to check out your disk drives. (Hour 13, "Fine-Tuning Your PC," explains how to use ScanDisk to check your disk files.)

ScanDisk is not the only program on the startup disk. The following is a list of the programs you can run from the startup disk:

☐ **DriveSpace:** Makes it possible to access compressed drives that still work.

☐ **Format:** Lets you prepare new disks for data so that you can save information to disk from whichever hard disks still work.

Figure 14.2.

Get ready to create the
startup disk.

☐ **Sys:** Lets you create new boot disks.

☐ **FDisk:** Helps you partition new hard disk drives to prepare them for formatting.

☐ **Attrib:** Lets you change file attributes.

☐ **Edit:** Lets you create, edit, and view text files.

☐ **Regedit:** Lets you review and edit the Windows *Registry*. The Windows Registry is a database of Windows system and program information needed for proper Windows operation.

☐ **Debug:** Provides advanced disk- and file-editing capabilities.

☐ **Chkdsk:** An MS-DOS–based program that performs disk checking similar to the ScanDisk utility program. Although ScanDisk is more advanced, Chkdsk can sometimes run on disks that ScanDisk refuses to run on.

☐ **Uninstall:** Executes the uninstall utility that lets you remove some registered programs. If you've just installed an application or system utility, and running that newly installed program caused your system to crash, you might be able to remove that program to keep it from interfering with your PC's operation.

JUST A MINUTE

This 24-hour tutorial does not have time to delve into these MS-DOS–based programs. It takes a whole book to cover the MS-DOS commands. If you want more information on these utility programs, check out *Peter Norton's Inside the PC, 6th Edition*, from Sams Publishing.

Back Up Often

The Windows Backup program is a comprehensive backup program that you can use to save a copy of your disk files. The backup protects you against data loss. If your hard disk breaks down, once you fix or replace that hard disk you will then be able to restore the backup and resume your work. Without the backup, you would have to try to re-create the entire disk drive, which is often impossible because you will not have a copy of every transaction and document that you've created.

14

JUST A MINUTE

The Windows Backup program both creates and restores backups.

Many people back up regularly. Most of these people back up regularly because they once had a disk crash but did not have a backup. (The author is one of those guilty of losing a disk and all the data before learning to back up!) Please don't be one to learn the hard way. Learn to use the Windows Backup program and back up your files regularly.

Put It in Reverse—Back Up!

The first time you back up, you should back up your entire disk drive. After you have backed up the entire disk, you then can make subsequent daily or weekly backups and back up only the files that you've added or changed since the most recent backup.

The Windows Backup program can often compress files while backing them up so that you can back up large disk drives to other disks or tapes that would not normally be able to hold all the data. If you turn on the compression option, the backup should take less time and make the backups easier to do.

The Windows Backup program also lets you select which files you want to back up so that you can make a special backup of a few selected files. Windows Backup can create a *full backup* of your entire disk drive or a *differential backup* (or *incremental backup*), which backs up only the files that have changed since the most recent backup. Backup also lets you direct restored files to a different drive or directory from where they originated.

TIME SAVER

Take your home computer's backup files with you to work every day and bring your work's backup files home each night. If a terrible disaster happens at home or at work, such as a fire, you will be able to restore your data because the backups will not be destroyed.

You must decide on which *medium* you want to store the backup. The Windows Backup program creates backups on the following types of media:

- ☐ Network disks
- ☐ Hard disks
- ☐ Floppy disks

14

☐ High-capacity removable disks such as Zip and Jaz disks
☐ QIC 40, 80, and 3010 tapes

Caution

> If you back up to high-capacity disks, Backup does not let you swap disks if the first disk you insert cannot hold all the backed-up files.

Windows Backup uses the QIC-113 format, which means that it can back up and restore onto tapes and other media that other popular backup programs created. After you make a full backup, especially the very first time, you might also want to run Windows Backup's comparison option to make sure that the backup matches the original data.

The following steps describe how to back up a hard disk to floppy disks. Although a tape drive, high-capacity removable drive, or network drive makes backing up easier than backing up to floppy disks because you don't have to keep switching disks in and out of the drive, the majority of users today have only one hard disk and one floppy disk, so they must back up onto floppies. Such users generally only perform selected backups. As the following steps show, you can select only those files you want to back up.

Caution

> Backing up to disks can take a *lot* of disks! Even if you use Windows Backup's compression option, a large hard disk backup consumes many disks. If you have a backup tape drive and want to back up to your tape drive or high-capacity removable disk (you should do this if you have the hardware), select your tape drive or high-capacity drive instead of floppy disks as you follow these steps.

To back up your hard drive, follow these steps:

1. Select the Start menu's Programs | Accessories | System Tools | Backup menu item. Windows displays the Backup screen shown in Figure 14.3.

2. Backup is informing you of the *full system backup file set*. A *backup file set* (called a *backup job* in some Windows versions) is a predetermined list of files to back up that you can create. If you back up only a certain group of files on a regular basis, you can create a backup file set that tells Backup to back up only those files.

   The window is suggesting that you use the full system backup file set the first time you back up. You will now use that backup file set to back up your entire hard disk to floppy disks. Later, you can create your own backup file sets that describe certain differential backups or backups that will save only a certain set of files or folders.

14

Figure 14.3.

The opening Backup window for backing up a disk drive.

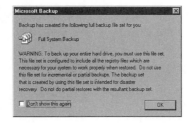

JUST A MINUTE

If you want to follow these steps but do not want to take the time right now to back up your entire hard disk to floppy disks, you'll be able to cancel the backup process after it starts.

3. If you don't want to see Figure 14.3's reminder window, you can check the Don't show this again option at the bottom of the screen to hide future displays of the window.

   Click OK now to continue with the backup process.

CAUTION

At this point, you might or might not get a cautionary window telling you that you do not have a tape drive or that Windows did not detect a tape drive. Backup assumes that you'll want to back up to a tape drive, even though many people have no tape drives. If you have no tape drive, click OK. If you do have one, close the window and exit Backup. Select the Control Panel's Add New Hardware icon to install the tape drive.

4. Backup does not start backing up right away because it still does not know the kind of backup you want to perform or the type of media to which you want the backup to go.

   Backup displays the window shown in Figure 14.4. The tabs at the top of the window let you select either a backup, restore, or comparison. For this exercise, you will keep the Backup tab selected. (You can look through the two other tabbed windows if you want to learn more about the other tasks Backup can perform.) All three tabbed windows work virtually the same except that the direction of the data flow is reversed using Backup and Restore, and the Compare tabbed dialog box does not back up or restore, but compares a backup to its original set of files to make sure the backup worked.

5. The Backup window contains two panes that work like the Explorer's screen. The window pane on the left describes the storage devices that you might want to back up. The right window pane describes the details of whatever device you select.

14

Figure 14.4.

Describe the details of the backup to the Backup program.

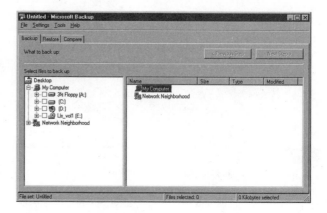

Although you are going to perform a full backup in this exercise, take a moment for a detour so you can learn something about creating a backup file set.

Select drive C by clicking on the button, and wait while Backup collects a list of all files on drive C. The collection takes a while. When it's finished, Backup displays a list of all files and folders from drive C, with a checkmark next to each. Backup assumes that you want to back up the entire drive C. If you don't care about backing up certain files, uncheck them.

6. Press the Next Step command button so that you can tell Backup the medium you want to use for the backup. Backup displays the screen shown in Figure 14.5.

Figure 14.5.

Tell Backup the backup's destination medium.

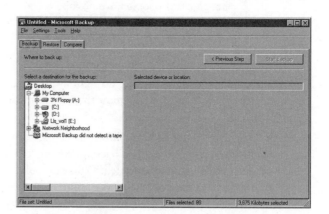

7. Select drive A. Now that Windows Backup knows the files to back up and the destination medium, you can save the backup file set that you've just designed (selected files from drive C backed up to drive A) by selecting File|Save and entering a name for the backup file set.

Instead of backing up just drive C, select the File|Open File Set command to display the backup file set's Open dialog box.

14

8. Select the Full System Backup. Backup then scans your computer and its files, looking for everything to back up as well as the hardware to which you can back up. If you have only one hard disk, the full system backup file set will be the same file selection as you would have if you'd selected all of drive C. If you have several hard disks, the full system backup file set will select every hard disk. Your only job left is to indicate the medium to which to back up.

JUST A MINUTE

> When you want to make a differential backup, select Settings | Options and click on the Backup tab of the dialog box. Click the option labeled Incremental backup of selected files that have changed since the last full backup.

9. Click the Next Step command button and then select drive A for the destination floppy disk (or your tape drive if you have one).

10. Click the Start Backup command button. Backup displays the Backup Set Label dialog box shown in Figure 14.6. The *backup set label* is a descriptive name that labels this particular backup. For example, you could name this backup *My first full backup.*

Figure 14.6.

Assign a label to this particular backup.

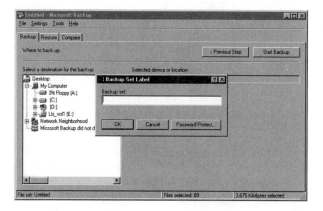

CAUTION

> If you back up sensitive data, you might want to add a password to the backup so that others will not get your backup files and restore the files onto their system. Before restoring a password-protected backup set, Windows Backup asks the user for the password and refuses to restore without the proper password. Be sure to store your password in a safe place so you can find it (but nobody else can) if you forget the password.

Backup displays a dialog box that illustrates the backup procedure. Your entire hard disk will probably not fit on a single disk, so Backup will ask you to insert the next disk in drive A after Backup fills the first one. If you are backing up to a tape, the entire hard disk might fit on the tape without your intervention.

TIME SAVER

Select Settings | Options from the menu bar and turn on the option Turn on audible prompts in the General tabbed dialog box so that Backup beeps when you need to insert the next disk.

11. When Backup finishes (click Cancel if you want to stop the backup early), select File | Exit. Put the backup disks (or tape) in a safe place and label the backup media so you'll know the backup is there.

Consider taking your backup disks or tapes with you when you leave home or the office. The off-site backup data that you take with you ensures that you can always restore your information even if something happens to destroy your PC. For example, a flood might get your PC, but it won't hurt your backups if you keep them off-site.

Internet Backups?

If you access the Internet by a modem, even a fast modem such as a 56Kbps modem, you already know that the modem is slow for today's information and that the Internet must get faster to make it a seamless integration of the PC environment. Many office-based PCs provide a T1 connection for faster access speeds up to 8 times that of a 56Kbps modem. In addition, some cities now offer cable Internet services. You access such services through a special *cable modem* that receives and sends Internet information on the same cable as your cable television wire.

Because some can access the Internet at relatively high speeds, and because cable modems and satellite access are paving the way for fast Internet access in the home, some companies are now offering Internet backup services. (At the present time, such services might be better suited for people who travel with laptops.) The idea is that you can set up your system to back up files to the hosting Internet service's disk drives. The backup operates in the background, as long as you're signed into the Internet, and sends files to your account when you change them. If a complete disaster occurs, the files are safely tucked away on a remote system for later recovery.

14

Inoculate Against Viruses

Perhaps you've heard horror stories about PC viruses. A PC *virus* is a program that, unknowingly to the PC user, attaches itself to other programs and to the operating system. At a later time, the virus leaves its dormant state and, at worst, it destroys the files and the operating system, requiring the user to reload the entire operating system and all programs and data. At best, a virus will display ornery messages to the PC user as he uses the machine.

JUST A MINUTE

> The reason for the time delay is that the virus author hopes the user will back up the system a few times before realizing the virus is there. The backups, then, are rendered worthless.

Although a virus *could* enter through the ranks of programmers at a software company, the chances of receiving a virus from a store-bought program are extremely small. As long as you stick with name-brand software, you should not have to worry about viruses from them.

Viruses could easily come from programs that others give to you. Perhaps someone gives you a copy of an electronic spreadsheet program "just to try out." Although the giver might not know of the virus if he got the program from someone else, you won't know if the software is virus-prone. Of course, if your friend loans you a program on CD-ROM, and the CD-ROM is an original manufacturer's CD-ROM, the CD-ROM probably won't contain a virus. You must guard against receiving programs on disks, however. In addition, drives that create CD-ROMs are becoming inexpensive and common, so you might get a virus even if you receive the program on a copy of a CD-ROM.

CAUTION

> If you borrow a program from another user and install that software on your disk drive without buying the program, you are in many cases violating copyright laws. When you purchase a program, you don't own the program; you only own the disks or CD-ROM as well as a license to use that program for your own use. A program's copyright laws almost always follow the treat-it-like-a-book rule; that is, you can install the program on several PCs if you have multiple PCs, but you can only use the program on one PC at a time, just as only one person can read a book at once. If two or more people, on two or more PCs, use the program, the program's copyright will be violated.

14

Be extremely careful when receiving programs in e-mail and from the Internet. The last part of this book discusses ways you can receive e-mail and programs from the Internet. Again, consider the source. If you download a program from a reputable software firm, you'll probably have no trouble. If, however, you receive the program from an unknown source or from a Web page not sponsored by a major software firm, you are opening yourself up to virus troubles.

JUST A MINUTE

Most Internet-access programs (called *browsers*, as you'll learn in the last part of this book) let you specify settings that guard against viruses. You can ask that the browser warn you if you ever receive a program, either through the Internet's sites or from e-mail. Once warned, you can consider the source and then decide if you want to install the program.

TIME SAVER

Make a complete backup before you download and install that program. Keep that backup safely tucked away until you know that the downloaded program is safe.

You can purchase virus-protection programs that constantly check your system for viruses and, in many cases, will eradicate any viruses found. You'll be able to update these virus-protection programs as new versions become available due to new viruses found. Most of the virus-protection software companies let you update your software from their company Internet site so you can keep your system up-to-date.

Protect Your Hardware

Hour 5, "Setting Up Your New PC," introduced you to hardware protection. In addition to the steps you can take to protect your software investment, you should protect your hardware as well. Keep your work area free from dust. Dust is deadly to PC equipment. Smoke can also harm disk drives and disks lying around. If you get a room air cleaner, both you and your PC can benefit from the cleaner air.

Your PC's memory and components are susceptible to power fluctuations. Consider purchasing a *surge protector*. When another appliance on the line goes on or off, the surge protector keeps your PC's power flow steady. Your electric company might be able to offer additional tips that will keep your electrical line clear, such as a lightning protector. Although a surge and lightning protector will never protect you from a direct hit, such protectors help render nearby strikes harmless.

Although *uninterruptible power supplies* (*UPS*) are more expensive than surge protectors, you will be glad you use a UPS if your power ever goes out while you are working on your PC.

14

The UPS stores electrical energy for just such an emergency. If the power goes out, the stored energy keeps your PC running for a few extra minutes—enough time for you to save your work and shut down Windows properly.

CAUTION

> The more you plug into a UPS, the less time the UPS can run without power. Don't plug your printer into a UPS. If the power goes out while you are printing, you can restart the print job later. If hooked up to the UPS, the printer will drain the reserve power, and you might not have enough time to save your work and shut down Windows properly if the UPS has to handle both your printer and your PC.

Summary

This hour explains how to use proper precautions to guard against data loss. In case your disk crashes, you will be able to restart your PC as long as you have made a startup disk. The startup disk lets you boot without a hard disk.

The Windows Backup program contains a complete set of backup, restore, and comparison features. The backup file sets make it easy to back up regularly because you can create backup file sets that describe different backup settings and open whatever backup file set you want to use. (The Windows Backup program supplies a full system backup set for you to use when you want to back up all hard disk drives.)

Hour 15, "Why and When to Upgrade," begins a new part of your 24-hour tutorial that explains how to upgrade your PC's hardware. If you use outdated equipment, you won't necessarily have to purchase a new computer; you can upgrade the components inside your old PC to bring it up-to-date.

Q&A

Q Which kind of backup, full or differential, should I perform?

A The first time you back up, you should make a full backup. After you make one full backup, you can make subsequent differential backups of only those files that have changed. Be sure that you save the full backup, however, so that you can restore everything if you need to. If you have a disk failure, you'll restore the entire full backup and then restore each differential backup set of files.

14

Q Does a full backup take longer than a differential backup?

A Yes. As mentioned in the first question, first perform one full backup and then, subsequently, you can perform the quicker differential backups.

After you've made several differential backups, you might want to make a full backup once again. By making a full backup every once in a while, you will be able to reuse your differential tapes or disks.

Q Other than full backups that I perform weekly, I want to back up only my three work folders every day. Should I take the time to create a backup file set that describes only those three folders?

A By all means, you should create a backup file set for those three folders. Although you must take a few moments to create the backup file set the first time, specifying exactly which folders you want to back up, subsequent backups will take less of your time. You'll thereafter only have to select the three-folder backup file set and start the backup.

PART
V

Improving Your PC

Hour

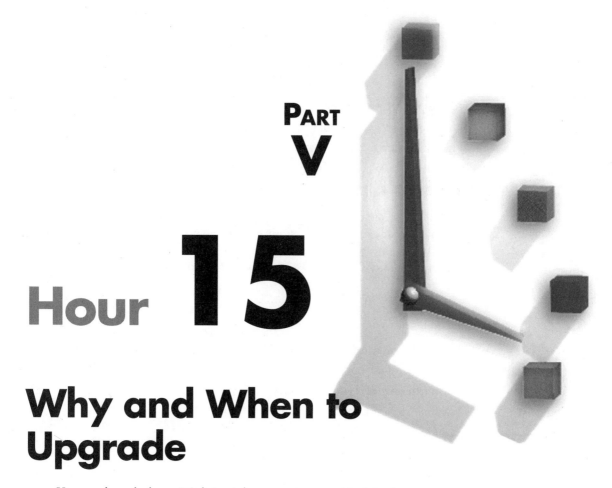

Hour 15

Why and When to Upgrade

You purchase the latest PC, bring it home, set it up, and look in the newspaper the next day only to find a more powerful computer selling at a lower price. What do you do after you finish sobbing? Read this and the next few hours' lessons to learn how to upgrade your PC to today's standards.

Although a PC that you buy today will almost surely be obsolete in a short time, obsolescence is relative. Just because a more powerful machine is for sale at a lower cost does not mean yours is scrap. PC users can get many years of good use from their systems if they buy a recent model when they do purchase a PC. As better hardware comes out, you can upgrade your PC to use the newer hardware. (If you buy an out-of-date model today, you could regret the purchase. Too many people save money by purchasing used PC equipment only to find that the PC will not run today's software adequately.)

The highlights of this hour include

- ☐ When to purchase and when to upgrade your PC
- ☐ Why you can open your PC without fear
- ☐ What expansion board standards exist

☐ How to prepare your system for upgrade

☐ Why Plug and Play does not always work

☐ Which hardware settings you must make

Making the Upgrade Decision

"Buy or upgrade?" is a question frequently asked of PC consultants. The decision is not always an easy one, but here's a general rule of thumb: Search your newspaper's Sunday supplements and create a list of the most standard, common systems you see. Rule out the most expensive, fastest, and largest PCs, and also the least expensive ones. Look for the typical computer, sold at an average cost.

After you have a good feel for the current PC standard, determine how your PC differs from that standard in the following ways:

☐ How much slower is your CPU?

☐ How much less memory do you have?

☐ How much smaller is your monitor?

☐ How much less disk space do you have?

☐ How much slower is your modem?

☐ How much slower is your printer?

☐ How much lower quality is your printer's output?

☐ How do your PC's multimedia qualities compare with the standard PC's?

Not all these questions will apply to everyone. For example, you might have a printer that still works great and is comparable to today's printers. (Printer speeds don't increase as quickly as PC and modem speeds.) You might not care about the quality of your PC's multimedia capabilities because you might use your PC strictly for word processing text documents. And your monitor's size does not keep you from using today's software; only your PC's system unit contains components (such as the CPU and memory) that might limit your use of software.

Make a list of answers to the questions that apply to your situation. Write down exactly what your PC needs to make it compatible with today's standard. Your list might include

☐ 16MB of memory

☐ A Pentium II processor that runs 30% faster than your current CPU

☐ A second disk drive that will double your current storage

Take your list to a PC store and price the upgrade components. If you can upgrade your PC for 25% less than you would need to buy a new PC, do the upgrade. It will bring new life

15

to your PC. If the new PC costs less than 25% of the upgrade price, consider giving your PC away to a charity and buying a new one.

Keep in mind that you don't have to purchase the upgrade components from the store where you bought your PC. Most stores sell upgrade equipment that is compatible with most PCs. You can even purchase the upgrade components through the mail, at discount prices, but you'll have to install the components yourself. If that frightens you, don't be alarmed; this and the next few hours explain how to upgrade your PC properly.

CAUTION

If your upgrade comes in the mail on a cold day, let the part warm to room temperature before you install the component. Condensation and sudden heat can harm a PC component.

Don't Fear Opening Your PC

Your PC was designed to be upgraded. In fact, it was designed for *you* to perform many of the upgrades! You will not, in virtually every instance, violate your PC's warranty by opening the system unit. Of course, not all upgrades require that you open your PC's system unit. If you change external modems, your upgrade requires only that you unplug your current modem, plug in your new one (into both the PC and the electrical source), and add the new modem to your operating system. In most cases, Windows will detect that you've changed hardware and can make the adjustment automatically when you start Windows.

CAUTION

Keep all upgrade components in their packaging, except to remove the instructions, until you are ready to install them. Static electricity can damage today's fragile memory chips, and the longer they are out of their anti-static packaging, the more prone they are to getting a static charge.

When you add any upgrade inside your system unit, follow these steps:

1. Properly shut down Windows.
2. Turn off all your equipment.
3. Touch a metal part of your PC, such as the back cover screws, for a moment before opening the system unit. You will ground yourself and help protect against static electricity.
4. Unplug all electrical cables.

5. Open your system unit. Keep the screws out of your system unit (they drop easily) but handy so you can replace them when you're finished. Never touch electrical parts except by their edges.

As Figure 15.1 shows, opening your system unit requires only that you remove eight or so screws on the back of your system unit. After you remove the screws, the system unit cover slides off.

Figure 15.1.

Unscrew the system unit screws and slide off the cover.

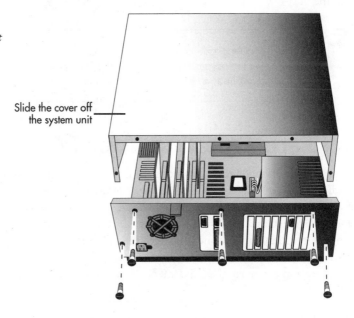

Slide the cover off
the system unit

Some system units include thumbscrews and slots you can depress to remove the system unit without a screwdriver.

JUST A MINUTE

When you complete the upgrade, you'll have to slide your system unit cover back onto the system unit carefully, watching all cables. Use kid gloves! If you have to force the cover on, a card or cable may be getting in the way. Correct the obstacle before you replace the cover.

Types of Interfaces

You must shop for upgrades that work with your PC. Although most components will work, you need to make sure that the interface your PC supports matches that of the upgrade. The interface becomes critical when you install expansion boards.

15

CAUTION

Upgrading PC equipment is not always straightforward. You don't have to know much about your PC's hardware to use the computer, but you must be very careful, and know more about hardware, if you upgrade your own PC. As you'll see in this section, the PC "standard" is not actually as standard as it could be. Over the years, PC makers have improved components, but had to change the interface as well.

15

Get your PC's owner's manual and look for one of the interface card standards shown in Table 15.1. When you purchase an expansion card, make sure the card works with your expansion slot type. Table 15.1 describes the *bus standards* that exist. A *bus* is the point of the interface where data flows to and from your PC and the expansion board.

Table 15.1. Interface standards for expansion cards must match your PC's interface type.

Type	Description
8-bit ISA	(*Industry Standard Architecture*) These are the slots that appeared in the first PC, the original IBM-PC. Therefore, most PCs include at least one ISA slot for compatibility with a large number of boards. If you buy an ISA board, you can insert that board into 16-bit ISA and EISA slots if your PC has those slots. If you have a choice, and if your PC supports a newer standard that appears throughout this table, stay away from 8-bit ISA cards because they are slow and limited.
16-bit ISA	These support boards that send data twice as fast through your system due to the wider data path. 16-bit ISA cards will not work in 8-bit slots, but will work in EISA slots.
EISA	(*Enhanced Industry Standard Architecture*) An EISA slot will accept both 8-bit and 16-bit ISA as well as EISA cards. EISA cards, however, only fit in EISA system unit slots. If your PC supports EISA, you would prefer to buy EISA cards over 8-bit and 16-bit ISA because EISA works faster, but EISA boards are sometimes difficult to find today.
MCA	(*Micro Channel Architecture*) IBM developed the MCA standard to improve (greatly) on the 8-bit ISA of the day and to compete with the 16-bit ISA released about the same time. Despite its superior design over the ISAs, MCA never became standard in anything but

continues

Table 15.1. continued

Type	Description
	IBM PCs and, eventually, even IBM abandoned the standard. If you have a PC with an MCA slot, you might have to order all expansion boards directly through IBM. Much of the newer hardware on the market will never be sold with an MCA interface.
VESA Local	(*Video Electronics Standards Association's Local Bus*) A video card interface that supports more efficient video cards than the other standards (except for PCI). If you have a VESA Local slot, look for a video card that is VESA-compatible. (The VESA slot will accept 8-bit and 16-bit boards, but not any other kind other than VESA.) The VESA Local bus is sometimes called *VL-Bus*.
PCI	(*Peripheral Component Interconnect*) The fastest interface around about a PCI board, a PCI card only works in a PCI slot, and a PCI slot only takes PCI cards. Installing PCI cards is often simpler than the other cards because the PCI can automatically adjust its own settings to work with your PC.

Figure 15.2 shows what's ahead if you install an expansion card into your system unit. The process basically involves aligning the board with the slot in which it goes, and then gently rocking the card into its slot. If the card is incompatible with the slot into which you are inserting it (that is, if the card is the wrong type for your PC), you won't find an expansion slot in your PC with a slot that matches the card's connector.

TIME SAVER

Subsequent hours describe, in more detail, the installation of expansion boards, so keep reading to get the specifics.

Not every upgrade comes on an expansion board. For example, if you upgrade your CPU, the new CPU will not come on an expansion board.

Windows can help you determine the kinds of hardware you have. From your Start menu, open the Control Panel and double-click on the System icon. Click on the tab marked Device Manager to display the Device Manager window shown in Figure 15.3. Click on the plus signs to expand the items in the list and view their descriptions. You can often tell the kind of interface being used by its description. For example, you might see a video display adapter named *PCI Genetron 4.5XL*. From that description you can glean that your PC supports PCI cards.

15

15

Figure 15.2.
You'll align the expansion board's edge connector to an appropriate slot.

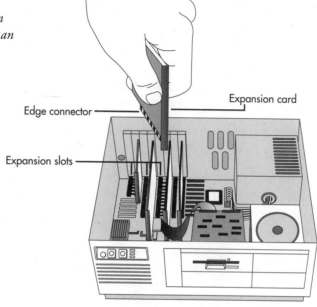

Expansion card

Edge connector

Expansion slots

Figure 15.3.
Let Windows tell you the kind of hardware your PC has.

JUST A MINUTE

All peripheral cards, or expansion boards, sold today should list on the box the card's interface type. Don't purchase a PCI card if your PC supports only a 16-bit ISA bus.

What to Expect

The next few hours explain how to upgrade different parts of your computer. You now know how to determine whether an expansion board is compatible with your PC. Before getting to the details, however, you need to understand another technical set of terms that affect almost all installations: *DMA channels*, *I/O port addresses*, and *IRQ*. When you install a new piece of hardware, you might have to make changes to these settings.

What About Plug and Play?

Beginning with Windows 95, PCs began supporting a new hardware installation standard called *Plug and Play*. In theory, Plug and Play is supposed to adjust all needed PC settings when you remove, replace, or install new hardware devices such as modems, expansion boards, and printers.

Unfortunately, Plug and Play works in theory but not always in practice. (Users have even resorted to *Plug and Pray* with more success than Plug and Play!) Not only must you run Windows 95 or later, but your PC must be new enough to support Plug and Play, and so should the hardware that you purchase.

When you buy new hardware, be sure the box says something about Plug and Play to help ensure that your installation woes will be minimal. Without Plug and Play, you can probably get the installation to work properly, but Plug-and-Play compatibility will help speed things along.

Note that all new hardware is Plug and Play, so you might have to install the old way and set the IRQ and other values yourself. Even if the new hardware is Plug and Play, your PC is Plug and Play, and you run Windows 95 or later, you *still* might have to make changes to the settings because things just don't always go as smoothly as Plug and Play promises.

A small number of today's expansion boards, and almost all older expansion boards, contain *jumpers* (see Figure 15.4). These jumpers are connectors that connect two pins together out of a series of three or more pins. In almost every case you can accept the manufacturer's jumper settings, but you might have to change the jumper settings yourself. When you connect a combination of the pins, the expansion board takes on one of several optional behaviors, such as determining which IRQ value to use inside your PC.

Before you install *any* device, read the installation instructions that come with that device. If the instructions require jumper settings, you'll have to make them yourself. If the instructions don't require jumper changes, you'll know that you can set the settings through software or that the hardware relies on Plug-and-Play technology (which might or might not still require software settings).

15

Figure 15.4.
*Your board's jumper
settings can specify
hardware values such as
the IRQ value.*

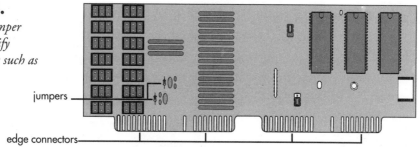

jumpers

edge connectors

The jumpers control these three setting values:

- [ ] **DMA (*Direct Memory Access*) channel:** Specifies the path to take to memory. Of the eight DMA channels available, two or more hardware devices might use the same DMA channel, *but not at the same time.* For example, a modem and a printer might share the same channel, but only one works at any given time.

- [ ] **I/O port address (I/O means *input/output*):** This address determines the memory location that will be dedicated to this hardware device. Hardware devices require their own memory locations.

- [ ] **IRQ (*Interrupt Request*) signal:** This signal tells your CPU that the device needs something. For example, if you've set up a modem for automatic answering of phone calls, the modem will interrupt the CPU, using the IRQ, to grab CPU resources for answering the phone.

The owner's manual that comes with your new hardware will often suggest setting values. If jumper settings are required, the manufacturer almost always sets the jumpers to the most common settings, so you might not need to change the hardware itself. You will, however, need to tell Windows about the settings (assuming Plug and Play does not take care of things for you). Therefore, after you install the new hardware, you'll often need to inform Windows of the hardware's values.

CAUTION

> Your current hardware settings might (and many times do) conflict with new hardware if your PC contains several components already. The more expansion boards, disks, video cards, CD-ROMs, and high-capacity removable drives in your system, the fewer resources are available and the more likely that a new device's default DMA channel, I/O port, or IRQ setting is already in use. Sometimes Plug and Play can resolve the conflict; sometimes you can resolve the conflict. In rare instances, your system might be full and offer no free IRQs.

Windows Helps

As you learn to install new equipment in the next few hours, you'll see that Windows provides help. Not only can you let Plug and Play attempt to detect and install your hardware's setting values, but you can run the Add New Hardware Wizard (whose opening window appears in Figure 15.5) to set up a new device.

Figure 15.5.

The Add New Hardware Wizard helps you install upgrades.

The Add New Hardware Wizard attempts to avoid IRQ and DMA conflicts as much as possible. After you run through the Add New Hardware Wizard's windows, if your upgraded hardware does not work properly, you might need to return to the Device Manager window (the dialog box you saw in Figure 15.3) and modify values yourself.

Summary

This hour's lesson is a little shorter than the others to give you a chance to familiarize yourself with installation requirements, expectations, and new terms. If the prospect of upgrading hardware frightens you a little, you'll see in subsequent hours that actual hardware upgrading can be simple. In most cases, you'll install a board or replace a device, plug in your PC, let Windows adjust to the new hardware, and be on your way.

Sometimes, problems will arise if you attempt to upgrade with incompatible hardware. This hour has taught you how to determine your PC's hardware bus type and how to use the Windows Device Manager window to determine your current hardware types.

The next hour begins discussing details needed for upgrading specific hardware components. The most challenging upgrade in most cases, the CPU or memory, is not too difficult as long as you are careful to follow this hour's precautions.

15

Q&A

Q How do I know if I have Plug and Play?

A If you have Windows 95 or later, installing hardware ought to be fairly simple as long as both your PC and the new hardware you're installing are also Plug-and-Play compatible. Perhaps the best way to see if you have Plug and Play is to plug the new device into the computer, power on your machine, and see what happens. (Of course, you should read the new hardware's installation instructions to learn the correct way to install the device.)

If you turn on your computer and the computer responds to the new device properly, you have, for all intents and purposes, all the Plug-and-Play compatibility you need. You have Plug and Play, at least, for that one device. Just because Windows and your hardware are Plug-and-Play compatible does not mean that the hardware you install will also be Plug-and-Play compatible. Some hardware might be Plug-and-Play compatible and some might not be.

15

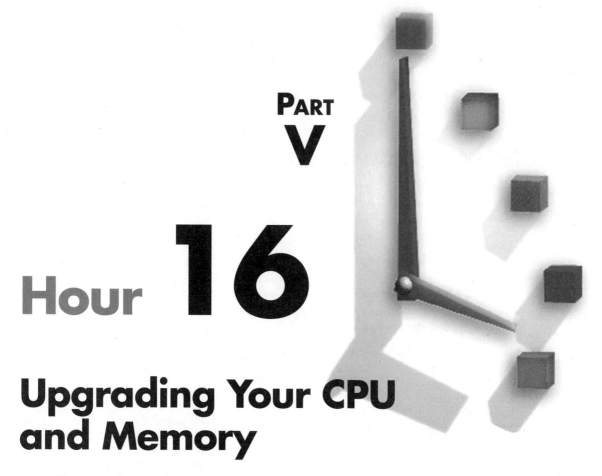

Hour 16

Upgrading Your CPU and Memory

When considering a faster PC, most people first attempt to speed up their current system. If you can save money and get a faster PC by upgrading your existing hardware, why not do it? You'll learn about CPU (central processing unit) and memory upgrades in this hour.

However, much of this hour attempts to talk you *out* of a CPU upgrade! Although adding RAM (random-access memory) is fairly routine, upgrading a CPU is often complex. If you are unsure about the CPU upgrade, you may want to upgrade your memory first and then, if your system has not speeded up to your satisfaction, consider the upgrade to the CPU.

The highlights of this hour include

☐ When to upgrade a CPU

☐ What tools an upgrader needs

☐ Why some CPUs require cooling fans

☐ How to install CPU upgrades

☐ How memory differs

☐ Why a memory mismatch causes system trouble

☐ What to do if your system has no room for additional memory

☐ How to install memory

CPU Upgrade Issues

Upgrading your CPU will improve your PC's speed and often costs much less than purchasing a new PC. By upgrading your CPU, you can extend your PC's usable life and make it compatible with software that it otherwise would not be able to run. Given these statements, why doesn't everybody upgrade their CPU?

Despite the lower cost of a new CPU over a new PC, new CPUs can run a few hundred dollars, so cost is still a factor. If your PC runs smoothly and doesn't balk at today's software, and if you are happy with your PC, you don't need to mess with an upgrade. Some PC users want to ride technology's *leading edge,* but they overdo it and end up on the *bleeding edge* when they look at their checkbook balance.

CAUTION

Often you cannot just remove your CPU and drop in another one to upgrade. Upgrading the CPU in some older systems requires that you completely replace the *motherboard* (the board inside the system unit that holds your memory and CPU). If your CPU is soldered to your PC's motherboard, as most 386 and earlier CPUs are, you'll need to replace your entire motherboard if you want a faster processor. Finding a motherboard with measurements and notches that match your system unit is the smallest problem you'll have. Replacing a motherboard can be tricky and is best left to professionals. Even replacing the CPU itself, if your system allows such an upgrade, is best left to service departments in many situations. Only those PC users who want the challenge should attempt a processor upgrade. The cost of a glitch is too much to gamble.

After you upgrade your CPU, your processor's speed will be limited to your motherboard's speed, your disk drives, and your memory speed. No matter how fast your new CPU is, the CPU's speed may seem limited by the speed of the rest of your system. Often, a CPU upgrade speeds up a PC somewhat but then the user wants completely new hardware to go along with the new CPU to get even more speed. This vicious cycle doesn't appear as often if you replace the entire PC instead of upgrading only the CPU. Therefore, think through your upgrade decision before you make the plunge.

Before heading into the CPU upgrade decision, know that upgrading your CPU is one of the most difficult upgrades you can make. In addition, even the fastest CPU upgrades will not help a slow disk drive. If your PC has too little RAM, try adding more memory before upgrading your CPU (as explained in this hour's final sections). Additional memory can often speed up a computer more than a CPU's moderate upgrade.

16

JUST A MINUTE

Don't get discouraged from upgrading your system's CPU despite the bleak picture being painted here! A faster CPU will make your graphics scream and your calculations fly. If you watch multimedia video, you'll be impressed with the faster and smoother playback that your upgraded CPU provides.

TIME SAVER

One of the best tools an upgrader can own is a *chip puller*. Some CPU upgrades, such as the 386 upgrade described in the next section, require that you remove the existing CPU chip from your unit. Without a chip puller, you could damage your old chip socket or motherboard. Most CPU upgrades come with their own chip puller, but higher quality chip pullers sold separately often perform better.

Some CPUs ride in a *ZIF* (*Zero Insertion Force*) socket that has a lever you press to lift the CPU out of its socket (see Figure 16.1). If you happen to be one of the fortunate who have a ZIF-based CPU, you won't need the chip puller because you'll be able to remove your existing CPU by pressing the CPU's ZIF lever.

Figure 16.1.

ZIF-based CPUs make chip removal as easy as pressing a lever.

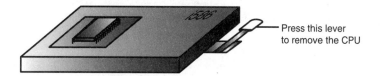

Press this lever to remove the CPU

Upgrading a CPU often requires that you know your existing CPU's brand and model. If you cannot glean this information from the PC's manuals, you'll have to sleuth around inside your PC. Remove your system unit's cover (by using the precautions described in the last hour) and locate the CPU on the motherboard. Look for a large chip with the name *Intel* or *Cyrix*. Sometimes the CPU houses a fan on top of or next to the large CPU chip. The CPU's model information should appear on top of the chip.

JUST A MINUTE

The CPU's fan keeps the chip running at an acceptable temperature. Heat builds up quickly in a CPU due to the tremendous number of components packed into the small space. Sometimes, you'll replace a fanless CPU with a fan-based CPU.

Upgrading a 386-Based PC

If you have a 386-based PC and want a 486-based PC, you have only one upgrade option: Buy a different PC. You'll be able to keep your monitor and modem, and if your video card is fairly new, you may want to transfer it to the new PC. In addition, the old PC's hard disks *may* work in your new one although new disks are inexpensive and your old drives are probably too obsolete to transfer. (The interface type, such as IDE, EIDE, PCI, and the others you read about in the last hour, dictate whether you can transfer your old PC's parts to your new PC.)

JUST A MINUTE

> You can replace a 386 PC's motherboard with a 486 motherboard but, as mentioned in the previous section, such an upgrade is difficult and costly.

You're not left in the cold if you have a 386 to upgrade because 386 upgrades are still available. Sometimes billed as a "486," such upgrades can't be true 486 chips because your 386 motherboard still operates only with a 386-based CPU. A CPU upgrade that you see in stores and in the catalogs replaces your CPU with a faster one. Therefore, you'll gain speed but not as much speed as a 486-based system gives you.

Before making the upgrade, back up your system completely. The upgrade is risky. Even if you send your PC to a service shop for the upgrade, back up before you send in the PC.

TIME SAVER

> No matter *why* you send in your PC to a repair center, whether you are upgrading a new CPU, memory, video card, or whatever, always make a complete system backup before it leaves your desktop. The service center won't make the backup for you (unless you pay them to do so) and hardware problems may arise when your system unit cover comes off. A backup can make a bad situation all right.

Although you may want to perform the CPU upgrade yourself, *get help* when selecting the upgrade chip. Not all 386 CPU chips are the same. They differ in speeds (such as 20MHz versus 25MHz) and type (a 386DX chip differs dramatically from a 386SX). Take your exact PC brand, manuals, and model number to the store where you will purchase the upgrade. If you purchase the upgrade by mail, be sure that you match the upgrade to the CPU inside your system unit.

The following steps outline the 386 upgrade process you can expect if you perform the upgrade yourself. Many of the upgrades differ, but these are the general guidelines you can

16

expect. Read and follow the specific instructions that come with your upgrade CPU when you're ready to replace it. The guidelines for the upgrade follow:

1. Ground yourself by touching your finger to a screw on the back of your system unit to discharge static electricity.

2. Unplug your system.

3. Remove your system unit's cover.

4. Locate your system's CPU. If an expansion board or cable covers the CPU, you may have to temporarily remove the card or cable. Be sure to note how the card or cable went in originally, so you can replace it after you finish the CPU upgrade. Double-check to ensure that you are replacing your existing CPU with the correct type of upgrade.

CAUTION

> At this point, you may face bad news. If your CPU is directly attached—by soldered connections—to your system's motherboard, you cannot upgrade the CPU. Close the cover, cry, and then be content with what you have until you purchase a new system.

5. Notice how the existing CPU sits in the socket. Look at the printing and remember the direction of the text. Also look for a notch or dot in one corner of the CPU; this notch or dot is called the *Pin 1 indicator*, and it orients the chip. One corner of the new CPU will also have a notch or dot, and you'll have to insert the new CPU the same way as the old one.

6. Gently remove the CPU by pressing the lever or by using a chip puller. Pull the CPU out of its socket but keep the socket attached to the motherboard. The socket is where the new CPU belongs, and if you dislodge the soldered socket, you will need to take your system to a service center to attempt a correction and complete the upgrade.

7. Insert the new CPU chip into the socket in the same direction as the original chip used. *Make sure every pin goes into a socket hole before pressing the chip into the socket.*

8. If the upgrade comes with a cooling fan or *heat sink*, you must install the extra hardware or your new CPU will overheat. Check your upgrade manual for the precise instructions for the fan or heat sink installation. The fan will need to plug into a power supply somewhere on your motherboard to run properly. The heat sink absorbs extra heat and looks somewhat like a small blank waffle iron atop your CPU.

9. Replace any dislodged cables and cards as well as the system unit. Plug your PC power cords back into the wall and turn on your system.

16

10. All may be well without further steps, but if your CPU comes with software, you'll have to install the software before your PC can properly use the CPU. For example, some 386 upgrades with fans require software to start the fan.

After you finish the upgrade, start your favorite game and have fun at the new speeds.

Upgrading a 486-Based PC with OverDrive

If you want to upgrade a 486 CPU, you can add an *OverDrive* processor or upgrade to a Pentium chip. The OverDrive is typically less expensive and is simple to install. The purpose of the OverDrive is to speed up your existing 486 CPU.

One of the nice features of the OverDrive is that you don't need to remove your existing CPU. You can install an OverDrive chip next to any 486 CPU that contains an OverDrive socket on the motherboard. The OverDrive socket sits next to your CPU and has holes where the OverDrive processor will sit. The OverDrive socket is approximately the same size as the socket in which your CPU fits. Your manual should tell whether an OverDrive socket exists, or you can check your motherboard to see if you can find an OverDrive socket.

JUST A MINUTE

In rare cases, the OverDrive CPU completely replaces the 486. If your motherboard doesn't have an OverDrive socket, you'll need to replace your 486 chip with an OverDrive/CPU combination. As with all CPU upgrades, you'll need to search your manuals and possibly remove your system unit to determine what your system currently contains. Be sure to read the back of the 486 upgrades to make sure you purchase one that works with your existing machine.

To install the OverDrive, follow these steps:

1. Ground yourself by touching a screw on the back of your system unit.

2. Unplug your system.

3. Remove your system unit's cover.

4. Locate your system's CPU. If an expansion board or cable covers the CPU, you may have to temporarily remove the card or cable. Be sure to note how the card or cable went in originally so that you can correctly replace it after you finish the CPU upgrade. Double-check to ensure that you are replacing your existing CPU with the correct kind of upgrade.

5. If your motherboard includes an OverDrive socket, plug the OverDrive into the socket, taking care that all pins go into their socket properly. If you must replace your 486 CPU with the upgraded 486 with OverDrive attached, follow the same steps as described in the previous section for a 386 upgrade.

Upgrading a 486-Based PC with a Pentium

If you're willing to spend some bucks, you can upgrade to a Pentium processor. Pentium upgrades cost almost twice as much as OverDrive processors for 486 PCs. Intel sells several versions of Pentium processors, including the Pentium, Pentium Pro, Pentium with MMX technology, and Pentium II. Although the Pentium's costs are dropping, such upgrades are still expensive. In addition, several kinds of upgrades exist and they install differently.

CAUTION

Some software today runs *only* on an MMX-based Pentium. Such software usually contains advanced multimedia operations. (The *MMX* in *Pentium MMX* stands for *MultiMedia eXtensions* because the Pentium with MMX runs multimedia applications more efficiently and more smoothly.)

A Pentium upgrade almost always requires a fan due to the extra heat the Pentium generates, so expect to install the CPU's fan (included with the upgrade) along with the chip itself.

The Pentium upgrades install differently from each other depending on the type your system requires—you'll have to read the details of the upgrade. For now, if you can justify the cost of the upgrade instead of buying a new Pentium-based PC, just remember that you'll replace your 486 chip, install a cooling fan, and install software. Read through the previous two sections to get an overview of the steps you'll probably take. The Pentium, however, requires careful attention in some cases to specific details that you'll learn about in the upgrade's instructions.

JUST A MINUTE

The CPU upgrade often comes with a boot disk that you'll have to insert into your disk drive right after you install the CPU upgrade and plug in all the cables. Your PC will boot from the floppy disk instead of the hard disk; the floppy disk ensures that the CPU is working by running a series of diagnostics before turning your PC operating system over to its new CPU.

Your PC's CMOS

CMOS (Complementary Metal-Oxide Semiconductor) memory is a special memory that holds information about your PC hardware. A battery keeps the CMOS contents stable even when you pull the PC's power plug from the wall. The following is a partial list of what CMOS tracks:

☐ The date and time

☐ Disk drive information such as size, speed, and type

☐ Memory size

☐ Existing ports (such as the printer port and the modem port)

When you change your PC's hardware, you may have to change a CMOS setting. Back in the old days, before Windows 95-compatible hardware, CMOS didn't always exist. The computer contained *DIP switches* and *jumper connectors* inside the system unit that often required you to make educated and uneducated guesses as to those settings. Figure 16.2 shows what DIP switches look like. Installing hardware such as memory and disk drives required getting the numerous switch setting combinations just right before your hardware booted properly.

Figure 16.2.

DIP switches and jumpers used to represent your computer's hardware.

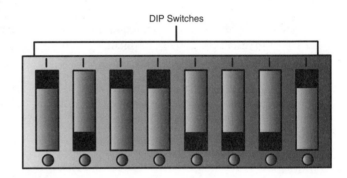
DIP Switches

Fortunately, today's PCs don't require such settings in most instances. You can set these required settings from the keyboard by using software that comes with every PC. Instead of putting the hardware configuration inside switches, the CMOS memory stores the information that can be altered by running a program.

JUST A MINUTE

Although the CMOS battery generally lasts three or more years, you may have to replace yours before you replace your PC. If your PC forgets the date and time and seems not to recognize your disk drives, you've lost your battery. Fortunately, the first time you look at your CMOS settings in the next few paragraphs, you'll record your current settings and safely tuck them away so that you can restore them when you replace your battery.

16

You can only access your CMOS settings when you first boot your computer. You'll probably see a message that appears for a couple of seconds that reads, Press F1 to Enter CMOS Setup. Instead of F1, some PCs use Ctrl+Alt+Insert, F10, and Delete. If you see no such message, you'll have to search your PC manuals or call the manufacturer.

The message only appears for a brief moment because if you don't enter the CMOS setup, your PC starts as normal and Windows appears. If, however, you trigger the CMOS screen, you'll see something like the CMOS setup area shown in Figure 16.3.

Figure 16.3.

Enter the CMOS area to adjust new hardware settings.

```
Main      Advanced      Security      Exit
---------------------------------------------
                  System Date   Oct 3, 1999
                  System Time   02:12:52

            Floppy Options   Press Enter for Menu

        Primary IDE Master   WDC AC33100H
         Primary IDE Slave   Not Installed
      Secondary IDE Master   TC209H
       Secondary IDE Slave   Not Installed
                  Language   English (US)
              Boot Options   Press Enter

                Video Mode   EGA/VGA
                     Mouse   Installed

               Base Memory   640K
           Extended Memory   317444KB

               BIOS Version   1.00.06.A

Press an arrow key to select. Press F10 to save and exit.
```

JUST A MINUTE

Please take a moment now to enter your CMOS and record all the values you see. Search all the menus to reach all the screens. Pay special attention to your memory and disk drive information such as type, cylinder count, and number of drive heads. You'll need to re-enter this information if your battery ever goes dead.

Fortunately, hardware is getting more intelligent. When you add memory or a new disk drive, you *may* not need to change the CMOS setting, but you probably will. Your new hardware upgrade should describe the CMOS setting you need to make.

If an error message appears when you first boot your system after installing or changing hardware, you'll need to enter the CMOS setup information and change the CMOS values to reflect your new hardware. If your system starts Windows as normal, you don't need to worry about the CMOS.

An Easy Upgrade: Extra Memory

One of the easiest upgrades you can make is adding more RAM to your PC. Windows works well with lots of RAM. With today's Windows versions (starting with Windows 95), your memory options are made simpler. In previous versions, with MS-DOS and Windows 3.1, PC users had to deal with special hardware issues that made memory expansion more difficult due to the number of options. If, however, you run Windows 95 or a later version, you

certainly don't have to worry about an IBM XT (a very old machine) because such a computer
doesn't run Windows 95.

JUST A MINUTE

If you want to add memory to an old computer, such as an XT, make sure
you still have the need for that hardware. Your money may be better spent
buying newer hardware. Some PC newcomers think an XT or something
else around that time period (such as a *PS/1* or *PC Jr.*, both IBM's early
attempts at the home market) are all they need to learn on, but such
machines make for more work than newer machines that support
Windows 95.

Ample memory is critical for good performance. Some 486s with a lot of memory run faster
than Pentiums with less memory. Memory is inexpensive and, unless you have 32MB or more
RAM, adding RAM is an economical and simple way to improve your system's performance.

The most important part of upgrading memory is purchasing the right memory for your
system. Fortunately, most memory upgrades list the systems with which they work on the
back of their package. Although too many PCs exist to list all of them, most manufacturer's
systems are listed on memory upgrades by model. The manufacturers provide this service
because of the critical nature of matching new memory to your existing memory. A memory
mismatch causes severe problems—in fact, your PC won't even boot properly.

CAUTION

Don't just find memory that works in your brand of computer, but be sure
you match the model number as well. The same PC manufacturer makes
PCs with several types of memory.

The memory match is so critical that you should probably check with a repair center—
especially one inside the store where you will purchase the memory—to ensure that the
upgraded memory works on your model. The store will probably install the memory for a
small fee, but memory upgrades are fairly easy to install yourself.

When looking through the memory options, you'll run across several new terms related to
memory that are explained in Table 16.1. When you locate memory designed for your PC's
model, you are actually ensuring that the new memory's specifics from Table 16.1 match the
memory already in your system unit. Some rules-of-thumb you can go by are as follows:

☐ If you use a 486-based PC, you will *probably* upgrade memory by using four
memory SIMMs at a time.

☐ If you use a Pentium-based PC, you will *probably* upgrade memory by using two memory SIMMs at a time. Never mix memory in their pair or quad formations. In other words, never install two SIMMs that differ in capacity.

CAUTION

Read this entire section before buying memory, including the steps required to install memory that come later in this section. You'll need to understand the memory inside your PC before you can properly upgrade it and know the memory capacity you'll need to purchase. Therefore, open your PC before you purchase memory so you'll know what to buy after reading through the rest of this section.

16

Table 16.1. You'll run across these terms when shopping for a memory upgrade.

Term	Description
DIPs/SIPs	(*Dual Inline Packages* and *Single Inline Packages*) Memory chips used in older pre-486 PCs. These memory chips must be installed one at a time onto the motherboard or onto a memory card.
SIMMs/DIMMs	(*Single Inline Memory Modules* and *Dual Inline Memory Modules*) A small board that contains a row of memory chips (usually nine chips reside on the board). Figure 16.4 shows a sample SIMM. Instead of inserting several memory chips into sockets, you need to install only two or four SIMMs (DIMMs hold twice as much memory as SIMMs but are still not as common as SIMMs). SIMMs and DIMMs come with 30-pins or 72-pins, and you must match your PC's memory socket requirements.
Parity	Memory is made either with *parity*, meaning automatic error checking occurs, or *non-parity*, meaning that no automatic error checking can take place. If your system requires parity memory, or if your system already contains parity memory, the replacement or upgrade memory must also contain parity support.
Gold and Tin	Some PCs require tin-based or gold-based memory SIMMs, so be sure to match the memory with your PC's requirements. (Often, however, the type of metal does not make a difference.)

continues

Table 16.1. continued

Term	Description
Speed	Memory speed is measured in *nanoseconds* (billionths of seconds), and the fewer nanoseconds the chip can operate, the faster the memory; hence, a lower speed setting is better than a higher speed setting. Always purchase as fast or faster memory than currently resides in your PC. A faster memory does not offer noticeable performance improvement, but each hardware model requires a minimum memory speed. Almost all new PCs require memory speeds of 60- to 70-nanoseconds and faster.

Figure 16.4.

Plug two or four SIMMs into your PC to upgrade memory.

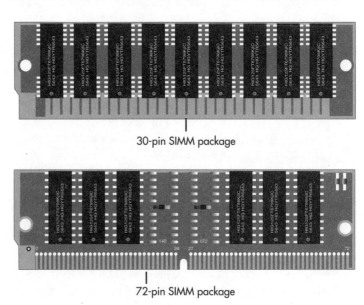

30-pin SIMM package

72-pin SIMM package

You must do some math. If you want to upgrade your 16MB PC to 32MB, you must purchase enough SIMM memory to boost your memory by 16MB. If you find 4MB SIMMs that work in your model, however, you'll need to purchase four sets of the 4MB SIMMs to do the job. If your existing PC does not have enough SIMM sockets, you'll need to remove your existing lower-memory SIMMs (assuming your PC supports various SIMM quantities, as many do) and upgrade your original SIMMs with a higher capacity. Your resulting memory might then include eight banks of 4MB SIMMs. You could probably save money and time if you purchased more expensive 8MB SIMMs and installed only four of them. Although DIMMs are more expensive than SIMMs, you need only one DIMM for every two SIMMs, and you

16

may not have enough empty sockets to fill your memory requirements without using DIMMs.

CAUTION

> Some PCs support a maximum memory limit. Make sure that you don't attempt to upgrade more than your PC can handle. Check your PC's owner manual to see whether the vendor published a maximum memory limit for your machine.

After you purchase the correct memory for your PC, follow these steps to install the new memory:

1. Ground yourself by touching a screw on the back of your system unit.
2. Unplug your system.
3. Remove your system unit's cover.
4. Find the empty SIMM sockets. Figure 16.5 shows sample sockets. You do have empty SIMM sockets, don't you? If not, you'll have to remove lower-capacity SIMMs and install high-capacity SIMMs to upgrade your system memory. (Yes, you may be going back to the store to switch memory at least once. Keep in mind that the store can perform the upgrade and you can let them worry about these issues.) Read through the rest of these instructions to learn how to install SIMMs *before* you remove existing SIMMs. You'll need to gently pry open two tabs holding the SIMMs before you can remove existing SIMMs.

Figure 16.5.

SIMMs go in SIMM sockets, and you'll need two or more empty sockets to upgrade memory.

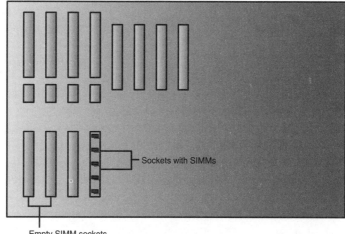

5. Carefully look at the SIMM placement details that you'll find in the memory's instructions. You'll need to locate the slot at one corner of the SIMM and drop that corner into the socket that requires the notch. (You can see the notch catcher inside the socket before you install the SIMM.)

6. Insert the SIMM into the socket either straight up and down or at an angle depending on the socket type (the memory instructions will direct you). When the SIMM reaches its full seated location, rock the SIMM toward the metal tabs that will grab the SIMM and hold it in place. The SIMM will rock only one direction (don't force anything) and you'll feel and probably hear the locking tabs after they grab the SIMM.

7. Repeat this procedure for the remaining SIMMs you want to install.

8. Look over the SIMMs to see if they all reside in parallel without any one tilting differently from the others. Tilt any SIMMs not yet locked into place. All the SIMMs should form a military-like line of similarly placed memory modules.

9. Replace your system unit cover and power cables and plug your power cords into the wall.

10. Turn on your PC. Windows should automatically detect your new memory and adjust the operating system to the new measurements.

JUST A MINUTE

If an error appears instead of Windows, you'll need to enter your PC's CMOS screen and adjust the memory setting there.

When you first work on your PC with the added memory, you will almost certainly notice a speed improvement. As memory sizes get larger and prices go down, memory upgrades are becoming one of the most common upgrades being performed by both service shops and individual PC owners. You'll be glad you upgraded the moment you turn on your PC.

Summary

This hour taught you a lot about CPU and memory hardware. The major challenge when upgrading such components is not in the upgrade itself, but in the purchase. You've got to buy the proper CPU or memory upgrade that works with your hardware or the upgrade won't work. After you buy the right hardware, you can usually perform the upgrade yourself. Although this hour could only show you an overview and not give the specifics for each manufacturer, you now know exactly what to expect in 99 percent of all CPU and memory upgrades. You now have enough ammunition to decide if you want to perform the upgrade yourself or if you want to pay a service center to do it for you.

16

When it comes to upgrading your CPU, you'll want to make sure the cost of the upgrade justifies the upgrade over a new purchase. Upgrading a CPU will boost your computer's performance, but the upgrade is often expensive and you are putting a better CPU into a computer with, probably in today's terms, slow disk drives and slow memory. Upgrading memory is not questionable. In general, the more memory your PC contains, up to at least 32MB, the faster your PC will operate. Memory is inexpensive—make sure you have enough.

The next hour explains how to upgrade your PC's multimedia hardware to take advantage of the multimedia-based software and data that today's PCs support.

16

Q&A

Q Can you have too much memory?

A If your PC supports a memory limit, you cannot go past that limit. Therefore, you can install only as much memory as your PC allows. The PC's memory limit, however, is rarely reached. PCs purchased in the past few years allow at least 64MB of memory and few users, even the power users, have more than 32MB.

Windows 95 actually does slow down if you put more than 64MB of RAM into the machine. You probably won't notice this slowdown, but more than 64MB does little good if you run Windows 95. Windows 95 uses memory to store instructions and to read ahead from the disk drive. Too much memory to fill can sometimes cause a bookkeeping overhead for Windows 95 that actually slows performance.

Hour 17

Upgrading Your Disk and CD-ROM Storage

One never seems to have enough disk space. When you purchase a PC, it seems that you fill space faster and faster. In reality, you probably do. Applications continue to get bigger as their feature sets grow. In addition, accessing the Internet often gobbles up disk space because an Internet program stores Internet pages on your PC so that subsequent access takes less time. The more free disk space you can get, the better. As this hour shows, if you don't have enough disk space, you can add more.

In addition to hard disk drives, you may want to add a second CD-ROM drive or even a CD-ROM changer that keeps five or more CD-ROMs ready for your computer's access. Rewriteable CD drives now exist so you can create your own CDs. The new large capacity removable drives offer not only storage options but great backup solutions as well. This hour describes how to install all these expansion storage devices.

The highlights of this hour include

☐ Which kinds of disk drive upgrades are available

☐ Why you may need to purchase a controller card for your disk drive upgrade

☐ How to install new disk drives

☐ When to select an external or internal removable disk drive

☐ How to install a tape backup drive

Hard Disk Upgrades

Hour 4 discussed the kinds of hard disks you'll find, including the IDE, EIDE, and SCSI types. These acronyms actually describe the disk's interface type to your computer. If you purchase a new disk drive, your choices today basically fall into these two categories:

☐ **EIDE (Enhanced Integrated Drive Electronics):** Drives that hold more than 1GB of information.

☐ **SCSI (Pronounced *scuzzy* and stands for *Small Computer System Interface*):** Drives and other expansion hardware that you can link together into something called a *daisy chain*.

> You can still purchase IDE drives at a lower cost than EIDE drives, but IDE drives cannot hold a gigabyte of information.

The SCSI drives are faster, more expensive, and harder to install and set up than EIDE drives. Nevertheless, SCSI offers the advantage of being able to support non-disk peripherals, such as tape backups. Despite the SCSI standard, different SCSI cards and drives require different setup details. If you select a SCSI drive, you have to follow the manufacturer's installation instructions carefully.

If you are running Windows 95 or later on an older PC, such as an early 486, you may have to replace your current drive if you want an IDE or EIDE drive. The following drives don't work together with IDE or EIDE drives: *ST506, ESDI, MFM* (for *Modified Frequency Modulation*), or *RLL* (for *Run-Length Limited*). The huge storage capacities of the new drives make replacement of your old one trivial anyway. (Just be sure you make a full backup first, so that you can restore the backup when you replace the drive, especially the boot drive.)

Heard of a *Controller Card*?

A *controller card* is an expansion card that older disk drives, such as the ST506 drives of the early PCs, required. The drive plugged into the controller card and the controller card plugged into the motherboard.

Today's newer PC technology does not require controller cards because support for IDE and EIDE drives is often built right into the motherboard. If you want to put a new drive into an older PC, however, you have to purchase a disk controller card that handles IDE or EIDE disk drives—your controller card certainly won't be able to handle the new technology. Such controller cards are inexpensive and drop into an empty slot in your PC.

17

JUST A MINUTE

If you're replacing an older drive with an IDE or, preferably, an EIDE drive, your new drive becomes your boot drive (called the *master*). If you add a second drive, the second drive becomes the *slave*. Check your disk drive's instructions to determine how to set one drive as the master and one as the slave. This generally requires positioning a jumper to indicate the boot drive.

TIME SAVER

Before you install any disk drive, make a system startup floppy disk (see Hour 13). If the worst case happens and you can't boot your PC, you'll be able to boot with the startup disk in the floppy drive and attempt to determine why the problem exists. Even if you don't have problems, you need the startup disk if you install a new boot disk, so make one now.

Installing an additional disk drive requires at least one open *drive bay*. A drive bay, such as the one shown in Figure 17.1, is the place inside your system unit where disk drives and CD-ROMs reside. If your bays are full and you have two floppy disk drives, you need to remove one to make room for the new drive. Special combo drives exist that let you insert two disks into a single drive, but you rarely need more than one disk drive.

Making the Upgrade

As with CPU and memory upgrades, most IDE and EIDE drives install the same way *except* for a few *gotchas* due to small manufacturing differences. Just as you did in the previous hour, you need to read through the following instructions to learn what's in store for your hard disk upgrade and *then* read your manufacturer's instructions for the details specific to your drive. More than likely, you'll find that these instructions are *much* easier to follow than the manufacturer's, so you'll be glad you read this first.

Figure 17.1.

Plastic drive bay covers hide empty slots where you can install additional disk drives.

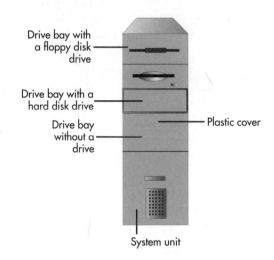

Drive bay with a floppy disk drive

Drive bay with a hard disk drive

Drive bay without a drive

Plastic cover

System unit

CAUTION

Have you recorded all your CMOS information? (See Hour 16.) If not, please do so now.

To install an IDE or EIDE hard disk, follow these instructions:

1. Ground yourself to a screw on the back of the system unit, shut down your PC, and unplug all the power cables.

2. Remove your system unit's cover.

3. If you are replacing an existing drive, remove the cables plugged into the drive. The drive will have a power cable and a data cable (called a *ribbon cable*). The ribbon cable should have plugs for additional drives. If another drive is plugged into the ribbon cable, keep that drive plugged in unless you are replacing both drives. Figure 17.2 shows the cables attached to a typical disk drive. Be very careful when you pull the ribbon cable off the drive; pull by the plug and don't tug the cable by the ribbon because the ribbon wires can come out easily. (If this happens, you'll need to purchase a new cable.)

4. If you are replacing a non-IDE or non-EIDE drive with an IDE or EIDE drive, you need to replace the controller card with one that supports your new drives. Follow the old disk drive cable to the controller card. Unplug the cables from the

17

controller card, unscrew the screw holding the controller card in place, and rock the card upward until you unseat the card from the motherboard. Gently insert the new IDE or EIDE controller card in its place (gently press downward until the gold connectors insert into their slots) and screw it in. Figure 17.3 shows a controller card installed in a system.

Figure 17.2.

Disk drives need a power cable as well as a ribbon cable for data transfer.

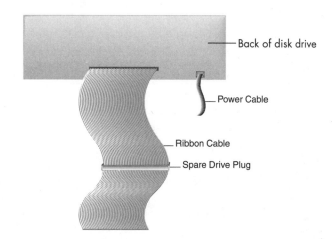

Back of disk drive

Power Cable

Ribbon Cable

Spare Drive Plug

17

Figure 17.3.

You'll have to replace your controller card if you are installing an IDE or EIDE drive in an older system.

Holding screw

Disk's ribbon cable

5. If you are replacing a drive and you've unplugged the cables, you need to remove the old drive from the system. Play detective and determine how the drive is held into place. Drives generally have two or more screws—one or more on each side, and sometimes one in front. You may have to take an access panel off your system unit to get to the drive. If you can't figure out how the drive is secured, or if you can't get access to one of the screws, you've got to hope the PC manuals will give you a hint. After they're unscrewed, some drives slide out the front of the system unit and some slide into the center of the system unit.

TIME SAVER

Drives are held into place by *drive rails*, which are long plastic or metal guides attached to the disk drive that hold the drive correctly in the drive bay. After you slide your disk drive out of the system unit, check your new drive to see whether it has drive rails. If it doesn't, unscrew the two rails from the sides of your old drive and attach them to your new drive so that your new drive will stay inside its drive bay properly. Rail sizes are standard and work between different drive brands and types. If you are adding a second drive and the drive does not contain drive rails, you have to purchase them at a local computer store (look in the cable and accessories section) before you can install the drive.

6. If you are installing a second drive, you need to open a slot for the new drive. Often, this means you have to pry off a plastic cover from an empty drive bay. Slide your new drive into its empty slot from the front of the system unit and screw it into place from inside the open system unit cover.

7. Attach the ribbon and power cables to your new drive. The cables should plug in only one way. Either attach the same cables you removed from an old drive or plug the spare plug from your existing ribbon cable into your drive and plug a power cable into the drive.

   An unused spare power cable will be coming from your power supply, the silver box in the back of your system unit. The power cable's red cord goes into the power slot marked with a number 1.

CAUTION

If you cannot find a spare power cable, you need to purchase a Y-adapter cable from your local PC store and share power with another drive. Unplug the power connector going into an existing drive and plug your new Y-adapter cable into the old power cable's connector. You've in effect split the single power cable into two. Now, you can plug the two cables into two drives; previously, the cable powered a single drive.

   Be sure to plug the cables into the controller card if you installed a new controller card.

8. Recheck that both ends of the ribbon are plugged in, make sure the power cable is snug, replace your system unit's cover, and plug in the power cords.

9. Today's new drives come with a setup disk. The Windows *Disk Wizard* program not only sets up your CMOS, but also tells Windows about the new drive and its proper settings. If all works fine, take a break. If not, you may need to start at the beginning and modify your CMOS settings. Remember, a trip to the repair center might save you a lot of headaches.

17

10. After the Disk Wizard program completes, you'll need to restore your backup so you can use your system with the new drive.

TIME SAVER

> If you have trouble with your newly installed drive, check out the final answer in this hour's Q&A section for some troubleshooting tips.

Installing CD Drives

Whether you're installing a CD-ROM, a writeable CD-ROM, or a multi-disc CD changer, you follow the same installation procedures. CD-ROMs, both internal and external, almost always require a controller card and they should come with one. Make sure you have an empty expansion slot before you purchase the CD-ROM.

17

TIME SAVER

> Look for a CD-ROM that is *Kodak Photo CD-compatible*. You can now get pictures developed (pictures from a regular camera, not just a modern digital camera) onto CD-ROM. A CD-ROM that's Kodak Photo CD-compatible can display those pictures. Fortunately, most CD-ROMs are Kodak Photo CD-compatible these days.

You may want to add a second CD-ROM to your system that already has one CD-ROM. If the CD-ROM is the same type or brand as your existing CD-ROM, you don't need to add the CD-ROM controller card. CD-ROM controller cards support at least two CD-ROM drives. A second CD-ROM comes in handy when you access some of today's multi-CD reference applications and games.

JUST A MINUTE

> If your CD-ROM doesn't come with a controller card, it might plug directly into your motherboard. Of course, you need a PC that's new enough to supply a motherboard-based IDE connection. If your PC's manual does not mention motherboard support for a CD-ROM, purchase a CD-ROM with a controller card.

If you already have a SCSI card, you *may* be able to plug a SCSI-based CD-ROM into the SCSI connector or into the back of another SCSI device. The problem is that not all SCSI devices are standard. Generally, two different SCSI cards don't get along with each other. Ask the store or mail-order company to check whether your SCSI card's brand works with the SCSI CD-ROM. If they don't know, ask them to contact the manufacturer for you to see whether your SCSI card works with the CD-ROM. If it does, you don't need to install the CD-ROM's controller card because you plug the CD-ROM into your SCSI card connector.

Fortunately, installing a CD-ROM is much easier than installing a disk drive. Although internal CD-ROMs take just as long to install, you don't need to mess with CMOS; you don't need to tell Windows (Windows 95 and later) about the new drive because Windows detects it automatically; and you don't have to restore any backup files as you do with boot hard drives. Follow these steps to install your new drive:

1. Ground yourself to a screw on the back of the system unit, shut down your PC, and unplug all the power cables.

2. Remove your system unit's cover.

3. Install the CD-ROM controller card into an empty slot. Unscrew the screw from an empty expansion slot cover, remove the silver cover, and gently push the controller card into the slot. Make sure the card is seated firmly and evenly.

4. If you're installing an internal CD-ROM drive, remove a plastic cover from an empty drive bay. (The cover keeps you from peering into an empty drive slot from the outside of the system unit.) You may have to pry the plastic cover off with a small screwdriver. Slide the CD-ROM drive into the bay and secure the drive with screws. Connect the included cable into the controller card and run the cable to the back of the CD-ROM.

5. Replace your system unit cover.

6. If you're installing an external CD-ROM, plug the included cable into the CD-ROM and the other end into the controller card's connector at the back of the system unit. Plug the power cord into a power outlet.

7. Windows 95 and later versions are great at recognizing new CD-ROM drives. As soon as you boot your PC, the Plug and Play intelligence will probably recognize the new drive. If not, you will have to run the setup software that comes with the CD-ROM drive.

17

Installing a High-Capacity Removable Drive

Companies such as Iomega, SyQuest, and Epson now make high-capacity removable disk drives. These removable disk drives offer a mixture of hard disk access and speed with the convenience of floppy disks. These drives start at 100MB of storage and reach capacities over 2GB. You have an almost unlimited storage capacity as long as you keep purchasing the disk cartridges. Although these removable disk cartridges cost much more than floppy disks, they cost much less than a hard disk of the same capacity.

These drives often come in three versions: internal, external to parallel, and external to SCSI. The parallel port is the port into which you plug your printer. If you purchase an external parallel removable drive, the only three steps required to install the drive are as follows:

1. Unplug your printer and plug the removable drive's cable into your printer port.

2. On top of the cable's connector is another printer port into which you can plug your printer. These connectors are called *pass through connectors*, meaning that your printer gets all the signals it needs and the removable drive gets all the signals it needs to do its job. You now have a CD-ROM cable as well as the printer cable coming out of your printer port.

3. Plug the power supply into the wall and you're ready to run the drive's setup program that comes with the drive.

CAUTION

The parallel version is much slower than the SCSI version. Although the parallel version works well for mass backups, you won't want to use it as a secondary hard disk because its speed rivals that of floppy disks only.

TIME SAVER

If you use a parallel drive, you can move the drive from PC to PC. You can back up every PC in the office, your PC at home, and your laptop simply by moving the drive to the next machine and plugging it into the printer's parallel port.

If you install an internal or external SCSI removable drive, you need to open your system unit and install both the SCSI board as well as the internal removable drive if you bought an internal drive. You can follow the same installation procedure that you read about in the previous section for an internal disk drive with controller. You won't have to make CMOS

17

settings, however, because the setup disk that comes with your removable drive will take care of letting Windows know all about the new hardware.

Installing a Tape Backup Drive

Tape backup drives are made that can back up everything from the largest disk drives sold today to a single tape cartridge. (Removable drives can back up only about 2GB per cartridge.) Although you can't use the files on a tape drive as if they were stored on a removable disk, you can back up and restore very easily. You don't have to sit in front of the PC changing removable drives to back up your entire disk. You can start the Windows Scheduler program to automate tape backups in the middle of the night.

Installing an external tape backup requires only that you plug the drive's connector into your system unit's printer port and then plug the printer into the tape drive's connector. If you purchase an internal tape drive, follow these steps to install the drive:

1. Ground yourself to a screw on the back of the system unit, shut down your PC, and unplug all the power cables.

2. Remove your system unit's cover.

3. Remove a cover from an empty drive bay. (The cover keeps you from peering into an empty drive slot from the outside of the system unit.) You may have to pry the plastic cover off with a small screwdriver.

4. Slide the tape drive into the bay and secure the drive with screws.

5. Attach the cables to your new drive. Plug a spare power cable into your tape backup drive. Your tape backup drive uses the same ribbon cable as your floppy disk drive. The floppy disk's ribbon cable includes a spare connector where a second drive normally goes. Plug that space connector into your drive.

JUST A MINUTE

> If you already have two floppy disk drives in your system, you need to remove one for the tape backup. Remove the second (B) drive and plug its ribbon connector into the tape drive. When you restart your PC, you have to inform the CMOS about the lack of a second disk drive.

6. Recheck that both ends of the ribbon are plugged in, make sure the power cable is snug, and replace your system unit's cover and plug in the power cords.

7. Start your PC and install the tape setup software that came with your tape drive. You don't have to tell the CMOS about the tape drive because your backup software should be able to find the tape drive when needed.

17

Summary

This hour showed you what's in store when you upgrade your PC with disks, CDs, and tape drives. Most of these drives install in a similar manner. The disk drives take the most care because of their required CMOS change and because you might be replacing your boot drive. Fortunately, today's drives come with self-installing software that takes care of both your CMOS and Windows.

Despite today's improved installation routines, most PCs have a limited number of drive bays. If you have two floppy disk drives but also want a tape drive, you have to purchase an external parallel-port drive unless you're willing to give up one disk drive.

The next hour explains how to upgrade your printer's capabilities or select a second printer.

Q&A

17

Q What can I do if I have no free expansion slots?

A If you have no expansion slots for a disk drive controller card or for any other upgrade you want to make, your options are certainly limited. The first thing to do is take an inventory of your current system's expansion cards. Do you have a game card (for a joystick) as well as a sound card? Most sound cards now have game ports, so you can replace your two existing cards with a single card. Combining existing cards to make room for a new expansion card, such as for a new disk drive controller card, gets expensive and begins to make the upgrade too costly.

Therefore, unless you want to upgrade your sound card to a newer technology or convert an internal modem card to an external modem to free a slot, you may have to consider an external disk drive upgrade that plugs into your parallel port. The external drives are usually more expensive and slower than internal drives, but such drives may be your only solution until you replace your system with a new PC.

Q How do I install a DVD (Digital Video Disk) drive?

A It depends, because no true DVD standards have yet to emerge. Each DVD standard installs differently. Due to the tremendous capacity and the growing number of software titles that take advantage of DVD technology, these drive standards should settle shortly. For now, you are on your own with the manuals that come with the drive. You may want to ask your PC store about the installation or read the instructions in the store before purchasing the DVD drive to make sure you want to tackle the install yourself. Perhaps you should wait a while before purchasing a DVD drive, if you have not bought one already. Within a year or so, a better DVD standard should show itself and become common.

Q **Can I add a new IDE drive to my system and still keep my old MFM or RLL drives for extra disk space?**

A Unfortunately, no. You cannot mix these older drives with IDE drives. Newer disk drive controller cards are incompatible with the older MFM and RLL technology. The newer drives, even the least expensive ones today, offer so much more drive space and speed than MFM and RLL drives that you would gain very little by trying to combine those drives with newer disk drives.

Q **Why do disk upgrades seem so difficult?**

A One of the most difficult upgrades to make to a PC is a disk drive upgrade. Often, you can upgrade a PC's CPU quicker than its disk drives. Vendors label CPU upgrades with specific CPUs they upgrade, often along with PC models that accept the upgrade. It is true that a disk drive upgrade can be much more tedious and difficult than a CPU upgrade.

The upgrade difficulty, of course, does not mean that you should *not* upgrade your system's disk drive, because such an upgrade can extend the life of your system by a year or more. Nevertheless, you learned throughout this hour how difficult such an upgrade can be. Although this hour explained the highlights, you might run across more problems not discussed here. This chapter prepares you with the overview you need to decide if you want to make the upgrade but also lets you know what's in store. Be sure to read your new drive's upgrade instructions carefully though; some drives require special settings before a PC can recognize them. Those settings often depend on your current drives, your controller card type, and the order in which you want your PC to recognize your new drive.

Q **I installed a new drive but it doesn't work. What can I try?**

A Unplug your power cord, remove your system unit cover, and check all connectors. The ribbon cable sometimes looks plugged in when it's only partially plugged in. Make sure the power cable is secure and check the controller card for snug connections. Is your controller card fully seated in its slot? Make sure.

You may have a master/slave conflict. Be sure that your boot drive is set for master, and if you have a second drive, make sure it's set to be the slave. Remember that you have to adjust jumper settings for the master/slave specification.

If all looks good, display your CMOS screen once more and check the drive settings. Be sure that the drive configuration looks good. Make sure that your CMOS knows the correct drive capacity and properly designates the master and slave if you've got two drives. (If you have only one drive, the one drive must be the master.)

If you've installed a second non-boot drive, and your system boots properly but you can't access the drive, try to ask Windows for help once again. Run the

17

Control Panel's Add New Hardware program and let the program search your PC for the proper drive setting. Windows, starting with Windows 95, has become more intelligent when it comes to recognizing hardware.

If all looks fine but the drive still refuses to work, you may have to take your PC to the repair center to see what they can do.

17

Hour 18

Upgrading Your Printer

Your printer is your PC's printed voice to the world. The output that you produce, whether it looks good or bad, reflects the quality of your work. If you use an old printer, your PC's output will not look as if you put effort into your work. Upgrading your printer is one of the easiest and least expensive upgrades you can perform to improve your PC's output.

Although you may replace your entire PC several times over the years, you can keep the same printer through several generations of PCs. If you have a high-quality printer, it may last for years and produce great output. Although manufacturers improve printers every year, printer technology doesn't change as rapidly as other PC technology, so you get more life out of your printer. Your printer's manufacturer does not have to match your PC manufacturer.

The highlights of this hour include

- [ ] When to buy a new printer
- [ ] Why you might want two printers
- [ ] How to switch between two printers
- [ ] When to install a second printer port card inside your system unit

☐ How to take care of your new printer
☐ How to tell Windows about your new printer
☐ When to remove the Windows printer driver software
☐ How to upgrade your printer's hardware

When to Upgrade Your Printer

If you're happy with your printer, you probably don't want to run down to your local PC store and purchase another one. Nevertheless, printer technology is getting more interesting and your work requirements may dictate getting a new printer. (You may want to review Hour 4 to learn about the various printers available.)

If you still use a dot-matrix printer, you probably will be pleased if you change to a newer inkjet printer. The inkjet produces beautiful output and most inkjets produce color as easily as black-and-white. Inkjet printers cost very little (probably less than you paid for your dot-matrix printer years ago).

CAUTION

The inkjet cartridges can get expensive, especially the color ones.

One reason to buy a new printer is that your old one stops working correctly. If you've had the same printer for a few years and the printer breaks down, it's probably time to buy another. The cost of repairing printers is often high compared to the cost of a new one. Printers contain many moving parts that can break and repairing them can be labor-intensive.

Properly Maintain Your Printer

Due to the printer's physical make-up, it's important to keep your printer as clean as possible. You can find dust covers for almost every kind of printer. (Make sure you remove the dust cover every time you turn on the printer or the printer will overheat.) Even with a dust cover, the constant paper that moves through your printer leaves a build-up of paper fragments throughout the inside of your printer. Check your printer's manual for instructions about opening the printer (most printers have access covers) and keep the inside clear from dust and paper particles. One tool to keep handy is a spray can of highly compressed air you can use to blow away dust and debris.

Keep new toner cartridges (for laser printers) and ink cartridges (for inkjet printers) in their original packaging until you are ready to replace them. Many printers

---

18

contain LCD readouts that warn you when the toner or ink gets close to empty. If you know that you won't be printing for a while, perhaps because of an extended trip, you may want to return the ink cartridges to the sealed capsule that comes with many inkjet printers to keep the ink from drying.

TIME SAVER

When your laser printer first warns you about low toner, purchase a new toner cartridge right away but *don't install it yet*. Remove your existing toner cartridge and *gently* shake the cartridge for a few seconds; hold one end in each hand so that the cartridge is lengthwise parallel to your waist, and move the cartridge left and right, dispersing the toner that's left evenly across the bottom of the cartridge. Replace the cartridge and the warning may go away for a few days or weeks. Be careful, because the next time that warning appears, you'll have only a page or two of output before the toner is truly out. That's why you should purchase a toner cartridge when you see the warning the first time.

Take care of your printer and you'll extend its already long life. Of course, a broken printer is not the only reason to upgrade. Perhaps you need the features found only on a newer printer. Instead of replacing your first printer; however, you may want to add a second printer and keep your first one. Many of today's PC users work with two (or more) printers connected to their systems.

18

Why Have Two Printers?

Many PC users have second printers. Your needs may change to require a second one yourself. Some great uses for a second printer are

- [ ] You use your PC for business and want to dedicate a printer for check printing. By keeping the checks in the printer at all times, you can use your first printer for routine printing and reserve the second one for checks.

- [ ] Your first printer may not produce good enough output for your needs or may be too slow. Many all-in-one PC deals come with cheap printers. Although your PC's printer might work just fine, a second printer will be more sturdy, produce better output, and probably be faster than one you purchased as part of a package deal.

- [ ] Your children want color output. Perhaps your primary printer is a single color (black) laser printer. You can connect a second color printer for your children to use.

JUST A MINUTE

Color printers can print onto some very interesting output. Some of today's color inkjet printers produce T-shirt iron-ons and your kids will *love* designing their own shirts. Color printers often output well on overhead transparencies too, so your kids' school presentations will guarantee them an A+.

☐ You use an old printer for personal use, such as printing banners for your children, but you want a better printer, perhaps a high-speed laser printer, for special reports and for high-quantity output. You'll save on power bills and you'll save wear and tear on the new laser printer if you use the older printer for your own output. (Don't get the impression, however, that laser printers can't take wear and tear. As a matter of fact, laser printers probably produce like-new output longer than any other printer.)

☐ You share a PC with another and each of you prefers a different kind of printer. Perhaps one of you uses a color inkjet printer and the other prefers a high-speed laser.

Working with Two Printers

A second printer does pose one minor problem: How do you direct specific output to one printer or the other? If you use a check printer, how does your checkbook software know to print to the printer and how does your word processor know to print to the other printer?

The worst case, although it will work, is to use the same printer cable for both printers. Before you print you make sure the PC's printer cable is plugged into the correct printer. Using the same printer cable for both printers is the least costly of all multiple printer solutions. Unfortunately, it's also the biggest pain.

JUST A MINUTE

Printers don't come with cables. You'll have to purchase a cable every time you purchase a printer. The total cable length between your PC and the printer cannot exceed 20 feet because the print signal does not travel well at long distances (not unlike the Mir space station). Make sure your cable on either side of the switchbox does not exceed 20 feet. Most printer cables are 6-feet long, so two 6-foot cables with a switchbox between them should pose no problem.

Invariably, you'll forget to switch the cable, and output that's supposed to go to one printer goes to the other. This can cause headaches, especially if you sent a lot of output to the wrong printer and that printer is turned on.

Printers support special printer codes that Windows knows all about. Suppose that you draw a color picture with Windows Paint and want to print the picture. You'll select the File | Print menu option to start the printing. Windows, however, adds printer-specific information to that picture's data to produce the picture properly on your printer. Therefore, the data stream that Windows sends to a color inkjet printer differs dramatically from the data stream Windows sends to a laser printer, even though you printed the same picture and even though both printers produce the same picture. (The laser's picture will not be in color unless you spend $1.4 gazillion for a color laser.)

The problem occurs when you send output to the wrong printer; the codes for the *other* printer will confuse the connected printer and garbage will appear on the paper. In many cases, that garbage causes many pages to be ejected from the printer with perhaps only a little printing on each page before you get to the printer to turn it off.

A much better solution is to purchase a printer *switchbox*, sometimes called an *A-B switch*. The switchbox sits between your PC and the printers, as shown in Figure 18.1. You'll need to purchase two extra printer cables when you buy the switchbox. Connect the single printer connector to your PC and connect the dual printer connector to each of the printers.

Figure 18.1.

A printer switch enables you to select an output printer without changing cables.

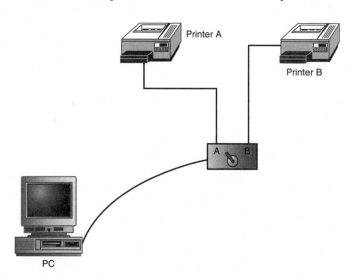

Before you print, simply make sure the switch is directed to the correct printer. The switchbox eliminates the need for swapping the printer cable (and possibly damaging the cable's connector through too much use), but you'll still need to change the switch before you print or you'll get garbage again as described earlier.

If You Print and Change your Mind

After you send something to be printed, Windows collects all the print output and begins routing that output to your printer. If you print to the wrong printer, or if you simply initiate a print job and decide you don't want to print, canceling the print job requires that you cancel printing from the Print Manager, which you learned in Hour 12.

To stop the output as much as possible (and to conserve expensive paper), as soon as you notice you've printed to the wrong printer, turn off the printer. (If you turn off the printer in the middle of printing on a piece of paper, you may have to pull the sheet manually out of the paper path in the printer.) After a brief pause, Windows displays the dialog box shown in Figure 18.2. Click Cancel to let Windows know you don't want anything else printed from that print job. You then can reroute the cable or switch to the proper printer and restart the printing.

Figure 18.2.

You can cancel the entire print job when Windows displays this dialog box.

JUST A MINUTE

If your printer runs out of paper, Windows also displays the dialog box shown previously in Figure 18.2. Instead of canceling the entire print job, turn off your printer and add more paper. When you turn on your printer again, click the dialog box's Retry button to resume the print job. (Often, Windows knows the printer is ready so you don't even need to click Retry to resume the printing.)

Some switchboxes are electronic and others are manual. (Some are not compatible with laser printers, but most are.) If you use a manual switchbox, you'll obviously have to make sure the switch points to the correct printer before you print. If you use an electronic switchbox, you'll set the correct printer from a program you install that comes with the switchbox. Either way, you must make sure that the printer on which you want to print is turned on before you send anything to it. So, unless you leave both printers on all the time, you'll manually be working with the two printers even if you use an electronic switchbox.

TIME SAVER

Some printers have the option of powering up as soon as data gets to them. That is, the printer stays off until you print to it. A sensor turns on the printer automatically and the output begins when the printer is ready. The printer's power stays on until a predetermined amount of time goes by without any printing. With such printers, you won't have to turn on the selected printer. Such printers also save on energy bills, but many users don't like them because they aren't always ready to print as soon as the user is. Think things through before you purchase such a printer. If you print one item an hour, you'll have to wait for the printer to power-up before each print job. If you could leave the printer turned on, the printer is ready to begin printing as soon as you direct a print job to it.

One of the simplest and least expensive ways to connect two printers to one PC is to insert a new printer card into your system so that your PC has two printer ports. Such printer expansion cards (often called *parallel port expansion cards*) are cheap, probably less than $30. You'll never print to the wrong printer because Windows will assign a different printer port to each printer. Your financial manager program always prints to the check printer connected to one of the ports, and your word processor and other programs would print to your *default printer* connected to the other printer port.

Depending on the kinds of printers you've attached, you may want to print to one or the other from the same program. Perhaps you normally print to a laser printer from your word processor but you want to print to a color inkjet some of the time. When you select File | Print, the Print dialog box enables you to select the printer to which you want to print as shown in Figure 18.3. Because each printer is connected to a different port, the output goes to the correct printer. (If you use a switchbox, Windows thinks both printers appear on the same port, which is actually true because your switchbox is connected to a single port.)

Figure 18.3.

You can select a printer to which to print in the Print dialog box.

Click to display your printers

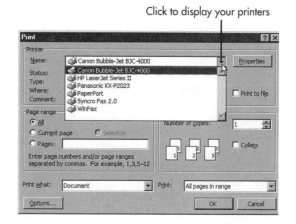

Setting Up a Printer

When you add a printer, whether that printer is a replacement printer or a new printer, you'll need to follow the same basic procedure. Fortunately, today's Plug-and-Play technology makes installing a printer relatively simple in most cases. To install a new printer, follow these steps:

1. Select Settings|Printers from your Start menu to display the Printers window.

2. Select Add Printer to start the New Printer Wizard.

3. Click the Next button and choose the Local Printer option. (To set up a networked printer you would select Network Printer.)

4. Click the Next button to display the list of printers as shown in Figure 18.4. You'll need to select your printer's manufacturer in the left column and then select the specific printer model in the right column.

Figure 18.4.

Select the printer you want to install.

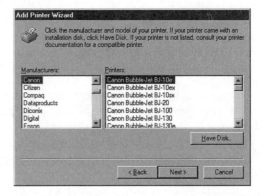

CAUTION

If you can't find your printer, Windows doesn't know about the printer because, perhaps, the printer was recently released. Your new printer will come with a disk or CD-ROM with the appropriate *driver software* (the code needed to make Windows recognize your printer). Insert that disk or CD-ROM and click the Have Disk button to let Windows know the driver is on the disk or CD-ROM. You'll have to select the correct disk or CD-ROM drive name so the New Printer Wizard knows where to look.

5. Click Next to display the dialog box in Figure 18.5. The text box shows all available devices on your system where a printer might go. In most cases, the printer device you want to select will be the printer port listed as LPT1:. If you have two printer ports, you'll need to decide if this printer will go on the printer port

18

listed as LPT2:. The port you assign to the printer stays with that printer, so don't plug the printer into another port without changing the printer's port properties. (Right-click over the printer's name in the Printers window to change its properties after you finish setting up the printer.)

Figure 18.5.

You must tell Windows where you have attached the printer.

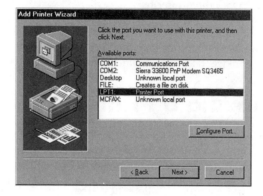

JUST A MINUTE

Some older printers, although rare, use the serial port (COM1 or COM2). If you have a modem connected to your serial port as well as a serial mouse, you will have to add another expansion card to gain a third serial port (COM3). If you need such a card, however, you'll begin to run short on IRQs and I/O addresses (even with Plug and Play). Opt for a parallel port-based printer when you have a choice.

6. Click Next to assign the printer a new name. For example, you may want to name your printer that contains checks, *Check Printer*. The name you assign (by overriding the printer's default name that includes the printer's make and model) appears in all Print dialog boxes when you select from the printer list.

7. If you want the printer to be the default Windows printer, meaning that Windows always routes all output to this printer unless you select a different printer before printing, select the Yes option and click the Next button.

8. To make sure the printer works, turn on the printer and select Yes to print a test page. When you click the Finish button, the test page will print and the printer will be set up.

If your test page does not print properly, look for the following problems:

☐ Did you turn on the printer?

☐ Is the printer online (often indicated by an *Online* or *Ready* light that you select by pressing a button on the printer)?

☐ Did you plug the printer into the same printer port you attached to the printer in the New Printer Wizard?

☐ Have you switched the switchbox or run the program to switch the electronic switchbox to the new printer?

☐ Does the printer have paper?

☐ Are the printer cables plugged in snugly?

☐ Has the printer had time to warm up after you powered it on? (Lasers and some inkjets take a few moments to get ready after you turn them on.)

Removing a Printer

If you replace a printer, not only will you need to unplug the printer from your system, but you'll also have to let Windows know that you've removed the printer. Otherwise, the printer will continue to show up on Print dialog box listings and in the Printers window.

To remove a printer, follow these steps:

1. Select Settings|Printers from your Start menu to display the Printers window.

2. Select the printer you want to remove.

3. Press the Delete key (or right-click and select Delete from the menu) to remove the printer.

4. Click Yes to confirm the removal of the printer and the printer's associated files.

Improving Your Current Printer

One of the easiest ways to improve your current printer's output is to purchase better-quality paper. Today's paper companies produce several hundred kinds of paper and paper products. Output printed on cheap paper looks terrible next to that same output printed on high-quality paper using the same printer. If you're unhappy with your output, try a few different kinds of paper to find one that works well with your printer. The office supply stores sell paper for specific kinds of printers, so if you use an inkjet printer look for inkjet paper.

Some printers, especially laser printers, support expansion through cartridges. The cartridges might contain extra fonts, memory, or even *PostScript emulation*. PostScript is a special printer language that some desktop publishing software accesses to produce special effects on paper, such as printed watermarks on the background of the page. Check your printer's manual for the kinds of cartridges that are available.

JUST A MINUTE

Today's PC stores rarely carry printer cartridges, so you may have to contact your printer's manufacturer for a list of cartridges you can buy to upgrade your printer's capabilities.

Printers often contain memory. The memory is basically the same kind of RAM as that inside your PC. (You cannot interchange both kinds, however; make sure you use memory designed for your printer only.) The memory speeds up your printer and, more importantly, often enables your printer to print more graphics. If you find that you cannot get a full page of graphics onto a printed page, your printer needs more memory.

TIME SAVER

When looking for a new printer, you might want to check out the multi-purpose printers hitting the store shelves. These printers do more than print. They also accept faxes, make copies, and hold multiple paper trays so several kinds of paper and envelopes can be ready for printing at any time. These multi-purpose printers save room because you don't need a separate printer, fax machine, and copier as you'd otherwise have. If these multi-purpose printers have any problem, however, you'll lose all the printer's functions while they're being repaired. In addition, most multi-purpose printers don't do everything well; their output may be more than adequate, but you'll find more dedicated printer features and, usually, better quality, in a standalone printer.

18

Summary

You now know what's in store if you want to upgrade your printer or add a second printer. Printers are easy to upgrade because you don't have to open your system unit (unless you install a second parallel or serial card for the printer). Unplug your old printer and plug in the new one when you want a new one. You'll need to update the Windows print driver software to support the new printer.

It's not always necessary to replace an existing printer when you buy a second one. Many PC users work with two printers. A second printer adds some printer-selection problems, but a switchbox makes switching between the two printers simple. If you add a second system unit card to support both printers at once, you'll never have to worry about switching between the printers as needed.

The next hour explains how to upgrade the rest of your system. Your monitor, video card, sound card, and other peripheral devices need replacing every once in a while as technology improves.

Q&A

Q How does more memory speed up my printer?

A Technically, your printer prints at the same speed no matter how much memory is in your printer. The extra memory acts as a buffer, or a holding area, that captures PC output to be printed. After your printer's buffer collects all the PC's output, your PC is freed up faster for other tasks.

With Windows, it's difficult to distinguish between the print spooler that you learned about in Hour 12 and the printer's own physical memory. Your application is released so you can do something else after printing as soon as Windows collects all the application's printer output. Windows then spools the output, in the background, to the printer while you do something else. The more printer memory your printer has, the faster Windows can spool that output to the printer. Although the printer has not yet printed all the output, Windows knows that all the output arrived at the printer. Windows can free up its print spooler resources and can then do something else.

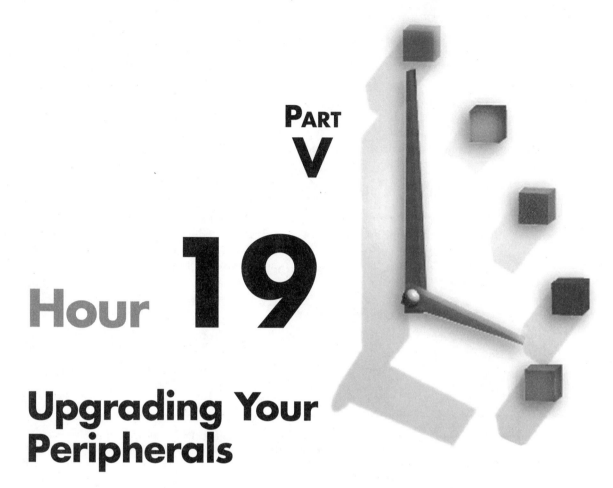

Hour 19

Upgrading Your Peripherals

This hour shows you how to upgrade the peripheral components of your PC. Perhaps you need a new keyboard or mouse. You'll be surprised at the variety of peripherals out there and you'll learn what's involved in changing your current device to a newer one.

Whereas *you'll* notice a difference when you upgrade your CPU or memory, *everybody* will notice a difference if you upgrade your PC's multimedia hardware. Multimedia makes a PC fun, especially the games, because of smoother animation and better sound quality. (Of course, your business presentations to upper-levels of management will become more effective too.)

The highlights of this hour include

☐ What you must do to upgrade your PC's video quality

☐ What to look for in a new monitor

☐ How resolution affects your video card purchase

☐ How to install a new video card

☐ How to shop for sound cards

☐ Which new keyboard features make you work more efficiently

☐ What differences exist among PC mice

☐ How to upgrade your modem

Upgrading Video

When you want better video, you have three choices: upgrade your monitor, upgrade your video card, or upgrade both. Older video cards don't produce enough resolution at enough speed to produce today's multimedia game output. Small monitors (those measuring less than 15-inches diagonally) don't provide enough screen size to read much of a word processor or electronic worksheet document.

Replacing Your Monitor

A larger screen is generally better than a smaller one. The minimum diagonal screen size you should accept is 15 inches. The largest PC monitors run 21 inches diagonally. (Larger monitors exist for specialized applications.) The most popular sizes are 15-inch, 17-inch, 19-inch, and 21-inch. The cost goes up with the size.

CAUTION

Be careful, however, because some manufacturers sell 15-inch screens but the actual output only comprises 13 or 14 inches of that 15-inch diagonal area.

The larger monitor does not just give you larger and more readable text. The larger screen enables you to comfortably view two or more open windows at one time. If you work with only one program at any one time, the multiple windows may not come in handy now, but they may later. Even if you do only one task at a time, the larger screen lets you view almost a complete word processing page at one time. Imagine being able to view an entire page at once in your word processor. In addition to more windows, the larger screen size lets you more comfortably read whatever you view at a finer resolution. The text will be larger and more readable. If you access the Internet, you'll appreciate the larger Web page viewing area that a larger screen provides.

A general-purpose monitor today runs 15-inches, but you may want to consider upgrading to a 17-inch monitor. If you purchase a new system, you can often pay the upgrade fee to get a larger monitor if a 15-inch monitor comes bundled with the system. If you commonly work with large spreadsheets or high-quality graphics, look at larger monitors if they fit your budget. The stores will let you view monitors side-by-side. No matter what the technical specifications say, one monitor may just produce output better, in your opinion, than another next to it. Pay attention to the monitor you like best.

19

In addition to output quality, look for a monitor that has easy-to-reach controls. A front-panel power switch and set of adjustment controls is great because you don't have to reach around the screen to adjust the brightness.

Some bells and whistles that make your monitor purchase even better include

- ☐ **Speakers**: Some of today's monitors include speakers attached to their sides that produce good-quality sound. That way, you don't need a set of speakers sitting elsewhere.

- ☐ **Television**: Some monitors include television tuners so you can watch both TV and work with your PC. (A television video card often is required as well.)

- ☐ **USB (Universal Serial Bus) Connection**: A new connection standard that lets you plug other USB devices into a USB connection without having to worry about IRQs, DMA channels, I/O addresses, or any other issues about which you've been reading the past several hours. Some of the newer monitors include several USB ports so you can easily expand your PC without opening your system unit or reaching around to the back of your PC. Only USB devices attach to the USB ports, however, and such devices are not yet as common as non-USB devices.

- ☐ **Footprint**: The monitor should not consume a lot of desk space no matter how big it is. Some flat-screen monitors (they are expensive compared to regular CRT-based monitors) take little depth, making them great for cramped desks.

- ☐ **Easy adjustable stand**: Make sure you can easily tilt the monitor to any angle.

If you choose a 17-inch or larger monitor that looks good, you'll be happy with it. These extra features are icing on the cake. Technically, you'll want a monitor with a refresh rate between 70–75Hz to reduce flicker that can occur on some monitors. The monitor's dot-pitch (the distance between two dots on the screen) should measure 0.27mm or less.

TIME SAVER

If light glare poses a problem, you can purchase a glare screen cover that attaches to your monitor and helps to reduce the glare. Many new monitors come with a built-in glare guard.

Replacing Your Video Card

Modern video cards are faster than older cards, provide higher resolution and more colors, and add internal support for three-dimensional graphics to 3D programs (such as virtual reality worlds and games). By replacing a video card, you will gain better graphics no matter what kind of monitor you use. If nothing else, your new video card will display graphics and text faster than your old card did.

JUST A MINUTE

Don't play games? Then why do you need to worry about graphics? Remember that the Internet is becoming more and more popular every day. The Internet is graphical in nature and you'll appreciate the higher resolutions, better color, and better support for speedy graphics that a new video card will provide.

As with monitors, video cards support rates and you need a 72Hz or faster refresh rate. Video cards also contain special RAM, called VRAM (*Video Random Access Memory*). The more VRAM your video card holds, the better your card works and the more colors it can display. Most video cards come with 2MB of VRAM and you can usually upgrade the card to 4MB or more.

Almost all video cards now handle resolutions at 1,024×768 pixels and higher. The new video cards also support 256 and more colors. After you install the new card, you can adjust the video's resolution and color display by right-clicking the Windows desktop screen, selecting Properties, and clicking on the Settings tab to display the Display Properties dialog box shown in Figure 19.1. Increase the resolution and colors until you can see as much information on your screen as you are comfortable with.

Figure 19.1.

Try new video settings after you install a new video card.

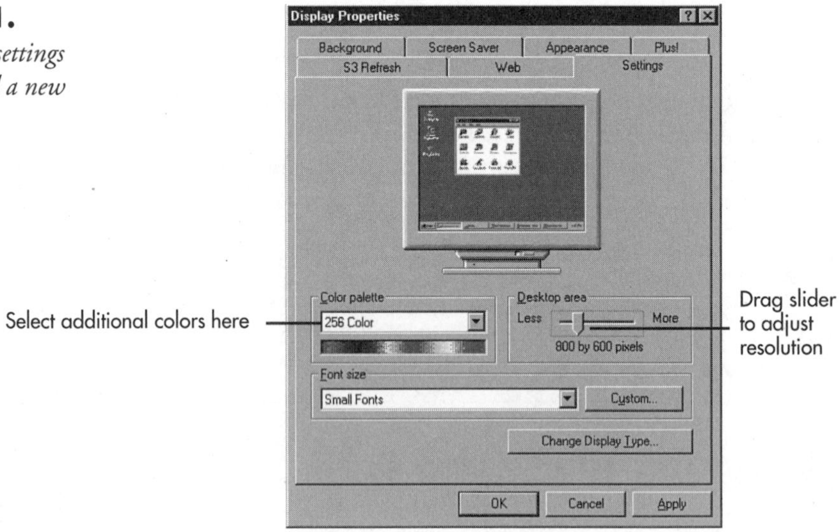

Select additional colors here ⎯⎯⎯

Drag slider to adjust resolution

19

CAUTION

If you set your video card's resolution too high, the text will be too small to read. A larger monitor helps, but does not always solve the problem. Before decreasing your resolution, select Large Fonts from the Font Size drop-down list on the Display Properties Settings page.

To install a new card, follow these steps:

1. Shut down Windows and unplug the power cables.

2. Unplug the monitor cable from the back of your PC.

3. Remove the system unit cover.

4. Locate the video card by finding the card into which you plug your monitor cable. Unscrew the seating screw and gently rock the old card out of the system unit. (Hour 17, "Upgrading Your Disk and CD-ROM Storage," explains how to replace expansion cards in detail.)

5. Insert the new video card into the slot and screw in the seat screw to set the card.

6. Replace your system unit cover and replace all cables.

7. Turn on your PC. Windows will probably recognize the new video card and adjust the settings accordingly. Plug and Play seems to work better for new video cards than any other hardware upgrade. Windows may require the disk or CD-ROM that came with your video card, however, so have it handy. If Windows does not recognize your video card, you need to run the Add New Hardware Wizard from the Control Panel window and let Windows search for the new card. If Windows fails to find the card, you may have to run the wizard again and click Have Disk to enable the wizard to access the disk or CD-ROM that came with your card.

Your video card, just like your monitor, can support several resolutions. Certain resolutions work best for specific monitor sizes. Table 19.1 lists the best resolutions for the most popular monitor sizes. After you properly install the new card, adjust your display property resolution to one of the sizes in Table 19.1.

Table 19.1. Locate your monitor size and adjust the video's resolution to the recommended sizes listed here.

Monitor size	Adjust your resolution to this
15-inch (or lower)	800×600
17-inch	1,024×768
19-inch	1,024×768 or 1,152×864
21-inch	1,280×1,024 or 1,600×1,200

JUST A MINUTE

Some newer video cards capture still-digital camera images as well as video from a video camera. You can use the pictures and video in documents that you send to others or on Internet Web pages you produce. If the card outputs moving video and sound, you can also print your own slides and pictures with special printers or produce edited video.

Upgrading Your PC's Sound

If you've attached inexpensive speakers to your PC, the sound card won't make much difference. If you want to upgrade your multimedia sound, you'll need to update both your sound card and your speakers.

TIME SAVER

Many multimedia upgrade kits now come with speakers, a sound card, and a CD-ROM. If your CD-ROM is slow (6X speed or less), your speakers need some improvement, and your sound card is old, such a kit will save you a lot of money. The sound card acts as a controller card for the CD-ROM. If you don't need all three units in the kit, however, you'll save money by purchasing your sound card and speakers separately.

The PC industry often measures a sound card's quality by its data path size. 8-bit and 16-bit sound cards offer older technology that doesn't reproduce true audio as well as more modern sound cards. A 32-bit *wavetable* sound card can produce orchestra quality sound, so look for such a card. (64-bit versions are also available.)

Replacing the sound card requires only that you remove your current sound card and replace that card with the new one. Windows almost always recognizes the new sound cards sold today, but you'll need to supply Windows with the sound card's disk or CD-ROM when prompted. Sound card manufacturers constantly upgrade their driver software and Windows will need the new software. Today's sound card software, combined with Windows's Plug and Play technology, helps you deal with IRQ conflicts automatically (in many cases), whereas previous sound cards caused little more than setup anguish.

Sound cards come with plenty of auxiliary I/O support. As Figure 19.2 shows, the back of your sound card contains jacks where you can plug in speakers, a microphone, and an auxiliary cable that you run to your stereo's in-jack if you want to amplify your PC's sound through your stereo.

Figure 19.2.

You can plug several devices into your sound card.

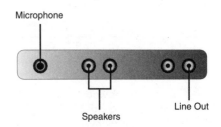

19

TIME SAVER

Use long speaker cables so your speakers can go on bookshelves or on stands on the walls left and right of your PC. You'll be in the middle of the sound action that way and the speakers will not be close enough on your desk that you'll be tempted to lay disks or tapes on them. (The magnets in the speakers will destroy magnetically recorded data on disks and tapes.)

If you replace your PC's speakers, you'll be surprised at the number of PC speaker systems sold at PC stores and in the PC catalogs. Some PC speakers are amplified. You'll be glad that you purchased amplified speakers that automatically power on when sound goes to them because otherwise, you'll run the risk of leaving the speakers turned on and running down the batteries. Most PC speakers contain a Y-cable that sends both speaker cables to a single cable that you plug into your sound card.

Upgrading Your Keyboard

As with speakers, the keyboards that come with most PC package systems are inexpensive, but they do hold up well if you stick with them. In addition, they offer few bells and whistles. Although it's true that a keyboard is fairly basic, some keyboards are better than others and people prefer the different key layouts.

For example, do you like your keyboard to produce an audible *click* as you type or do you want a quiet keyboard? The cheaper keyboards don't really do either but offer a high-pitched but small click when you press a key. Keyboards exist that are quiet or that return forceful and audible keystroke feedback if you want it.

TIME SAVER

Just like monitors, you'll want to try several keyboards in the store before you purchase one. Make sure you like the keyboard's overall feel.

Keyboards are getting more powerful. The standard key layout has changed little in the past several years, with the exception of a special Windows key or two that now appears on most keyboards that lets you display the Start menu with a single keypress. (A second Windows key simulates clicking the right mouse button.)

Some keyboards come with a touchpad mouse (see Figure 19.3) that enables you to save desk space. Instead of using a separate mouse, you only have to run your finger across the pad to move the mouse cursor on the screen. Tap or double-tap the pad to perform a single or double mouse click. (The pad usually has buttons above or below the touchpad area if you want the security of buttons.) Touchpad mice do take some getting used to. If you work with a traditional mouse and then move to a keyboard-based touchpad, you will have to practice a while before you learn to use the touchpad well.

Figure 19.3.

Keyboards sometimes come with a touchpad mouse.

Touch here to
start moving mouse
pointer

Just a Minute

> Instead of a touchpad, many keyboards now include a built-in trackball.
> You roll the trackball around to move the onscreen mouse cursor.

If you really want to save desk space and you'd like a scanner, new keyboards are now available that have a rolling-pin like scanner at the top of the keyboard. The combination keyboard/scanner lets you scan business cards, articles, and paper without having to take up desk space with a separate scanner. The rolling-pin scanner cannot scan book pages unless you tear out the pages and scan them separately.

Fortunately, keyboards require no special installation on your part except for unplugging the old one (*after* you turn off your PC) and plugging in the new one. If the keyboard includes a scanner or touchpad mouse, Windows may need to adjust its settings or you may need to run software that came with the keyboard before you get the keyboard's full functionality. If you replace the keyboard on an older PC, you may need to get an adapter cable to make today's keyboards work on your PC. Check your current keyboard cord before purchasing a new one. To ensure that you get the correct keyboard or adapter, take your old keyboard with you when you purchase a new one.

Although you'll laugh at first, check out the new ergonomic keyboards such as the one shown in Figure 19.4. These keyboards are said to lessen wrist pain that can come after days, weeks, months, and years of typing. Perhaps surprisingly, these keyboards work well and take almost no getting used to.

Improve Your Mouse

Mice aren't just for cats anymore. (I know, PC mouse jokes are passé in the late 1990s.) PC mice need replacing in many situations. Perhaps the mouse that came packaged with your PC is cheap. If so, the mouse may not roll smoothly and may feel awkward in your hands

19

compared to more modern (and more pricey) mice. Perhaps your mouse just doesn't work consistently. Over time, dust and grime infiltrate the mouse and the mouse stops working properly.

Figure 19.4.

Want to type faster and with less effort? Some people prefer ergonomically designed keyboards.

JUST A MINUTE

You can remove the underside cover and ball from most mice to clean them. Don't use soap and water. A damp cloth usually works well. Some of the newer mice are *optical* or attached to *feet* that eliminate dust build-up and reduce your maintenance chores.

Mice connect to your PC by using one of these three methods:

- ☐ **PS/2**: Almost every PC these days contains a PS/2 mouse port. Originally offered on IBM's PS/2 line of PCs, other manufacturers began offering PS/2 connections so your mouse does not take up a serial port. If you have a choice, and if your PC contains a PS/2 mouse port, purchase a PS/2 mouse.

- ☐ **Serial**: The mouse has a serial cable attached to plug into one of your PC's serial ports.

- ☐ **Bus**: The least common mouse today, bus mice require their own controller card. Although they don't consume one of your serial ports, they do take over an expansion slot in your PC.

After you decide on the mouse port, you've got to decide on the type of mouse you want. Two buttons are all you'll need because most software today ignores the third button and that trend will probably continue. If the mouse contains a roller or rocker button, such as the Microsoft IntelliMouse mouse shown in Figure 19.5, the roller lets you scroll and zoom without moving the mouse or adjusting a scrollbar within those programs that now support IntelliMouse technology.

A trackball saves desk space because you don't have to roll it around your desk. The base stays put and you roll the ball. Trackballs often have buttons on either side of the ball to emulate regular mouse buttons. Newer trackballs include the IntelliMouse-like roller.

19

Figure 19.5.

*Do more than move
and point with the
IntelliMouse.*

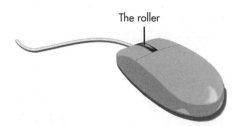

The roller

> ### What About Joysticks?
>
> Generally, the more you pay for a joystick, the better its quality. Joysticks do not replace mice, but work as input devices to control games. Your PC requires a game port (if your PC doesn't have one, you'll have to install a game card into an empty expansion slot) for this to work.
>
> When you shop for a joystick, keep in mind that today's games require that you control several kinds of action. Some joysticks do more than let you control a single rudder. Joysticks come with buttons and extra firing controls that advanced games need. No matter how many controls the joystick offers, however, you'll need to make your final purchase decision based on the joystick with which you feel most comfortable. Try them out; many PC stores let you test their joysticks before you purchase one.
>
> Before you make a decision, make sure you test a *force feedback* joystick. These joysticks, such as Microsoft's Sidewinder Force Feedback Pro joystick, change the way you play games. These sticks actually jolt when you crash, shake when you rumble, and jerk when you fire to give you the true feel for playing the game.

Modems Galore

Perhaps no other upgrade decision is more difficult than a new modem purchase. So many different modems exist that selecting one is not easy. Winners of PC magazine modem reviews often are losers in other magazines due to the technical nature of modems and the inconsistent phone lines the magazines used to test modems. Fortunately, even the most expensive modems are rarely more than $250, and many high-speed modems now cost less than $100. In addition to their low price, most modems perform at *roughly* the same levels. A generic modem rarely poses problems that a name-brand modem user would not also encounter.

If you use a modem with a speed lower than 28.8K, you need to upgrade to a faster modem. Although some users get by with slower modems, the Internet is becoming such a computing staple that you'll want to take as much advantage of it as you can, and that means faster access. The Internet gets heavier with sound and video, and faster access will enable you to take advantage of the Internet's capabilities. Don't settle for less than 28.8K.

JUST A MINUTE

Many of today's modems rate at a speed of 33.6K, although your phone line quality may slow that down somewhat. If you use a 28.8K modem, check with your modem's manufacturer (or their Web site) to see if an upgrade exists with which you can convert your 28.8K modem to 33.6K. Often, such an upgrade requires only a software patch. Most online services automatically connect you at 33.6K if you have a modem that supports that speed.

All of today's modems support the sending and receiving of faxes. Of course, the fax information must already reside in your PC as would be the case for a word-processed document you want to fax to someone. If you want to fax an article from your PC, you'll either need to type the article's text into your word processor or scan the article with a scanner. The File | Print option of most software packages enables you to select a fax modem for the output device as easily as you can select a different printer.

When you upgrade your modem, you'll have to decide whether you want an internal or an external modem. If you have a free serial port, an external modem is much easier to install because, as with a printer, you simply plug the modem's cable into the back of your PC. Windows will recognize the new modem in most instances the next time you reboot your PC, and Windows will either know about the modem and its model number or you'll have to supply the disk or CD-ROM that came with the modem so Windows can get the driver software.

19

JUST A MINUTE

External modems cost more than internal modems. External modems, however, are easier to install and display lights that indicate modem activity. Sometimes the lights come in handy when you don't know if a modem is receiving data (indicated with blinking lights) or sitting idle. An external modem's volume control is also handier than reaching around the back of your PC to adjust the volume. (The volume control is handy when you want to hear the connection being made.) External modems, however, have on and off switches that you must remember to shut off if you want to save on power, whereas your internal modem always powers off with your PC.

Some of the biggest problems with internal modems are their conflicts with other devices. The IRQ, I/O address, and DMA channels taken up by other devices almost always cause some kind of conflict with a new internal modem. You'll have to adjust settings until you find the correct ones (see your modem's manual) unless the modem and your PC are fully Plug-and-Play compatible.

After you install the modem, you'll connect one phone connector to your phone's wall jack and the other modem phone connector to your phone. Your phone works normally until you use the modem to dial another computer or fax.

JUST A MINUTE

Some modems are known as *voice modems*. With these modems, you can talk to someone and communicate with that person's computer in the same phone call. The drawback is that the other computer must also use a voice modem. In addition to voice modems, you may see *ISDN modems* (*Integrated Services Digital Network*) and *cable modems*. If your phone company provides ISDN service (a call to the local office will tell you), you can install an ISDN line and get faster modem access than you can get with a regular line. If your cable company offers cable modem access, as some are starting to do, you will need a cable modem to access that service, but the result will be extremely quick Internet access.

The 56K Speed Debate

You'll find modems advertised that support speeds as fast as 56K. Be careful before you buy these modems because, unlike the 28.8K and 33.6K modems, not all 56K modems are compatible with other 56K modems or services. Online services don't yet support 56K speeds in most cities. In addition, even if you connect with an online service that supports 56K, the actual transfer speed slows down considerably if your phone line does not stay perfectly clear during your modem sessions.

Part of the problem with 56K modems is that *two* standards exist not unlike the early VCR days where Betamax battled VHS. These standards are called *56KFlex* and *56K*. Online services and Internet providers often don't want to spend money on supporting both standards until one becomes the *true* de facto standard. The problem is that until online services select a standard, a standard will not fall out any time soon.

If you don't mind paying a premium for this modem, check with your Internet provider or online service to see which standard you can use. If your provider or service supports neither, put off your buying decision for a while. If you need a modem, you'll do just fine with a 28.8K or 33.6K modem.

19

Modems come in laptop versions as well. Most laptop modems come on a PC card (also called a *PCMCIA card*) like the one shown in Figure 19.6. You'll need to be careful when you plug the phone line into the PC card, however, because such connections are often fragile. That's a shame because, if you travel a lot, you'll be frequently using the modem.

Figure 19.6.

Modems slide into laptops on a PC card.

TIME SAVER

New laptop modems are out now that enable you to connect your laptop to a wireless, digital phone. You can send and receive data transmissions, connect to the Internet, send and receive e-mail, and send and receive faxes even when no phone jack is handy. The digital signal keeps the line clearer than analog cellular phone signals so you'll have little to no data loss.

19

Summary

This hour showed you what's in store if you want to upgrade your peripheral devices to take advantage of newer hardware advances or to add new devices to your current PC. Peripherals differ in the way you install them. Some, such as external modems, require little effort on your part physically, although their setup may take some time depending on your PC's compatibility with true Plug and Play.

The next hour explains the other side of upgrades: software upgrades. Today's PC user must ensure that he uses the latest and greatest software versions to reduce the chance of bugs and to effectively use new hardware.

Q&A

Q Can I talk and transfer data at the same time with a voice modem?

A Sadly, no. You must dedicate your phone line to your PC after you initiate a PC transfer to another modem, and your PC must release you so you can talk with the modem when you're ready. Remember, too, that the modem on the other end must also be a voice modem; otherwise, you can only transfer data or talk but not both on the same phone call.

Voice modems are helpful for after-sale support. If you have a PC problem, you can call the service center and they can then, after you set things up, use their computer to analyze yours and determine what may be wrong with software or with a hardware installation.

By the way, look at your office supply store or mail-order catalog for a new device that sits next to your office phone and blinks while someone talks on an extension. You'll know whenever someone else is on the line, and in those cases you won't dial with your PC to mess up the connection. Be sure to get the blinking light for all extensions so others won't pick up the phone during your PC's data transfer.

Q How can I install new hardware when I seem to have used up all my IRQ values?

A If your system is full of expansion cards and you have multiple parallel and serial ports, you'll have a hard time expanding. The USB standard was created to eliminate such conflicts, but your current hardware, most or all of which will not be USB-ready, needs to fight for resources such as the IRQ and I/O address values discussed in Hour 15, "Why and When to Upgrade."

If you want to keep your PC a while longer, you may need to upgrade some of your peripherals to PCI if your PC contains PCI expansion cards. The PCI devices are much friendlier with each other than pre-PCI hardware. In addition, you might need to install a SCSI card in your system and replace your hard drives with SCSI drives. Such a procedure is expensive, but you'll probably transfer the drives to your next PC due to their speed.

19

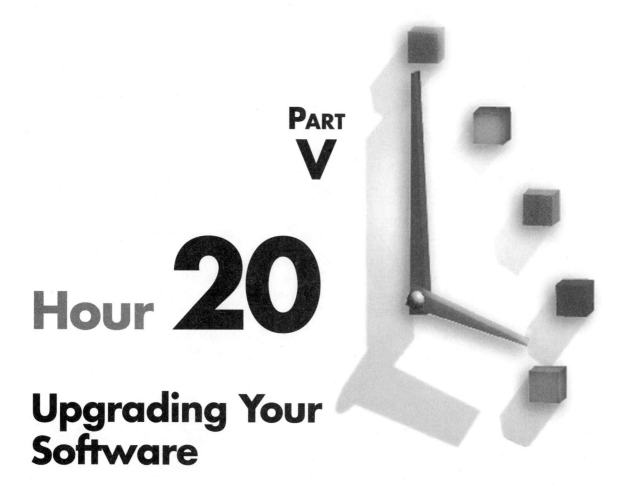

Hour 20

Upgrading Your Software

This hour shows you how to upgrade both your application software and your system software (including Windows and the system utility programs that you use to manage your PC resources, such as fragmented disk space). Several issues arise when using software. One of the most common reasons software stops working after a while is that the user didn't upgrade to a later software version and now the software doesn't work with a new operating system or new hardware.

Several methods for updating software exist. Many companies automatically send their customers new releases free of charge or for a nominal processing fee. Other companies seem to forget they have current customers and *never* let the customers know about the new releases; it's up to the customer to do the leg work and keep up with the updates.

The highlights of this hour include

- ☐ What you actually buy when you purchase programs
- ☐ Why new versions of software come out so quickly
- ☐ How software companies test their programs before they sell them
- ☐ Why you should register your software

☐ How to find the version number of software you use

☐ Where to go to locate software updates

☐ How to use the Internet to update software automatically

Multiple Upgrades

You do not own software; when you buy a program, you actually buy only the right, or the *license*, to use that program. You cannot, for example, alter and redistribute the program.

One problem with software is that you have to keep buying the same program (as you now know, that means buying a new license) when the software company puts out a new version. Although the original version you purchased might work well and do exactly what you want it to do, the newer version works well with newer hardware and operating system versions.

Of course, the continual purchasing and updating of programs gets costly. Nothing mandates that you buy a new version (unless new hardware keeps the software from working properly), but the new version's features often add value to the product. If you like the program in its original version and the company then adds to the feature set, the company deserves income for distributing that update to you.

JUST A MINUTE

Often, new hardware and operating systems don't outdate all your software. Most software works through new hardware changes and operating system updates. Some software, however, such as MS-DOS–based games, doesn't work well under some versions of Windows, so an update that makes the software work better under Windows saves you a lot of time. One of the most famous, best-selling games in the history of PCs is Microsoft's *Flight Simulator* which, until late 1996, was an MS-DOS-based game only. Microsoft's own program *refused* to run under Microsoft's Windows operating system! After Microsoft finally released a Windows 95 version, many Windows users who played the game upgraded immediately because they could finally run Windows *and* their favorite game at the same time.

Do Vendors Sell Bugs?

A major debate now travels through the PC industry regarding software updates. Many feel that software companies release programs too soon without enough testing. Others say that this form of "industry testing" is needed due to the complexity and size of today's software projects.

If a company waited to release a software product until *all* the bugs were out, *no* software products would be sold. Despite extensive testing, one cannot ensure that all bugs are out. Companies have a good reason to do the best they can, however; they want you to buy more products, and if you battle bugs you are less likely to purchase something from that company in the future.

Some companies are giving away their early test releases of software as *beta release* in hopes that those who use the product will let the company know about problems that do arise. After extensive beta testing, a company needs to decide just how much testing is enough. The good thing about software is that a company *can* easily release an update to correct the problem, a feat not possible with most other products such as automobiles or airplanes.

Given this explanation, you can better understand why companies release software updates so quickly and often. The industry moves so fast that software must keep up with hardware, causing bugs to enter the picture. Of course, as an end user, you want to know about all updates and you want those updates as quickly and as inexpensively as possible.

Update Hardware Drivers

One kind of update, called a *hardware driver update*, is a new version of a software program that makes your hardware work better. Often, hardware vendors release new hardware drivers for their hardware to correct bugs and to respond to other newly released hardware. For example, video card manufacturers often supply disks or CD-ROMs with software drivers that may or may not come with Windows. If a new kind of monitor is announced that will not work correctly with the video card, the video card manufacturer might release a new software driver to work with the new monitor.

Learning About Updates

20

How do you learn about software updates? One thing you can do is fill out *all* registration cards that come with your hardware and software. Sure, they are a pain and they often ask nosy questions (you don't have to answer *all* the questions, just the ones that you think are their business), but by filling them out you get on the software vendor's mailing lists so you'll be told about new software versions or hardware drives that the manufacturer has released.

Sending in the registration cards doesn't ensure that the vendor will keep you posted of new software and driver updates, but many vendors use the mailing lists to mail update notices.

JUST A MINUTE

Some vendors (the good ones) automatically send *free* updates for a specific time period, such as a year, after the initial purchase. When you buy software from those vendors, you know that you'll have the latest version for up to a year.

Many software programs enable you to register online. You fill out an onscreen registration form, such as the one in Figure 20.1. Then, the programs use your modem to dial the company and send in the registration information. The registration is quick and toll-free in virtually all cases (the software will warn you if it's a toll call), and it saves you the time of filling out and mailing a card.

Figure 20.1.

Some software enables you to register online for quick, toll-free software registration.

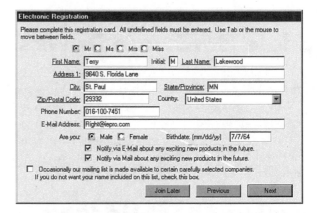

JUST A MINUTE

Some software automatically downloads an update while you register electronically. By registering, you ensure that you have the latest version.

You can subscribe to some update plans, so that after you purchase the software, you get newly revised updates at least yearly. Many of the electronic encyclopedias and CD-ROM–based phone books offer such a subscription service so that you can update the information with current data. After you pay for the subscription, you get the updates when the company releases them and you won't have to worry about locating the update or learning when the update is released.

The registration does not guarantee that the vendor informs you about software updates. Some vendors simply don't tell you personally when an upgrade occurs. (Microsoft is one such example.) You'll have to learn on your own if an update is available. Magazines often inform the public when an update is released. If you upgrade certain hardware and a program stops working, that program's vendor may have an update that corrects the problem. If you think an update is due, you might want to call the vendor to see whether a new release is out.

Of course, one of the best ways to stay abreast of software versions is to check the software vendor's Internet site for information. Most companies maintain Internet sites that describe the latest versions of each program the company sells. The next part of this book contains several hours of lessons that teach you about navigating the Internet. The next section describes how you can update software on the Internet; if you've never used the Internet, you may want to come back to this section after you learn how to go online.

TIME SAVER

To learn the version number of your software, you can often click Help | About to open the program's About box, such as the one in Figure 20.2. Sometimes, software comes with a major and minor version number, each separated by a period. If you see *2.03* in the About box, you know that the software has had two major releases and three minor releases. The major releases often contain new features and the minor releases often correct bugs or add minor features.

Figure 20.2.

Check the software's About box to learn which version you're currently running.

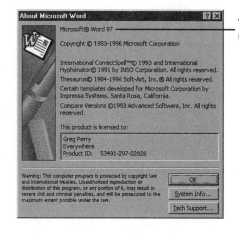

Version number

20

One way to learn about software updates is to walk through software retail stores and glance through software catalogs. Software vendors often sell software updates through these outlets. The update costs much less than the full product. You may have to show proof of ownership of the original product (rare) or, more likely, the update won't work on your PC unless you have the original software, but that's not a problem as long as you have something to update.

Before buying a software update at the store or through a mail-order outlet, check to make sure that the same update is not free on the Internet. Companies that offer updates for sale sometimes provide them free online. The price of the update is required to pay for the distribution channels at the stores and in the mail-order houses, so you may save that cost if you get the software online as described in the next section.

TIME SAVER

Before buying *any* product, make sure a less expensive update does not exist. For example, some companies let you purchase a software update that actually includes the full retail version of a product as long as you have a similar product from that company or a competitor. Instead of buying Microsoft Word, for example, you can save money by buying Word's update software if you already have one of several companies' word processors on your computer when you install the update. The update is actually the full retail version of Word with code that makes sure you are updating from some word processor.

Updating Software on the Internet

One of the benefits the Internet offers you is the capability to *download*, or transfer to your PC via the phone lines, software updates when the company releases them without waiting on the post office. (Postal mail is called *snail mail* by the computer industry because of the latter's quick and cheap e-mail system.)

JUST A MINUTE

If you don't have Internet access, some companies still offer electronic *bulletin board systems* (*BBS*s) that you can dial from your PC to retrieve software up dates by phone. Check your software manual's Technical Support section to determine if the company maintains a BBS.

Suppose that you bought the latest word processor nine or ten months ago and you read in a magazine about a patch the company is releasing on their Internet site. (A software *patch* is a small update, perhaps one that fixes a minor bug but doesn't add significant features.) You can go to that site and download the software. The site will offer instructions to help you through the download and software update process, and when you finish, you'll be using the latest version.

20

CAUTION

Most Internet software warns you about potential virus harm before letting you download software from the Internet. If you download from a reputable software firm, one whose software you've purchased through a retail or major mail order outlet, you'll have very little risk of downloading a virus.

Automatic Updates

New software now exists that regularly checks all the software on your PC and then goes to the Internet and looks for updates. CyberMedia's *Oil Change*, for example, shown in Figure 20.3, takes an inventory of your PC and then goes to the Internet looking at each site related to each program on your computer.

Figure 20.3.

Software, such as Oil Change, *can automatically update all software on your PC from the Internet.*

JUST A MINUTE

Companies that sell programs that automatically retrieve software updates and install them from the Internet usually require an annual subscription. The price of the software usually includes the first year, but requires a subscription to the service in subsequent years. The subscription payments enable the company to continue operating and updating software.

20

CAUTION

> Software, such as *Oil Change*, does its best to update all your software, but doing so is not always possible. If a company does not offer a software update on the Internet, *Oil Change* can't do anything to get the update. You'll have to call the company.

More and more companies are adding support for these software update programs. Update programs like *Oil Change* cannot always update software from the Internet even if the update resides on the Internet because a software vendor must make its update available to the update program. If a company releases a software update on the Internet using its own download method that does not match *Oil Change*'s required download standard, for example, *Oil Change* cannot make the update.

One potential problem is that an update won't install correctly. An invalid update can be caused by many things, and the result could mean that your original software (the program you wanted to update) will no longer work—and neither will the update!

Fortunately, such programs offer an automatic *undo* feature that reverses the Internet program update so that your system returns to its original state before you attempted the update. The Internet sites that offer software updates *must* make the undo feature available to programs such as *Oil Change* or the update cannot be undone except manually, which is often difficult or impossible. Therefore, before updating from the Internet, determine whether the site offers an undo feature. If it doesn't, decide whether the update is worth the potential risk of not being able to reverse the update easily if you are unhappy with it.

TIME SAVER

> Before you start a program update from the Internet, either from a site you've gone to yourself or from using an automatic update program, make a backup of your system. The time you spend backing up will reap dividends if the update has a problem and you cannot undo it.

In the past, if an update failed, restoring your original program was not as troublesome as it is today. Before the Internet, companies could not offer updates as easily, or as rapidly, as they can today. Therefore, an update would come out every year or two with the major release with an interim update occurring only to correct serious bugs. If an update failed, you could easily reinstall the pre-update program from the disk or CD-ROM on which the original program came. Suppose, however, that you purchased a program two years ago on CD-ROM and have updated it four times from interim versions released to you on the Internet. If the last update did not work properly, and if the last update keeps you from using the program (even in its pre-update form), how do you restore the last version you had without a backup? You would have to find the original CD-ROM and somehow locate the three updates you applied from the Internet to get back to where you were. Back up your system often—especially before updating software.

Updating Your Operating System

Although your application programs are your most important programs because they perform the work you need, such as accounting and word processing, your operating system keeps things running smoothly. If your operating system, such as Windows, has a bug, everything can be affected. That's why you need to stay aware of operating system updates when they appear and update your system as needed.

Each major release of an operating system, such as the update from Windows 3.1 to Windows 95, appears in the press long before the actual release. You have plenty of warning and you'll be kept abreast of the release date through many sources. The interim operating system updates, however, do not seem to garner that much press attention. A large percentage of current Windows 95 users, those who installed Windows 95 when Microsoft first released it, have no idea that two interim releases have quietly been around for a couple of years. Microsoft offers the update on its Internet site, but the update doesn't offer a lot of new bells and whistles, so the press doesn't bother too much with it.

Check your system software sites as often as you can to read about software updates and patches.

JUST A MINUTE

> Fortunately, Microsoft is adding automatic updates to its operating systems in the future so that you can click a single button and the operating system will go to an Internet site and update itself with the latest patches.

Summary

This hour taught you how to update your software. Software companies try to write bug-free software, but that goal is virtually impossible given the complexity of today's software. Therefore, companies attempt to get users to test programs by releasing beta versions of the software in hopes that bugs will be found early in the testing process before the final release is sold.

Given that bugs do exist, software companies want you to register your software, not so you get on a bunch of mailing lists (although that's a secondary reason), but so the company can contact you if your software needs to be updated. Some companies mail updates free, others charge a small update fee, and some offer updates on the Internet that you can download.

20

You can purchase update software that automatically scans your computer and updates all the software that's possible to update from the Internet. Such utility programs help ensure that you have the latest software available. Even your operating system has the capability to go to the Internet and download patches and updates.

The next hour starts the final, and perhaps most important, part of your 24-hour tutorial by introducing you to the details of the Internet and by explaining what you must do to get Internet access.

Q&A

Q When I buy software, how do I know if I have the latest version?

A Call the company or go to the software company's Internet site and check for the latest version. Either the sales or technical support staff should be able to tell you the latest version shipping. Then, start the program and select Help|About as described in this hour. Your software version should appear somewhere on the About dialog box.

Here's a tip: If you see a button on the About box labeled System Info, click the button and you'll see helpful information about your computer in the resulting dialog box. The System Information dialog box lists all vital statistics about your PC, such as your CPU model, disk capacity, memory, and Windows version.

The About boxes often offer the System Info button because it provides helpful information if you call the software company's technical support staff for help. The About dialog box describes the version number of the program you are running. In addition, the support staff may need to know about the kind of computer you are running. Some problems arise because of the lack of a disk or memory space, and the System Info button tells the staff what you have.

Q Why should I pay for updates?

A Many updates are bug fixes and you have good reason to be wary of paying for corrections to something that should have been right from the start. Rarely will a company charge you for a software update that only fixes bugs. If the bugs are minor, the company might charge you for postage and handling (assuming you order the software on disk or on CD-ROM), but they won't charge you for anything else.

New features do come with many software updates, however, and not just bug corrections. If you are happy with your software version, you may not need the new features. You should learn what those new features are before you make a decision to upgrade; a new feature might save you time and make the upgrade price worthwhile.

20

Q Can anti-virus programs protect me from downloading virus-laden software updates?

A Anti-virus programs work any number of ways. Most rely on your Internet software to warn you when you're about to download software. The Internet programs (called *browsers* as you'll see in Hour 21) do a good job of warning you that you're about to download software that could contain a virus. As long as you download from trusted sites, you shouldn't have to worry too much about such a warning.

After you decide to download an update, your virus program can scan your PC and look for viruses that may be present, possibly from the download. Many times, the anti-virus program can safely remove the virus and return your system to a normal state. It's interesting to note that anti-virus programs are some of the programs that need updating the most frequently. New viruses appear all the time, so the anti-virus companies are busy locating the new kinds of virus programs and writing code to detect and remove the viruses from systems. If you buy an anti-virus program that offers an update subscription service, either by mail or by the Internet, be sure to subscribe so you'll always be able to combat the latest virus that appears.

20

PART
VI

Connecting to the World

Hour

Hour **21**

Enter the Internet

In today's world, the Internet is much more a part of computer users' lives than ever before. Windows includes Internet Explorer, an Internet *browser* that lets you access the Internet from within Windows. This hour introduces the Internet and shows you just some of the ways Windows integrates itself with the Internet. You'll learn how to access the Internet with Internet Explorer.

The highlights of this hour include

- [ ] What makes the Internet such an important online tool
- [ ] Why modern Internet access techniques, such as Web pages, make the Internet more manageable
- [ ] How to start and use Internet Explorer to surf the Internet
- [ ] How you can navigate the Internet and view the multimedia information you find there
- [ ] Where you must go to obtain Internet access
- [ ] How to specify search criteria so that you can locate the exact Internet information you need

The Internet

The *Internet* is a worldwide system of interconnected computers. Whereas your desktop computer is a standalone machine, and a network of computers is tied together by wires, the Internet is a worldwide online network of computers connected to standalone computers through modems. Hardly anyone understands everything on the Internet because the Internet is not one system but a conglomeration of systems.

The Internet began as a government and university-linked system of computers, but it has now grown to a business and personal system that contains almost an infinite amount of information. The Internet is so vast that nobody would be able to access all its information today.

JUST A MINUTE

> No central Internet computer exists; instead, the Internet is a system of connected computers. *Internet* is the term given to the entire system. *Web* is the term given to the interconnected system of Internet information pages that you can access to read specific information, as described throughout this hour.

TIME SAVER

> After you master this part of your 24-hour tutorial, you might want to learn more about the Internet. For an in-depth look, you might want to read *The Internet Unleashed, 1997 Edition* (ISBN 1-57521-185-8), published by Sams.net.

The Internet's vastness almost caused its downfall. How does one access or find information on the Internet? Fortunately, Internet technicians began standardizing Internet information when it became apparent that the Internet was growing and becoming a major information provider.

The World Wide Web

The *World Wide Web, or WWW,* or just *Web,* is a collection of Internet pages of information. Web pages can contain text, graphics, sound, and video. Figure 21.1 shows a sample Web page. As you can see, the Web page's graphics and text organize information into a magazine-like readable and appealing format.

21

Figure 21.1.

*Web pages provide
Internet information
in a nice format.*

Generally, a Web site might contain more information than will fit easily on a single Web page. Therefore, many Web pages contain links to additional extended pages, as well as other linked Web pages that may be related to the original topic. The first page you view is called the *home page*, and from the home page you can view other pages of information.

JUST A MINUTE

Each Web page has a unique location that includes the source computer and the location on that computer. Such locations are difficult to keep track of. Therefore, the Internet has standardized Web page locations with a series of addresses called *URLs*, or *Uniform Resource Locator* addresses. You can view any Web page if you know its URL. If you do not know the URL, the Internet provides several *search engines* that find Web pages when you search for topics.

TIME SAVER

Surely you've run across computer addresses that look like this: www.microsoft.com and www.mcp.com; these are URLs that access the Web pages. These two happen to be the respective URLs for Microsoft Corporation and Macmillan Computer Publishing.

21

Introducing the Internet Explorer Web Browser

Before you can access and view Web information, you need a program that can display Web page information, including text, graphics, audio, and video. The program you need is called a *Web browser,* or just a *browser.* Although several companies offer browsers, Windows provides one of the best Web-browsing programs, called *Internet Explorer.*

This book uses Internet Explorer in the figures and descriptions. Some people prefer to use a competing Web browser, such as *Netscape Navigator,* and you can use one of these competing browsers from Windows to access Web pages. Internet Explorer, however, integrates the best with Windows (because Microsoft wrote both products). Also, because Internet Explorer comes with every copy of Windows, Internet Explorer is the obvious choice to use in a book on PCs that run the Windows operating environment.

Before you can access the Internet's Web pages, you'll need to get Internet access through an *ISP,* or *Internet service provider.* Hour 22, "Online Services," describes various services you can use to connect to the Internet. If you want Internet access through another ISP, such as a local Internet provider in your town, your provider will tell you how to use Internet Explorer or another Web browser to access the ISP's Internet system.

Starting Internet Explorer

Internet Explorer is easy to start. You can access the Internet with one or two clicks by running Internet Explorer. You must already have Internet access through the Microsoft Network or another provider, and you must know the phone number to that provider. (Your provider will have to give you the specific access and setup details.) To access the Internet with Internet Explorer, follow these steps:

1. Double-click on the Windows desktop icon labeled The Internet. If you get an Internet Connection Wizard dialog box, you must contact your service provider to learn how to hook up Internet Explorer to the Internet.

2. If you access the Internet through the Microsoft Network provider, you'll see the dialog box shown in Figure 21.2. If you use an alternative provider, you will see a different dialog box. Some providers, including some versions of Microsoft Network, don't require that you wait for such a dialog box when you indicate you want access to the Internet. Some providers sign you into the Internet automatically if you've already entered sign-in information.

   If required, enter your Internet ID and password and click Connect to dial up the Internet.

21

Figure 21.2.

You might need to log in to your Internet provider to use Internet Explorer.

3. Assuming that you have Internet access and you've been set up with a provider, Internet Explorer will dial your provider and display the page set up to be your initial browser's home page. Depending on the amount of information and graphics on the page, the display might take a few moments or might display right away.

JUST A MINUTE

> Internet Explorer's Home toolbar button displays your browser's opening home page. At any time during your Internet browsing, you can return to Internet Explorer's home page by clicking this Home button. You can change your browser's home page address by entering a new home page address within the View | Options dialog box's Navigation page. When you enter a new home page URL in the Address field, Internet Explorer returns to that page whenever you click the Home toolbar button or when you start Internet Explorer in a subsequent session.

As you can see, using Internet Explorer to access the Internet and Web pages requires just one or two clicks. Internet Explorer automatically displays an initial start Web page from which you then can access additional Web pages and surf the Internet.

Managing the Internet Explorer Screen

Internet Explorer makes it easy to navigate Web pages. Before looking at a lot of Internet information, take a few minutes to familiarize yourself with the Internet Explorer screen by following these steps:

1. Study Figure 21.3 to learn the parts of the Internet Explorer screen. Internet Explorer will display your home page and will list the home page's address in the address area. Depending on your version of Windows, you might see a different version of Internet Explorer, but the primary screen components stay the same.

21

Figure 21.3.

Learn the Internet Explorer screen so that you can maximize the Internet Explorer browser.

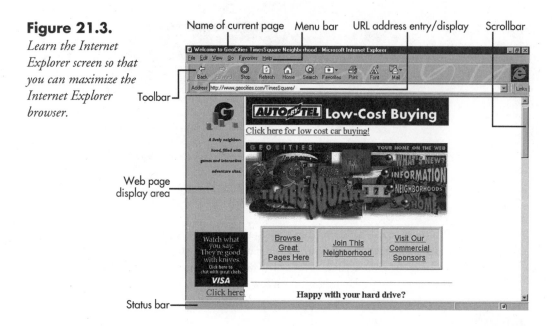

2. Some Web site addresses are lengthy. Drag the Address text box left or right (giving more or less room to the link buttons) to adjust the address display width. The more room you give to the Address text box, the less room you have for the other toolbar buttons. You can maximize and minimize the Address text box by clicking its slider control.

3. Click the down arrow at the right of the address entry to open a list of recently traversed site addresses. If this is the first time you or anyone has used your computer's Internet Explorer, you might not see sites other than the current start page sites. The Go|Open History Folder menu option (or clicking the toolbar's History button, if one exists) opens the window shown in Figure 21.4, which lets you return to previous sites you've gone to in past Internet visits. If you click any of the sites, the Web page's display area updates to show that site.

4. Click the scrollbar to see more of the page. Most Web pages take more room than will fit on one screen.

5. Select View|Toolbar and View|Status Bar to dedicate more of your screen to the Web page.

6. Select View|Toolbar and View|Status Bar once again to return the toolbar and status bar to your Web page.

Familiarize yourself with Internet Explorer's screen elements. As you traverse the Internet, Internet Explorer will aid you—as you'll see throughout the rest of this chapter. By adjusting the screen's elements, you can see more or less of large Web pages you encounter.

21

Figure 21.4.

*You can view a history of
Web sites you've visited.*

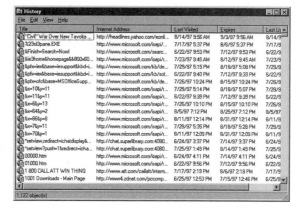

Surfing the Internet

Remember that the Internet's Web is a collection of interconnected Web pages. Almost every Web page contains links to other sites. These links (often called *hot links* or *hypertext links*) are often underlined. You'll be able to locate these links by moving your mouse cursor over the underlined description. If the mouse cursor changes to a hand, you can click the hand to move to that page. After a brief pause, your Web browser will display the page.

TIME SAVER

A link is nothing more than a URL address to another Web site. The link often displays a description, not a technical URL. (As you move your mouse cursor over a link, your Web browser's status bar displays the actual URL to the link.) Therefore, you can traverse related Web pages without worrying about addresses; just click link descriptions to move to those sites.

Suppose that you view the home page of your financial broker. The page might include links to other related pages, such as stock quotation pages, company financial informational pages, and order-entry pages in which you can enter your own stock purchase requests.

One of the most useful features of Internet Explorer and every other Web browser is the browser's capability to return to sites you've visited, both in the current session and in former sessions. The toolbar's Back button takes you back to a site you just visited and you can keep clicking the Back button to return to pages you've visited this session. The Forward button returns you to pages from where you've backed up.

Keep in mind that you can click the Address drop-down list box to see a list of URLs you've visited. In the History window, you'll find addresses from the current as well as previous Internet Explorer Web sessions.

21

If you know the address of a Web site you want to view, you can type the site's address directly in the Address text box. When you press Enter, Internet Explorer takes you to that site and displays the Web page. In addition, you can select File | Open to display a URL dialog box and enter an address in the dialog box. When you click OK, Internet Explorer displays the page associated with that address. From the Start menu, you can even enter a URL from the Start menu's Run dialog box to see any page on the Web.

If you find a location you really like, save that location in Internet Explorer's Favorites list. For example, if you run across a site that discusses your favorite television show and you want to return to that site again quickly, click the Favorites toolbar button and add the site to your Favorites list. The Address history does not keep track of many recently visited addresses; you can, however, store your favorite sites in the Favorites folders so that you can quickly access them during another Internet session.

Time Saver

Many non-browser products, such as Microsoft Office 97, let you add Web links to non-Internet documents such as Word documents. When you type a URL in Word, Word underlines the address. If you—or someone who reads your document from within Word—clicks on the URL link, Word automatically starts Internet Explorer (or whatever browser you use); as soon as Internet Explorer locates the page, it appears onscreen.

Moving Between Pages

Using the Internet requires that you move from Web page to Web page to view the information. After you visit a site, you can return to that site very simply. To traverse the Internet's Web pages, follow these steps:

1. If you have not started Internet Explorer, start it and log on to the Internet.

2. Click in the Address list box to highlight your start page's URL address.

3. Type the following Web page address: http://www.mcp.com. You'll see Macmillan Publishing's home page appear, as shown in Figure 21.5. (Depending on the changes that have been made to the site recently, the site might not match Figure 21.5 exactly.)

Caution

Often, you'll see Web addresses prefaced with the text http://. This prefix lets both you and your browser know that the address to the right of the second slash is a Web page's URL. Internet Explorer does not require the http:// prefix before URLs. Be sure to type forward slashes and not backslashes (\).

21

Figure 21.5.

Macmillan Publishing's home page.

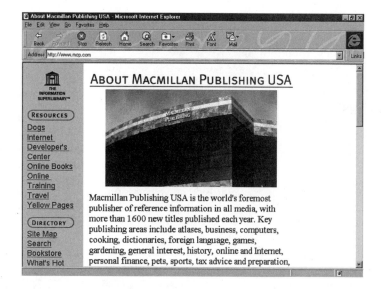

4. Click any link on the page. After a brief pause, you'll see the linked Web page.

5. Click the toolbar's Back button. Almost instantly, the first page appears.

JUST A MINUTE

Internet Explorer (as well as most browsers) keeps a history of Web page content in memory and on your disk. Therefore, if you revisit a Web site that you've recently viewed, your browser will most likely still have that site in its storage buffer. Instead of waiting for a long download once again, the page appears quickly because your browser actually reloads the page from memory and not from the original site. While waiting on non-buffered sites, the Internet Explorer status bar shows you the progress of the page's loading.

6. After you're back at Macmillan Publishing's home page, practice building a favorite site list by clicking the Favorites toolbar button.

7. Select the Favorites|Add To Favorites menu option. Internet Explorer displays the Add to Favorites dialog box.

8. Enter a description for the page. Make the description something memorable (such as `Macmillan Computer Book Publishing`).

9. Click OK.

10. Click the Favorites toolbar button once again. You'll see the new entry. When you select the favorite entry, Internet Explorer will look up that entry's stored URL and will go to that Web page.

21

The toolbar makes it easy to visit and revisit Web sites that interest you. You can return to previous sites and move forward once again. The Favorites toolbar button lets you add descriptions to your favorite Web sites so that you can return to those sites by clicking your mouse over the site's description in the Favorites list.

JUST A MINUTE

If you add too many favorites, your favorites list might become unmanageable. When you add to your favorites list, you'll be able to create folders by clicking the Create In button in the Add to Favorites dialog box. By setting up a series of folders named by subject, you can group your favorite Web sites so you can find them easily. Some versions of Internet Explorer (starting with version 4) add a Favorites list to the left of the Web page, as shown in Figure 21.6. The list stays on your screen so that you can select other favorite sites until you click the Favorites area Close button.

Figure 21.6.

Some browsers place the Favorites list to the left of the Web page.

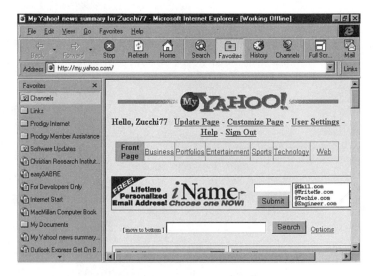

TIME SAVER

Visit Microsoft's site often. Microsoft will give you advanced information on Windows and Internet Explorer.

Speeding Up Web Displays

You'll find that some Web pages take a long time to display. Often, Web pages contain a lot of text and graphics, and that data takes time to arrive on your computer. Therefore, you might click to a favorite Web site but have to wait a minute or longer to see the entire site.

To speed things, Internet Explorer attempts to show as much of the page as possible, especially the text on the page, before downloading the graphics images. Internet Explorer puts placeholders where the graphics images are to appear. For example, Figure 21.7 shows a Web page with placeholders. This page appears quickly. If you view this page for a few moments, the placeholder images begin to appear until the final page displays in its entirety, as in Figure 21.8.

Figure 21.7.

Placeholders let you see the overall Web page design and text.

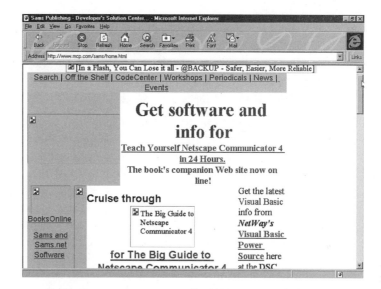

Figure 21.8.

After all the images arrive, the placeholders turn into graphics images.

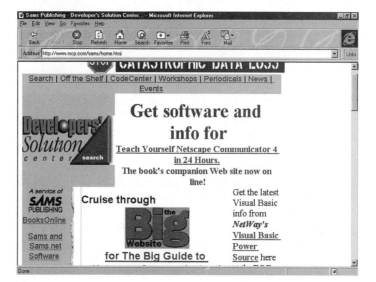

As you learned in the previous section, Internet Explorer saves the contents of Web pages you've been to recently in a memory buffer. Therefore, even if a Web page contains lots of information and requires a minute or longer to load, if you return to that page in a subsequent session, your browser will often display the in-memory Web page. Although the memory buffer speeds things, you might not want to see the buffer's Web page. You might, instead, want to see the original page in case the site has changed since your last visit, as described in these steps:

1. Return to Macmillan Publishing's Web site once again (http://www.mcp.com, in case you did not save the site).

2. Click on a link from that site.

3. Click the Back button to go right back. The site should appear almost instantly because you are actually viewing the site from your stored memory buffer.

4. Suppose that you suspect data has changed on the site and you want to see the real address site once again. Click the toolbar's Refresh button. Internet Explorer reloads the Web page from its original location. After the page loads, you see the page once again with any updates that might have been applied since your last visit.

5. Click the Refresh button once again to redisplay the page, but then immediately click the toolbar's Stop button. Instantly, Internet Explorer stops refreshing the page. Any graphics images not yet loaded will remain as placeholders and will not appear regardless of how long you view the page. The Stop button is useful for stopping the loading of a slow-loading Web page. If you have no need to see the images but are only interested in the text that quickly appears, you can reduce the Internet traffic by stopping the page before it completely loads. Obviously, you will not want to stop the loading process unless you are familiar with the page's contents. Some Web pages contain videos and sound files that can take a while to load.

6. If you want to limit the type of content sent from the Internet to Internet Explorer to speed your Web page surfing, select View|Options and click on the General tab in the dialog box. Uncheck the options under the Multimedia entry to limit pictures, videos, or sounds from coming into your browser when you reach a Web page.

Searching for the Information You Need

How can you expect to find information on a vast network of networks such as the Internet? Web pages offer linked sites in an appealing format that lets you comfortably view information and see related pages, but you must know the location of one of the site's pages before the links can help.

21

Fortunately, Internet Explorer (as well as most Internet Web browsers) offers a searching mechanism that helps you locate information on the Web. By clicking the Search toolbar button, you select one of several search engines and enter your search value.

The search Web page offers the benefit of multiple *search engines*. A search engine is a Web program that lets you enter words and phrases to search, and then the search engine scans the vast information on the Web to locate sites that contain the phrase. The accuracy of the search depends on the words and phrases you enter, as well as the capability of the search engine. For example, some search engines from which you can choose search only Web pages, whereas others search *newsgroups* (discussion areas that hold files and messages related to topics).

After the search page concludes the search, Internet Explorer displays from zero to several address links on which you can click to find information about your topic. For example, Figure 21.9 shows the result of one search. By scrolling down the page (and by clicking the additional pages of links if your search turns up several sites), you can read the descriptions of the pages (the descriptions often contain the first few lines of the located Web page text). When you click a search result, that result's Web page appears in your browser.

Figure 21.9.

The results of a search might produce several pages of Web sites.

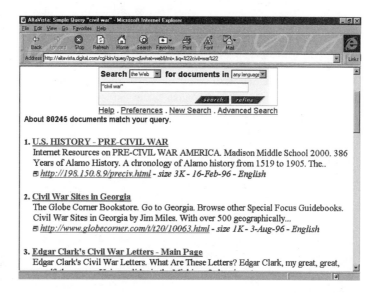

Each search engine locates information differently, and each has its own rules for the words and phrases you enter. Keep in mind that the more specific your search phrase is, the more accurately the search engine can find information that will help you.

21

TIME SAVER

If your search failed to locate information you think is on the Web, or if the search turned up too many sites and you want to narrow the search, you can often click the site Options button or More Information button to read the search criteria rules for that search engine. You then can refine your search and look for more specific information.

Generally, you can use these guidelines with most search engines:

☐ Enclose a multiple-word phrase in quotation marks if you want the search engine to search for those words in the order you list. For example, if you enter `"Bill Clinton"`, the search engine searches for that specific name. If, however, you enter `Bill Clinton` (without the quotes), most search engines locate every site that contains the word Bill and every site that contains the word Clinton, most of which would have nothing to do with the man you originally wanted to locate.

☐ Place a plus sign before each word or quoted phrase when you want to search for Web sites that contain every word and phrase in the list. For example, entering `+"Rush Limbaugh" +Congress` would find only those sites that contain both the name Rush Limbaugh and the word Congress, but would not find sites that listed only one or the other.

☐ Place the word `OR` between the words or quoted phrases if you want to search for sites that contain one or more of your words and phrases. For example, entering `"Bill Clinton" OR "Rush Limbaugh"` would locate any and every site that contains the name Bill Clinton or that contains the name Rush Limbaugh or that contains both names.

Remember that these search-criteria rules are only guidelines. Some of the search engines follow slightly different rules; you'll have to look up each search engine page's help references for specific information if the previous rules do not seem to work the way you expect.

JUST A MINUTE

Most of the search engines are case-sensitive when you mix uppercase and lowercase characters in your search; that is, you need to type words and phrases exactly as you expect them to appear if you want the search to match your search case exactly. Otherwise, if you enter a search criterion in all lowercase letters, the search engines generally do not base the match on case. Therefore, if you want to locate the city named Flint (in Michigan), enter `Flint`. Otherwise, if you enter the name in all lowercase letters, the search engine will probably search both for the city name as well as the rock.

21

Summary

This hour introduced you to the Internet. The Internet is a vast collection of interrelated computers all around the world. You can access the Internet as long as you have access through an Internet service provider. Although Internet information appears in many forms, the most useful information often appears on Web pages that contain text, graphics, sound, and video.

Windows supports the Internet Explorer Web browser, with which you can view Web pages. Internet Explorer includes searching tools as well as a history system that keeps track of recent Web pages. As the Internet becomes more organized and as Internet access gets faster and cheaper, you will make the Web browser more of your daily computing routine. One day, you'll find that you do most of your work from Web-browsing software such as Internet Explorer.

Q&A

Q I've clicked the Internet icon, but I don't see Web pages. What do I have to do to get on the Internet?

A Do you have Internet access from Microsoft Network or from another Internet service provider? Generally, unless you work for a company that offers Internet access to its employees, you'll have to sign up for Internet access, get the access phone number, pay a monthly fee (most ISPs offer unlimited access for a flat monthly rate), and set up your browser, such as Internet Explorer, to access that provider.

Q How do I know if I'm viewing a Web page from the memory buffer or from the actual site?

A If the page appears almost instantly after you enter the address, the chances are great that you are looking at the page from your browser's memory. In most cases, the memory's page will match the actual Web site. Nevertheless, if you want to make sure you're viewing the latest and greatest version of the Web page, click the Refresh toolbar button. Refresh forces Internet Explorer to reload the page from the site's actual address.

21

Hour 22

Using Online Services

This hour helps you locate an Internet Service Provider (ISP) by using one of the major online services. Depending on your Windows version, you may see a desktop folder named Online Services or something similar. Although you can sign up for Internet service through a local ISP and get only the Internet, you should consider one of the several popular online services that provide Internet capabilities as well as other kinds of online benefits.

The highlights of this hour include

☐ Why you should use an online service for your Internet Service Provider

☐ What advantages a service gives you over a straight ISP

☐ How to sign up for an online service

☐ Why you should sign up for trial memberships

Introduction to Online Services

The following lists some of the more popular online services that you're likely to hear about, and possibly see, when you open your Windows desktop folder labeled Online Services if you have such an icon:

☐ America Online (often called *AOL*)

☐ CompuServe

☐ Microsoft Network (often called *MSN*)

☐ Prodigy

In addition to these services, you may hear about the AT&T WorldNet and possibly see its icon in the Online Services window. Each of the services, with the exception of AT&T WorldNet, are more than just Internet providers; the services offer unique advantages for the Internet user who wants more than straight Internet Web access. If your Online Services window doesn't contain all these icons, try running Windows Setup from the Control Panel's Add/Remove Programs dialog box to see if the services are described there. In addition, if you've purchased a PC in the last few years, the vendor almost surely packaged online service CD-ROMs or disks with your PC's software.

All the services charge a fee for their access. Although they all offer somewhat different pricing plans, most services compete with one another well so you must decide which is right for you based on your needs, the reliability of the service, the capabilities each provides, and recommendations from others. If, for example, you have a new 56Kbps modem, you will probably want to use a service that supports your modem standard (as you learned in Hour 19, two 56Kbps standards exist and neither works with the other). You'll find that some services, such as AT&T WorldNet, don't offer ISDN lines for ISDN modem users at the time of this writing, so if you use an ISDN modem be sure to check out the service ahead of time.

Don't discount recommendations; if most of your co-workers and friends subscribe to a service, such as Prodigy, you should consider Prodigy because you'll communicate with other people without problems and they can help you get started more quickly. In addition, you can exchange tips and warnings to improve your group's efficiency with the service.

JUST A MINUTE

All the online services offer *flat-rate pricing plans* at the time of this writing. With a flat-rate plan you pay one monthly fee no matter how much (or how little) you use the service each month. Without a flat-rate plan, you'll pay a minimum monthly fee plus an additional charge for each hour you use the system over a preset minimum. In addition, the services provide local numbers to most areas so you won't have to pay long-distance charges.

The primary difference between using one of the Windows-supplied online services for your Internet connection and a local ISP that provides more of a generic Internet connection is that the online services offer unique content available only to their subscribers. Many of the online services also offer their own interface to the Internet and its content. The drawback

22

22

to online services is that they offer abundant advertisement at virtually every turn. These ads, as well as the extra graphics and menus they provide on their home pages, mean somewhat slower access in some cases than you would get from a standalone Internet service provider.

CAUTION

The companies that provide the online services want the services made available to as many users as possible. Therefore, they try to make these services simple to install. The very nature of online communications sometimes requires some fiddling even with the best of installation routines, but these services generally install without a lot of intervention on your part. However, if you use a local ISP and opt not to use one of the online services, you often face somewhat difficult setup routines and, depending on the quality (or lack) of support through your ISP, you may not get much help. These setup risks may not outweigh the lower cost of a local ISP, but you should consider the risks when shopping for a provider.

The growth of the Internet, with all its millions of Web sites, takes much of the uniqueness out of the *unique content* provided by online services. For example, CompuServe may offer movie reviews but so do a plethora of Web sites, many of which offer as many or more movie reviews as CompuServe. Most daily newspapers, magazines, and entertainment services now offer Web sites. If you're willing to search the Internet for a specific reviewer's take on a new movie, you can often get as good or even a better review somewhere other than your particular service provider's unique content.

However, one of the reasons online services, such as Microsoft Network, are successful is that they offer more than just unique content. The online services generally utilize a proprietary interface. Although you can often use the service in conjunction with Internet Explorer, for example, to access the Web, you also use the online service's customized interface to access information. The service's interface often provides more uniformity than the Web offers. For example, Figure 22.1 shows CompuServe's opening screen. From this screen you can access one of several categories easily whereas with a more generic Internet Service Provider, you would need to know the Web locations to find such information using Internet Explorer.

CAUTION

Prodigy is the only Windows full-service online service that does not offer its own Web-browsing interface. You use Internet Explorer or another Web browser to get to Prodigy's online features.

Figure 22.1.

Online service providers offer their own managed interface to the Internet and its information.

Newcomers to online technology often prefer the organized content available through an online service over that of a straight, Internet-only account. Setting up Internet Explorer or another browser is not always a trivial task with generic ISPs. In addition, the dedicated toolbar buttons and menu structure of the online services get the newcomer (as well as the pros in many cases) to their information destinations faster.

One of the benefits of using the supplied online service if you don't have an Internet provider or if you want to make a change is that all the software for the service setup comes with most copies of Windows and new PCs. You usually have everything you need to set up America Online, CompuServe, and the others from an Online Services folder, so you don't have to wait to get started.

If you can't seem to locate a folder called Online Services or something similar, and you can't locate one in Windows setup or on the software that came with your PC, you'll need to call one of the numbers below to request a free setup CD-ROM:

America Online: 1-800-827-6364, www.aol.com
AT&T WorldNet Service: 1-800-967-5363, www.att.com/worldnet
CompuServe: 1-800-524-3388, www.compuserve.com
Prodigy: 1-800-PRODIGY (1-800-776-3449), www.prodigy.com
Microsoft Network: 1-800-386-5550, www.msn.com

22

22

JUST A MINUTE

All copies of Windows include sign-up information for Microsoft Network. Therefore, if you have nothing else you can still try MSN.

JUST A MINUTE

You must have a credit card handy when signing up for a service.

One of the benefits of using Windows to set up an online service is that you can try a service free for a month before deciding if you want to keep it. The services compete heavily with one another and you, the user, benefit from that competition. Try all the services free for a month and explore their benefits before you decide which one is right for you. This hour's section entitled, "Comparing the Online Services," compares and contrasts all the services.

Setting Up CompuServe

When you choose which online service you want to try, you'll need to set up that service in Windows and subscribe to it. All the online services require that you set up the service before you can use it. Each service is compressed to save disk space until you are ready to use the service. You'll see here how to set up CompuServe, but you'll follow the same general setup guidelines to set up any of the services.

JUST A MINUTE

You'll generally only need to set up an online service once. Most of the services automatically download updates when needed. After you set up a service, if you need a new software update, the service will automatically download the update to your PC and update the software for you without requiring you to do anything.

Each Online Services folder icon starts a wizard that sets up one of the services. The wizard walks you through the CompuServe setup instructions and adds the appropriate service icons to your Start menu. Follow these steps to start the CompuServe Wizard:

1. Open your desktop's Online Services window or insert your CompuServe disk or CD-ROM into the drive.

2. Click on the CompuServe icon or select the Start menu's Run command and type **d:\Setup** (replace *d* with your CD-ROM or disk drive letter if you're installing from a non-Windows source). A dialog box makes sure that you want to continue by asking if you want to install CompuServe.

3. Click Yes to begin the wizard. After a brief pause, a CompuServe setup wizard begins.

4. Select your country and click the Next button. The online services are international, so the wizard needs to know your country to set up the appropriate service.

5. If you are setting up your first online service, select the Express install from the window shown in Figure 22.2. If you already have an ISP and want to access CompuServe from your existing connection, select Custom. (You will need to contact your ISP to determine which settings CompuServe needs before you can connect to CompuServe with this option.)

Figure 22.2.

Select the kind of CompuServe service connection that you want.

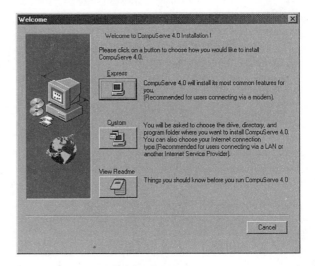

All the online services provide fairly adequate levels of security. Although no online service can ensure that your every keystroke's privacy is guarded, online services do provide more security than regular voice calls, credit card purchases in stores, and purchases you make by mail. The stories you may have heard about online privacy issues are generally overblown.

Use common sense when you provide information over an online service or over the Internet. If you order products from a reputable dealer, the odds are vastly in your favor that you'll have no security troubles. Almost every financial transaction made today over an online service uses a *secure connection;* meaning that, information you supply is encrypted on your end before being sent and then decrypted on the receiving end.

6. CompuServe displays the Create a Keyword dialog box shown in Figure 22.3.

22

Figure 22.3.

Your keyword provides security during your online sessions.

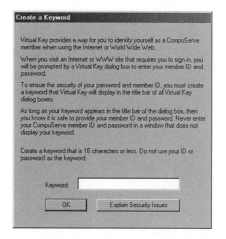

Enter a keyword, up to 16 characters, that acts as your security password. Although you'll need a password to sign in to CompuServe, the keyword offers yet another level of security for those times when you must provide information, such as a credit card number. Any time an online CompuServe screen asks you for secure information, you will be prompted to enter this keyword to help encrypt the information so it gets to CompuServe without security violation along the way. Select a keyword you can remember such as your mother's maiden name.

7. CompuServe requires that you restart your PC after you set up the CompuServe files. Click the Restart button.

8. After your PC restarts, you can select your Start menu's Programs | Online Services menu to see a new submenu called CompuServe. Select the entry named CompuServe 4.0 to complete your setup. If you don't have an Online Services menu, select the Start menu's Programs | CompuServe option to locate the program.

9. At the opening CompuServe screen, click Signup to sign up for a new CompuServe account. CompuServe requires a sign-in name, password (one that differs from your security keyword), personal information such as your name and address, as well as credit card information. Unless you cancel the service, CompuServe will bill your credit card monthly for the service.

10. When you first sign in, CompuServe enables you to select the phone number you want to use. If you've elected to use CompuServe in conjunction with an existing provider, you won't need to enter phone number information. When you select any service, CompuServe dials the Internet using your existing dial-up provider.

The previous information walked you through the preliminary steps needed to set up and access CompuServe, one of the online service providers available through Windows. After you set up a service, you can access that service's specialized areas as well as surf the Internet using the service's Internet browser. Some of the services enable you to use your own Web browser, such as Internet Explorer, if you don't want to use the proprietary browser that comes with the service.

Comparing the Online Services

Which online service is right for you? Only you can answer that question, but the following sections briefly explain advantages of each of Windows online services so you can better choose between them.

In comparing the services, keep in mind that competition makes all of them worthwhile contenders, and they each provide unique advantages over the others. All the services provide the typical Internet-based online service features described in Table 22.1. Each online service, however, goes about implementing the features in different ways.

Table 22.1. Look for these features in your online service provider.

Feature	Description
Chat	Enables you to interactively communicate with others who are signed on at the same time you are. All online services, including a straight Internet connection, provide text-based chats where you type messages back and forth to others who have joined your *chat room*. Chat rooms are areas of interest, sorted by topic such as *PC Support, Teen TV, Religious Talk, Windows Troubleshooting, Politics,* and *Movies*.
E-mail	Stands for *electronic mail* and describes the service with which you can transfer messages and files to other users on your online service and across the Internet. The receiving user does not have to be logged on to receive mail you send.
FTP	Stands for *File Transfer Protocol* and enables you to transfer files to and from other Internet-based computers. Online services almost always provide their own FTP alternative when you want to retrieve files from the service. Generally, a service will offer a file-search section where you can search for files of particular interest and download those files by clicking a button.
Internet Phone	If you have a multimedia PC (and who doesn't these days?) with a microphone and speaker, you can speak to others anywhere in the world. You aren't charged the long-distance connect rates, but only for your regular online service (some exceptions apply). Internet

22

Feature	Description
	Phone is not all peachy, however; the quality is sometimes low and both you and the other party must be signed on at the same time, and you both must know which Internet location the other will be at to connect. Internet Phone holds promise, but for now, not too many people use it despite its initial appeal.
Mailing Lists	Free (usually) subscription-based Internet services that send you any and all new messages and files posted to the mailing lists you choose via e-mail.
Newsgroups	An area of the Internet accessed through your online service that contains files and messages organized by topic that you can read, download, and send to. (Newsgroups have nothing to do with Web pages that contain news such as the world headlines.)
Web	Web pages you browse from your Windows desktop using Internet Explorer and your online service.

Keep in mind that you get the standard Internet service explained in Table 22.1 no matter to which online service provider you subscribe. In addition, if you prefer to subscribe to a local ISP that offers nothing but an Internet connection, you can access any of the services listed in Table 22.1. Remember, however, that most online services put a friendly interface in front of these Internet services that make the services much simpler to use. In addition, the online services provide you with support, news and current events, and entertainment areas that are more complete than you'll find with a straight Internet connection.

CAUTION

> Most online services provide nice, friendly interface layers between you and the Internet. In addition to the interface, each service provides unique content such as online magazines that you can't get elsewhere. Generally, an online service costs more than an Internet-only connection you can get locally, but you'll see a cost in another area as well: disk drive space. Most of the online services require between 30 and 50 megabytes of disk space. The unique content and interface requires a presence on your hard disk.

America Online (AOL)

AOL is the number one online service in use today. Its sheer number of users makes AOL a mixed blessing sometimes. Although AOL's content is some of the most complete and its service offers perhaps the largest selection of specialized benefits, some users have a difficult time getting onto the service during peak hours. In addition, AOL throws a lot of advertising at you while you use the service. This advertising keeps your costs down and the content massive.

JUST A MINUTE

> AOL is considered to be one of the easiest online services to use.

AOL's opening page, shown in Figure 22.4, offers a push button topic selection throughout its entire interface. When you want to access the Internet, you must use AOL's provided browser, which does not support the same features that Internet Explorer supports.

Figure 22.4.

AOL is one of the easiest online services to use.

AOL provides a wide variety of daily news, periodicals (newspapers and magazines), local weather, movie reviews and preview, and health forums.

TIME SAVER

> AOL enables you to sign on up to five members in your household. Each member can have his own distinct account and can send and receive e-mail separately from the primary account holder. You don't pay extra for the extra users, but only one user can be signed onto AOL at a time.

22

AOL enables you to send and receive e-mail between AOL and every other service and Internet user. The e-mail area is simple to use and you are nicely reminded, verbally through your speakers, when you have new e-mail (you can turn this off). Another AOL service that should weigh into your online selection is that AOL offers you up to 2MB of storage for your own personal home page. You'll have your own URL and be registered so that others on the Internet (both AOL and non-AOL users) can access your Web page.

AT&T WorldNet Service

AT&T WorldNet service is not a true online service with unique content, but an Internet Service Provider available from within Windows. Billing is simple for most customers because AT&T WorldNet Service bills through the AT&T long-distance service if you use AT&T. (If you have a credit card that offers extras such as airline miles, you may opt not to bill through your AT&T long-distance carrier, but select a credit card billing option to rack up those miles.)

AT&T WorldNet offers nothing fancy. You'll use Internet Explorer or another Web browser to surf the Internet, and the Microsoft Outlook e-mail and newsgroup reader works fine for the AT&T WorldNet access. AT&T WorldNet charges extra for 2–5MB of Web page storage if you want a Web page.

CompuServe

CompuServe has been around the longest of all the online services listed in most Online Services windows. Due to its maturity, CompuServe offers more depth of information and a wider selection of forums than any other service. Want information on travel to Jakarta? CompuServe probably has more information than the other services. Do you need help locating a replacement disk drive door for your 1953 IBM-PC? CompuServe's hardware forums probably have the address where you can buy one.

As Figure 22.5 shows, you can easily access CompuServe's areas of interest by selecting services similar to the way you traverse AOL's push button interface.

CompuServe uses a proprietary e-mail service, meaning that you cannot always send and receive e-mail to and from others who use different online services. You can send and receive regular Internet-ready e-mail so you can communicate with anyone else whose service also provides for pure Internet e-mail.

Despite its e-mail limitation, you can subscribe to various e-mail services through CompuServe that enable you to access your e-mail with a pager or listen to your CompuServe messages over a voice phone. Such services are vital if you travel without a laptop and need your messages. Although a CompuServe sign-in name and e-mail address is often cryptic (such as `420120,23433`) you can request a customized name such as `Casper` and people can get e-mail to you by sending your e-mail to `Casper@compuserve.com`.

Figure 22.5.

Access CompuServe's primary services through a selection interface not unlike that of AOL.

If you want a Web page, CompuServe gives you 5MB, more than twice AOL's 2MB storage limit, for the Web page you desire. For those who prefer Internet Explorer 4.0's active desktop features, CompuServe enables you to use Internet Explorer in place of the proprietary Web browser in CompuServe.

JUST A MINUTE

> AOL purchased CompuServe but promises (perhaps with fingers crossed) that the two services will retain their separate flavors and will continue to remain distinct entities.

Microsoft Network (MSN)

Microsoft Network offers the largest assortment of Microsoft-related sites and tools and seems to integrate more fully into Windows than the other online services. (One might expect this because both Windows and MSN are Microsoft products.)

MSN is known for its attempt to be *hip*. *MSN* sounds out jazz music and a video when you install and first sign in to MSN. MSN's black background adds an effectual interface that doesn't take itself too seriously and seems laid back. The Microsoft programmers seemed to create a service that they wanted and the results are fairly good. Figure 22.6 shows MSN's opening screen.

Figure 22.6.

The Microsoft Network screen offers a television-like six-channel interface for its topics.

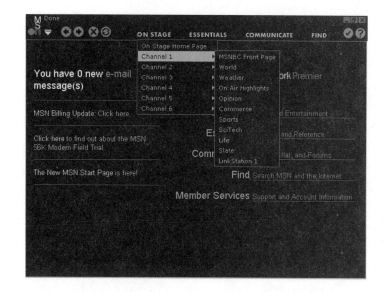

MSN's Web browser interface acts a lot like Internet Explorer 4, although you cannot directly send active content to your desktop unless you use Internet Explorer to access the Web after you've signed on to MSN. If you use the proprietary Web interface, you can select or enter URLs from the MSN screens and surf the Web with a surprisingly powerful (for a proprietary service) browser.

MSN takes advantage of the Windows environment and places an MSN icon on your taskbar when you install the MSN software. As Figure 22.7 shows, you can click the taskbar to display an MSN menu at any point during your MSN session or even when you aren't signed in.

Figure 22.7.

The Microsoft Network provides a taskbar icon you can click to display a menu.

As you use MSN, a timer pops up from the taskbar every few minutes to tell you how long you've been using MSN in that particular session. If you routinely chat with others, you can designate a list of online friends and the taskbar icon pops up to tell you which of your friends sign on during your MSN session. That way, you can contact them through a service to let them know you are signed on as well.

Prodigy

Prodigy's online service, now called *Prodigy Internet*, provides unique content over what you'll find on just the Internet, as the other services provide. However, Prodigy's interface takes place entirely within Internet Explorer 4, so you don't have to learn new commands to access the content Prodigy provides. Prodigy is more seamless than the other services and you can switch back and forth between Prodigy and the Internet's Web pages without as much distinction as you may feel in the other services.

JUST A MINUTE

> Prodigy adds a Prodigy-based toolbar to Internet Explorer so you'll have quick access to Prodigy's unique content.

Figure 22.8 shows the Prodigy opening screen that appears when you sign in to Prodigy for the first time. (The screen changes so yours will be different.) Prodigy adds an icon to your taskbar while you access Prodigy that, although not as full-featured as MSN's taskbar icon, helps give you Prodigy control when you're working with other applications.

Figure 22.8.

Prodigy uses the familiar Internet Explorer as its interface environment.

Prodigy gives you 2MB of storage for your own Web site, but you must use tools you find elsewhere to create your Web page. Prodigy supplies no Web site-creation programs. Windows comes with a Web page creation program called *FrontPage* that you can use to create a Web page. You can also use Word 97 to create Web pages or any number of Web page development programs on the market.

22

Prodigy's Internet Explorer interface enables you to use Outlook Express, the Internet Explorer 4.0 Newsreader and Internet Mail program, so you don't have to learn new commands to access newsgroups and e-mail. Hour 23, "Mail Without Stamps," explains how to use Microsoft Outlook Express to access e-mail and newsgroups from the Internet.

22

Summary

This hour explains how you can use one of the online services to access the Web, newsgroups, and e-mail if you don't already have access to a service. The online services, with the exception of AT&T WorldNet, provide unique content that you can't get from a Web ISP alone. You'll have access to forums, news, entertainment, and other links that offer a more structured content than an Internet-only ISP. In addition, the online services offer a simpler interface to Web services than you get from an ISP and a Web browser.

The next hour extends your Internet knowledge by showing you how to send and receive e-mail over the Internet.

Q&A

Q Should I subscribe to more than one service?

A Probably not, although you may want to sign up for multiple services for a month to try them out free during their free trial offers. The services compete with one another greatly and, although they differ, every one offers vast content as well as standard Web capabilities such as e-mail and newsgroup access. You can try them all during the trial and decide which one will best fill your needs.

If your service is frequently busy when you dial in, a secondary service offers a backup number so you can get to the Web when you need access. Too many busy signals for a certain service may make you decide against that service provider because you want to be able to access your service without the busy signals. Even with busy signals, however, a few dial-in attempts usually get you through if you're patient.

Q Do I have to provide my credit card number if I want to try the trial period?

A Unless you use AT&T WorldNet and bill to your AT&T long-distance carrier, you must provide a credit card number even if you sign up for a trial one-month period. The online service wants your business, and at the end of the trial period, they want your money also. By providing a credit card when you first sign up, the service can ensure that they'll get paid for each month you stay on the service. All the services offer e-mail to their customer support so you can let them know if you ever want to cancel the service.

Hour **23**

Mail Without Stamps

E-mail plays an important role in today's communications, rivaling that of even regular mail. E-mail's paperless aspect keeps your desk less cluttered, and it generally arrives at its destination within a few minutes to a few hours. Newsgroups offer a different kind of messaging center for messages you want to communicate publicly on a topic. You can post newsgroup topics, answers, and questions, as well as read responses from others interested in the same subject.

Starting with Internet Explorer 4, Microsoft offers a new program called *Outlook Express* that manages both e-mail and newsgroup information. Outlook Express replaces older Windows messaging programs called *Windows Messaging* and *Microsoft Exchange*. By combining a newsgroup reader with e-mail capabilities, you can manage more information easier than before.

The highlights of this hour include

- ☐ How Outlook Express enables you to view and send e-mail messages
- ☐ When to attach files to e-mail messages you send
- ☐ How to post and read newsgroup messages
- ☐ How to set up Outlook Express for multiple accounts

Internet Explorer

Internet Explorer gives you perhaps the most functional and powerful browser on the market and an active desktop so that you can place active Web content on your Windows desktop (such as a stock ticker). Internet Explorer also is *free*. If you use an older version of Internet Explorer, such as 3.02 (select Help | About to determine your Internet Explorer's version number), point your browser to Microsoft's Web site with the URL address www.microsoft.com/ ie/download/ and download Internet Explorer. The download is free, but you'll probably want to start the download before you go to bed because the file takes more than an hour to download (the file size is 7MB) on a 28.8K modem.

As you'll see in the rest of this hour, Internet Explorer 4 and its free Outlook Express complement program enable you to manage e-mail and newsgroups easily.

The E-Mail World

It's common for computer users to access more than one online service. Perhaps you work on the Internet and with the CompuServe information service. Each morning you might log in to the Internet to get incoming messages and send your outgoing Internet messages. After you're finished, you might log in to CompuServe to send and receive those messages. The burden of managing that electronic mail grows as more people sign up for more online services.

JUST A MINUTE

Are we living in a *paperless society*, as promised by the Management Information System gurus of the early 1970s? Not a chance. Computers help us use more paper and at a *faster* rate than ever before. It's often said in the computer industry that, despite the prevalence of e-mail, we'll have paperless bathrooms before we'll have a paperless society!

Wouldn't it be nice to tell your computer to send and receive all your e-mail without any intervention on your part? The computer could store all received mail in a central location; you could then manage, sort, print, respond to, or delete from there. Outlook Express provides that one-stop answer.

CAUTION

Outlook Express is not the same program as *Outlook* that comes with Office 97. It looks as if Outlook Express, or some form of Outlook Express, will replace Office 97's Outlook soon, perhaps by the time you read this.

23

Managing E-Mail with Outlook Express

Outlook Express offers benefits over previous e-mail programs because it supports several formats within an e-mail message. Although you could send text data, *binary data* (compressed data such as programs and graphics), sound files, and video as e-mail in previous programs, Outlook Express enables you to store HTML code inside your message so you can customize the look of your message. A message you send might look like a Web page. You can even send complete Web pages as e-mail inside Outlook Express. If you embed a URL inside an e-mail message, the recipient of your message can click that URL and go straight to that site on the Web.

23

Some additional features of Outlook Express's e-mail capabilities include

☐ View e-mail as text only to speed performance at the loss of seeing formatted messages.

☐ Attach files to your messages.

☐ Check spelling before you send a message.

☐ Reply to messages and forward messages to other recipients.

☐ Connect to Web-based e-mail address search engines, such as Four11, to find people's addresses (see Hour 10 for more information on Web searching).

☐ Connect to the Windows Address Book program. Address Book is compatible with several other address programs, such as Office 97's Outlook. You can load the Address Book program by traversing the Start menu or by looking at the addresses from within Outlook Express (see Hour 24 for more information on the Address Book).

☐ Send and receive mail from multiple Internet accounts.

Setting Up Outlook Express

If a wizard begins when you start Outlook Express the first time, you'll need to answer the wizard's prompts to set up your e-mail account. Most online services, such as Prodigy, automatically set up Outlook Express to work with that online service. However, if you see the wizard, you may need to contact your ISP to determine which settings are needed for Outlook Express to recognize your ISP-based e-mail account.

The following steps explain how to set up Outlook Express for use within Internet Explorer:

1. Start Internet Explorer and sign into your Internet account.

2. Select View | Internet Options and click on the Programs tab to display the Internet Options dialog box shown in Figure 23.1.

Figure 23.1.

Make sure Internet Explorer knows about Outlook Express.

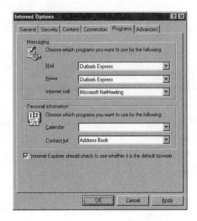

3. Select Outlook Express in both the Mail and News list boxes, as shown in Figure 23.1. (The third list box shows Microsoft NetMeeting, which enables you to contact other Internet users and set up chat- and voice-based meetings.)

4. Click OK to close the Internet Options dialog box. When you send or receive mail, Internet Explorer will now use Outlook Express as your e-mail program.

TIME SAVER

Outlook Express is smart and recognizes if you've already set up another e-mail program before installing Windows. You may see the Outlook Express Import dialog box (see Figure 23.2) the first time you use Outlook Express to send or receive a message, because Outlook Express offers to use your previous e-mail program's messages and addresses so you don't have to re-enter them in Outlook Express. Follow the wizard to load any or all of your previous program's options.

Figure 23.2.

Outlook Express will import your messages and addresses from your former e-mail program.

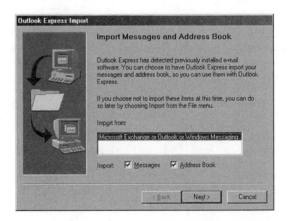

23

After you've told Internet Explorer that you want to use Outlook Express as your e-mail program, Internet Explorer remembers your setup and uses Outlook Express every time you send or receive e-mail.

Sending Mail with Outlook Express

Outlook Express has many options, but you can send e-mail messages and files to others very easily without worrying too much about what else Outlook Express offers. The following steps explain how to send various forms of e-mail to recipients:

1. Start Internet Explorer and sign in to your Internet account.
2. Click the toolbar's Mail button and select New Message from the menu that drops down. The New Message dialog box opens, as shown in Figure 23.3.

Figure 23.3.

You can now send a message to one or more recipients.

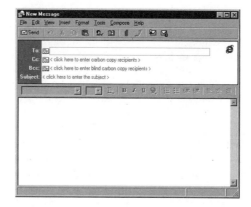

3. Enter your recipient's e-mail address in the To field or click the file card icon next to the To field to select the field. If you know the name under which you stored an e-mail address in the Address Book, you can type the name instead of the e-mail address in the To field.
4. Use the Cc field to send copies of your message to another recipient. The recipient will know the message was copied to him. If you enter an e-mail address in the Bcc field, your recipient won't know that others received the message.
5. Enter a subject line. Get in the habit of entering a subject so your recipients can file your messages by subject.
6. Press the Tab or Shift+Tab key to move from field to field. When you type the message in the message area, the scrollbar appears to enable you to scroll through messages that don't fit inside the window completely. Use the formatting toolbar above the message area to apply formatting, color, and even numbered and bulleted lists to your message.

7. If you want to attach one or more files to your message, click the Attach toolbar button (button with the paper clip) and select your file from the Insert Attachment dialog box that appears as shown in Figure 23.4.

Figure 23.4.

Select the file or files you want to send along with your message.

8. Select Tools | Set Priority | High if you want to send the message as a high-priority message. The receiver will see an alert icon next to the message in the Inbox when the message arrives.

9. To send the message, click the Send button (button with the flying envelope) and the message goes on its way toward the recipients.

Sending e-mail messages and files requires only that you know the person's e-mail address or that you've stored the address in your Address Book. Attach files of any type to your message and the recipient will receive the message and the files. Outlook Express imposes no limit on the size or number of attachments you can send.

Sending Web Pages as E-Mail

The following steps explain how to send Web pages to e-mail recipients:

1. Start Internet Explorer and sign in to your Internet account.

2. Display the Web page that you want to send. (You can send the page to your own e-mail account for this test.)

3. Click the Mail button on the toolbar.

4. Select Send Page. If the Web page is complicated, it may be considered a *read-only* Web page that cannot be edited. If so, Internet Explorer displays a message telling you that your recipient may receive the message as an attached file or as a read-only file. If you are sending the page to yourself or to someone who you know has Internet Explorer, send the page as a read-only page.

5. The e-mail window opens, so you can select a recipient and add copies to others if you like. You can see the Web page at the bottom of the window, as shown in Figure 23.5. Now *that's* quite a fancy e-mail message!

6. Click the Send button to send the Web page.

23

Figure 23.5.

The recipient will see the Web page when viewing this e-mail.

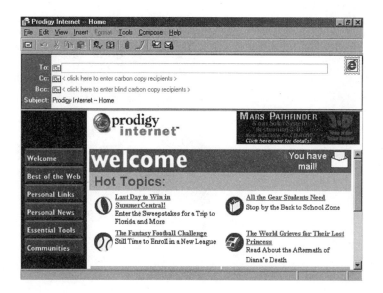

23

CAUTION

Your recipient must also use an e-mail program, such as Outlook Express, that can display HTML code or he will get a lot of garbage in the message. Your recipient will still be able to read the mail's text, but the e-mail will be messed up due to all the visible HTML formatting codes that are normally hidden. You can convert HTML pages to straight text from the Format menu.

If you locate a Web site you want someone else to see, send that site to the person via e-mail. Internet Explorer's Mail toolbar button contains a menu option that makes sending Web pages to others a breeze.

Receiving E-Mail

The following steps explain how to use Outlook Express to receive e-mail that people send to you:

1. Start Internet Explorer and sign in to your Internet account.

2. Click the Mail button on the toolbar.

3. Select Read Mail. Figure 23.6 shows the mail center window that appears.

Figure 23.6.

Check your e-mail from
this window.

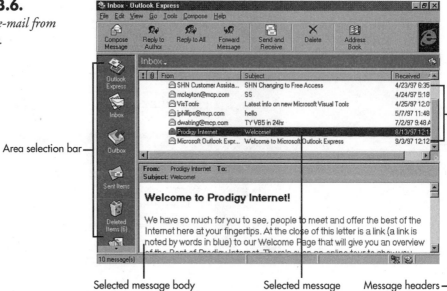

Area selection bar ——

Selected message body   Selected message   Message headers ——

E-mail comes to your *Inbox* (called the preview area) at regular intervals, but
Outlook Express doesn't constantly check for new mail—your Internet connection
would slow down due to the mail check. At any time, you can manually check for
new mail and send any that has yet to be sent by clicking the toolbar's Send and
Receive button. You don't have to be connected to the Internet to create e-mail.

TIME SAVER

> Select Tools | Options and enter a new time value for the Check for New
> Messages Every *10* Minutes option if you want Outlook Express to check
> for incoming e-mail more or less often than the 10 minute default.

The *Outbox* area (you can click on the Area selection bar to see your Outbox
contents) holds items that you've readied to send, but that haven't actually gone
out yet. When your Outbox contains unsent mail, the icon changes to show mail
in the Outbox.

4. As you click on the headers in the Inbox, a preview appears for that message in the
   lower pane. (Drag the center bar up or down to make more or less room for the
   headers.) If you double-click on an Inbox item, a window opens so you can view
   that message from a larger window without the other screen elements getting in
   the way.

23

5. Delete mail by selecting one or more message headers and dragging them to the Deleted Items icon. Deleted Items acts like the Windows Recycle Bin. Mail does not really go away until you delete items from the Deleted Items area by clicking on the Deleted Items icon and removing unwanted mail.

6. You can easily reply to a message's sender, or to the entire group if you were one of several sent mail, by clicking the Reply to Author or Reply to All toolbar button. In addition, when reading e-mail, you can compose a new message by clicking the Compose Message button on the toolbar.

23

TIME SAVER

Create new folders in the Area selection bar so you can organize your e-mail messages by business use, entertainment, stock trade confirmations, and other categories. Right-click over the bar and select New Folder. For example, you may want to create a new folder that holds business e-mail and another for personal e-mail. You can drag messages to either location to put mail together with others that match the same purpose.

As you can see, receiving e-mail with Outlook Express is easier than going to your front porch mailbox. From Internet Explorer you click the Mail icon and read your Inbox message *headers*. (A header is the sender ID and subject of the message that you see from the Inbox.)

TIME SAVER

When you're in Outlook Express, click the Outlook Express icon in the Area selection bar to see the one-click Outlook Express window shown in Figure 23.7. From this window you can easily read and compose e-mail, modify your Microsoft Address Book entries, locate people, and check newsgroups. (The next section describes newsgroup access.)

Figure 23.7.

The Outlook Express folder shows this one-step usage screen.

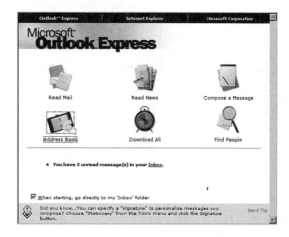

Using Newsgroups

In a way, a *newsgroup* acts like a combination of a slow e-mail program and a community bulletin board. Newsgroups have little or nothing to do with the daily news. Newsgroups are thousands of lists, arranged by subject, that hold messages and files you and others can post and read.

Suppose you are interested in rollerblading and want to trade the information you have with others who are interested in the sport. You could find one of the several newsgroups related to rollerblading and read the hundreds of messages and files posted to that newsgroup. Depending on the Internet service you use and the newsgroup filing rules, you may find messages months old or only from the past few days. Often, the larger newsgroups can keep only a limited number of days' worth of messages and files in the newsgroup.

This is how newsgroups act like slow e-mail services: If someone has posted a question you know the answer to, you can post a reply. Your reply will be seen by all in the newsgroup who want to read the reply. The person who submitted the question may never go back to the newsgroup to read the answer, but the postings are for anybody and everybody who are interested.

Each Internet ISP provides access to a different number of the thousands and thousands of newsgroups in existence. To see newsgroups available to your service, click the Mail button in Internet Explorer and select Read News. Although your ISP may give you access to thousands of newsgroups, you'll want to subscribe just to those that interest you. Click the Newsgroups button in Outlook Express to display the Newsgroups listing dialog box shown in Figure 23.8.

Figure 23.8.

Select the newsgroups to which you want to subscribe.

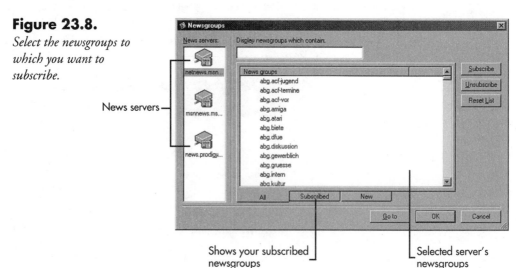

You may see one or more news servers in the left column. Each news server contains a different set of newsgroups. Your ISP determines the number of servers that appear in the news server column. When you click on a server, the list of newsgroups that reside on that server appears in the center of the window.

CAUTION

Some servers contain thousands of newsgroups that are downloaded into a list the first time you access a news server, so you can quickly scroll through the list in subsequent sessions. This download process may take a few minutes, as indicated by the dialog box that appears during the download.

23

Newsgroups have strange names such as `rec.pets.dogs` and `alt.algebra.help`. Table 23.1 describes what the more common newsgroup prefixes stand for. Somewhere else in the newsgroup name you can often glean more information about the newsgroup's primary topic; for example, a newsgroup named `rec.sport.skating.roller` would contain skating news and `alt.autos.italian` would contain files and messages pertaining to Italian cars.

Table 23.1. Common newsgroup prefixes describe the nature of the newsgroup.

Prefix	Description
alt	Groups that allow for informal content and are not necessarily as widely distributed as the other newsgroups
biz	Business-related newsgroups
comp	Computer-related newsgroups
gov	Government
misc	Random newsgroups
rec	Recreational and sporting newsgroups
rel	Religious
sci	Scientific newsgroups
soc	Social issue-related newsgroups
talk	Debate newsgroups

Scroll through the newsgroup list to find the newsgroups you want to see. When you find one or more newsgroups that interest you, subscribe to those newsgroups by double-clicking on the newsgroup name (or highlight the name and click Subscribe). If you click on the Subscribe tab, you'll see the list of newsgroups you've subscribed to. Click the OK button to close the Newsgroups window and prepare to read the news.

Enter a search topic in the text box at the top of the Newsgroups window to display newsgroups that contain that topic.

Reading and Posting Newsgroup News

Keep in mind that a message might be a short note or may be an entire file. As with e-mail, if a news posting contains a file, the file will come as an attachment to the message. The following steps explain how to read newsgroup messages and post messages to the newsgroups:

1. Start Internet Explorer and sign in to your Internet account.
2. Click the Mail button on the toolbar.
3. Select Read News. A list of your subscribed newsgroups appears as shown in Figure 23.9.

Figure 23.9.

Your subscribed newsgroup messages appear when you first request newsgroup access.

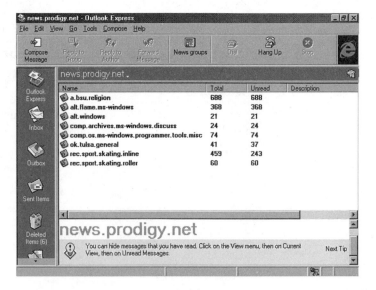

4. To read messages in a newsgroup, double-click on that newsgroup name. Figure 23.10 shows the newsgroups in the upper window and the text for the selected newsgroup in the lower window. Some long messages take awhile to arrive, and you won't see any of the message until the entire message downloads to your PC.

If a message has a plus sign next to it, click on the plus sign to open all related messages. If someone posts a question, for example, and several people reply to that posting, all those related messages group under the first question's message, and you

23

can see the replies only after you click the plus sign. The plus sign becomes a minus sign when you expand the newsgroup item, so you can collapse the item after you're finished with it.

Caution

> Some newsgroups are moderated better than others. You'll often find unrelated messages throughout all newsgroups that don't belong within that newsgroup.

23

Figure 23.10.

Scroll through the news message headers and see detail in the lower window.

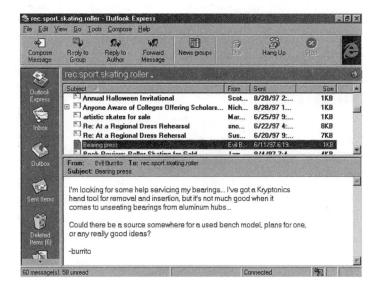

5. Check the Size column to determine whether you can read the message in the lower window or whether you should open up a new window to view the message. If a message is over 2KB or 3KB in size, you should probably double-click on the message header to view the message inside a scrollable window. The window contains a menu that enables you to save the message in a file on your disk for later retrieval. If a message has an attachment, you must open the message in a separate window to save the attachment as a file on your disk.

   After you've read a message inside the preview pane, you can click on another message header to view another message. If you view a message in a separate window, you can close the window to view a different message.

6. If you want to reply to a message, you have two options: Reply to the group, in which case everybody who subscribes to the newsgroup can read your reply (the general idea of newsgroups), or reply to the author privately via e-mail. The Reply

to Group and Reply to Author toolbar buttons accomplish this purpose. Each copies the original message at the bottom of your reply.

You don't have to reply to existing messages. You can also start a new message *thread* (related postings) by clicking the Compose Message button and typing a new message. Your message appears in the newsgroup as a new post and not part of a chain of previous postings.

Probably the biggest problem with newsgroups is the time you waste in them. You may hop over to a newsgroup to see if the group contains an answer you need and two hours later you're still reading the postings there. Newsgroups can provide a wealth of information on thousands and thousands of topics. Although the Web is great for organizing information into collections of pages, newsgroups are useful for the straight messages and files that people want to share with each other.

Summary

This hour explained how to use Outlook Express, Internet Explorer's e-mail program and newsgroup manager. E-mail is a major part of the Internet user's life today. You'll appreciate Outlook Express's advanced support and e-mail management simplicity.

If you want detailed information on a subject, you can search the Web for all kinds of data, but remember to look for related newsgroups as well. Whereas some Web sites are often consumer-related collections of merchandise and hype, newsgroups often contain thousands of messages from people such as yourself who have questions and answers to provide to others with the same interest.

Q&A

Q How can I get e-mail from my multiple Internet accounts?

A If you subscribe to multiple online services or to multiple ISPs, you can set up Outlook Express to send and retrieve e-mail from all your Internet accounts. Select Tools | Accounts to display the Internet Accounts dialog box. Select Add | Mail and follow the wizard to add your accounts to the e-mail. You will almost surely have to contact your ISP to get the information that the wizard will request. After you set up the accounts, Outlook Express will check each one when you request new mail.

Q I read a newsgroup message last month that I can no longer find in the newsgroup. How can I see old messages?

A Often you can't. Each news server holds a limited number of messages (your news server has only so much disk space). Outlook Express downloads at most 300

23

messages at any one time. Sometimes the server will have more than 300 messages that are available. To request that Outlook Express retrieve additional messages, select Tools | Get Next 300 Headers. If more than 300 messages are available, Outlook Express will download up to 300 more.

23

PART VI

Hour 24

A PC Communications Center

This hour broadens the discussion of remote PC communications by introducing you to the world of electronic faxing by using your PC. You'll learn how to expand the use of Windows to manage, send, and receive faxes directly from your PC. Most modems sold in the last five years have fax send and receive capabilities. You'll be able to find your faxing numbers quickly because the Windows Address Book program keeps track of your contacts.

To wrap up your 24-hour tutorial, this hour ends with a short discussion about networking. By communicating with other PCs through a network, you can share files and printers between two or more PCs. You'll gain efficiency and save on hardware costs by creating a network such as this.

The highlights of this hour include

- ☐ Where to access the Windows Address Book
- ☐ How to manage your Address Book contacts
- ☐ How to send faxes
- ☐ How to receive faxes
- ☐ What you need to network PCs

The Windows Address Book

The *Windows Address Book* is the central repository of name, address, e-mail, and phone information for Windows. You can store your contacts in the Address Book and then access that information from Outlook Express, the Microsoft Fax program, as well as other more advanced fax programs you add to your PC. (Microsoft Fax is discussed in the next section.)

JUST A MINUTE

> Not everyone uses the Windows Address Book for their PC contact information, but Microsoft seems to be moving users toward the Address Book for several reasons. By using the central repository of information, all programs that need access to your contact information will be able to look in one location for it. You won't have to maintain separate lists for your faxing software, your e-mail addresses, and your name and address mailing lists.

Access the Windows Address Book through the Start menu or from Outlook Express. Follow these steps to maintain your Address Book and make new entries in it:

1. If you have Outlook Express open, click on the top-level Outlook Express folder to display the overview menu and then click on the Address Book icon to start the Address Book program. Your Address Book will appear. Figure 24.1 shows an Address Book with several entries. (If this is the first time you or anyone else on your computer has accessed the Address Book, your Address Book will be empty).

Figure 24.1.

The Windows Address Book holds many details.

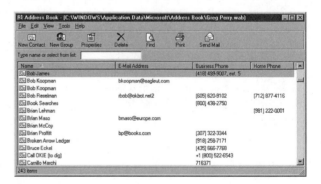

If you want, you can add information to your Address Book now. To get you started, the next few steps walk through the addition of a sample entry.

2. Click the left-hand toolbar button labeled New Contact. Address Book displays an empty, tabbed dialog box like the one in Figure 24.2. The tabs give you several fields of information for the contact you want to enter. You can track a contact's

24

personal and business numbers and addresses, e-mail addresses, and personal Web page if the contact has one. After you enter a contact, click OK to store that contact in the Address Book file. The contact will be available from both Outlook Express and from Windows' faxing programs that use the Address Book.

Figure 24.2.

You can enter a new contact's information.

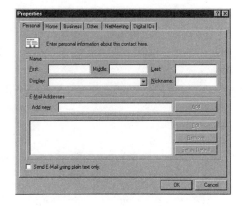

3. To edit a contact in the Address Book, double-click on the entry. The entry's information appears so that you can change or add new information. When you click OK, the change will appear in the Address Book files.

4. If you want to collect several entries into a *group*, click the toolbar's New Group button to display the group Properties dialog box, as shown in Figure 24.3. Suppose that you want the capability to send e-mail or faxes to all employees in your department. Enter your department name for the Group Name field and then select all the department's employees from the list that appears when you click the Select Members button. All members you send to the Members list box will appear in the group when you click OK. Subsequently, when you send a fax to all members of the group, you can send the fax to the group name instead to sending a separate fax to each department employee.

TIME SAVER

When entering a group's members, you may run across one or two names that you haven't entered into the underlying contact information. To add new contacts to the Address Book while working on new groups, click the New Contact button.

The Address Book is an integral part of the faxing and e-mail services for Windows. Not only does Outlook Express support the Address Book files, but also the Windows Phone Dialer and most other Windows-based communications applications on your system can read the Address Book. Over time, the information you store in the Address Book will be valuable because you'll use that information for so many things.

Figure 24.3.

Create groups of related
contacts.

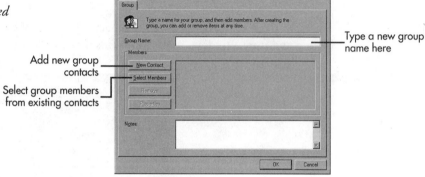

Type a new group
name here

Add new group
contacts

Select group members
from existing contacts

TIME SAVER

If you use Microsoft Word's mail merge capabilities, you can access the Address Book from within Word. That way you don't have to keep a separate address book for each program. Mail merge enables you to send a customized letter, based on a form letter that you create, to selected entries in your Address Book.

Introduction to Microsoft Fax

Microsoft Fax is capable of turning your computer into a fax command center as long as you have a combined fax and modem. When you install your fax/modem, you'll be able to select it instead of a printer from within your favorite Windows word processor.

If you send a document fax to another user who happens to have Windows answering his fax/modem, Microsoft Fax actually sends the document itself so that the receiver gets the fax in the form of a document file inside the Outlook Express Inbox. If the recipient has a standard fax machine or a computer fax that doesn't use Windows, the recipient gets a standard fax transmission.

TIME SAVER

As soon as you start using Microsoft Fax, Windows turns on the faxing support in the background. A fax machine will appear next to your taskbar's clock. You can click on the fax machine icon to see the fax options currently set.

24

JUST A MINUTE The Windows-based faxing service, Microsoft Fax, is by far *not* the best faxing program on the market. Its primary advantage is its cost—free. If you send and receive faxes quite a bit in your home or office, you'll want to invest in more powerful faxing software such as WinFax Pro. Such software enables you to edit received faxes onscreen, file faxes easily, and manage your faxes using much more power than is available in Microsoft Fax.

Faxing Easily

Much of the time, sending a fax means using your word processor to type what you want to send and then printing to the fax/modem connected to your computer. If the document is already saved to the disk, you can fax directly from within Microsoft Fax to any recipient in the Address Book. The following steps show you how easily you can fax from the Windows WordPad word processor:

1. Start WordPad and type a paragraph of text.
2. Select File | Print.
3. Display the drop-down list box labeled Name, and select Microsoft Fax for your destination printer. Microsoft Fax begins with the Compose New Fax window when you click OK.
4. Click the Next button to display the Compose New Fax dialog box, shown in Figure 24.4.

Figure 24.4.

Microsoft Fax is getting ready to send your fax.

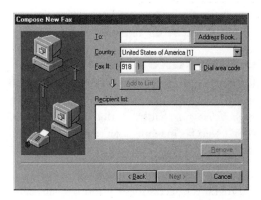

5. If the recipient's name and fax number appear in your Address Book, click the Address Book button to switch to the Address Book, and then select the name. Otherwise, type a name and number to whom you want to send the fax and click Add to List to add the name to the list of recipients at the bottom of the screen. You can enter additional recipients if you like.

6. Click the Next button and choose the cover page style that you want. Microsoft Fax includes several standard cover pages, or you can choose No to send only the document without a cover page. In addition, the Start menu's Fax menu includes a Cover Page Editor program. Use the Cover Page Editor to edit the cover pages that come with Microsoft Fax or create your own cover pages by using the text and drawing tools available in the program.

   If you want to send the fax sometime in the future, click the Options button to set the sending time (don't change the options now).

7. Click the Next and Finish buttons to send the fax. You can go on to your next task in Windows while Microsoft Fax sends the fax—you don't have to wait for it to send.

TIME SAVER

> If you want to fax an existing file directly from Microsoft Fax, select the Start menu and then choose Programs | Accessories | Fax | Compose New Fax. After the New Fax Wizard begins, you select or enter a fax recipient and the files you want to send. (To see the Fax menu, you must have installed Microsoft Fax previously, through the Control Panel Add/ Remove Windows Setup dialog box.)

8. Microsoft Fax tells you when the fax is finished. At that point, close the application or resend the fax if the line was busy or didn't answer. If the line was busy or didn't answer, double-click the fax sheet by the taskbar clock to send the fax again.

Microsoft Fax makes faxing almost as easy as printing a document on a printer. Fax all your documents and graphics files from Windows. If the recipient is also using Windows, the recipient will receive the file in its native format.

Receiving Faxes

Unless you are already set up to receive faxes, Windows doesn't make the procedure for receiving faxes obvious. To receive faxes, you must start another Windows program called *Windows Messaging*. Sadly, Outlook Express does not support faxing services at this time. If you don't see a fax machine icon to the left of your taskbar's clock, you cannot receive faxes. To set up your computer to receive faxes, follow these steps:

1. Start Windows Messaging by selecting the Start menu and then selecting Programs | Accessories | Windows Messaging program.

2. Select Tools | Microsoft Fax Tools | Options.

3. Click the Modem tab to display the Modem dialog box, shown in Figure 24.5.

24

Figure 24.5.

*Setting up the modem
to receive faxes.*

4. In the Available Fax Modems list, click your fax/modem to highlight the modem name if it's not already highlighted.

5. Click Properties to display the Properties dialog box.

6. To receive only faxes, click on the Answer After option and enter the number of rings you want to occur before Microsoft Fax receives the fax. (If you receive both faxes and voice calls on the line, click on the Manual option. When you get a call, Microsoft Fax will display a button that you can click to answer the fax, or you can pick up the phone if the call is a voice call. You'll have to know when you're expecting a fax to click when needed.) The Don't Answer option makes Microsoft Fax ignore all incoming calls.

7. Click OK twice to close the dialog boxes and return to Windows Messaging.

If you don't see a fax machine icon on your Windows taskbar, you will see the icon after you complete this task. The Microsoft Fax program sends and receives faxes, but you must load the program first.

TIME SAVER

If you've turned off the receipt of faxes, you can still receive a fax that you know is incoming by selecting Request a Fax from the Fax menu on the Accessories Start menu.

JUST A MINUTE

You might want to change the redial properties on the Microsoft Fax properties sheet's Dialing page. The redialing properties determine the number of retries to attempt when a faxed number is busy or does not answer and specifies the time to wait between retries.

Disable Call Waiting!

If you have call waiting, you'll need to disable it before using your modem for fax or data transmissions. Fortunately, you can disable call waiting very easily. Open the Modems dialog box from the Control Panel and click the Dialing Properties button to see the dialog box shown in Figure 24.6.

Click on the Disable Call Waiting by Dialing option, and then enter the code to disable your call waiting feature; this code is usually *#70*. When you close the Dialing Properties dialog box, Windows disables call waiting before each outgoing fax call.

Figure 24.6.

You can disable call waiting.

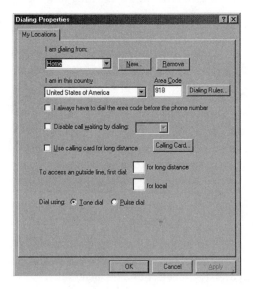

CAUTION

#70 usually, but not always, disables the call waiting feature. Check with your local phone company to make sure that you enter the correct code. Often, you'll find the code in the front of your phone book.

24

Introducing Networked PCs

Consider this scenario: You're tired of trying to run today's software on your slow PC. You go out and purchase the latest and greatest PC with a huge hard disk and lightening-fast video. What do you do with your old PC? If it runs today's software, albeit slowly, you don't just want to throw it away. Used PCs don't sell for much money. Why not network your two PCs?

Communication does not always happen over phone lines by voice and fax. When you network an office or even a home with multiple PCs, you can communicate among all the PCs by sending e-mail and files. One of the biggest benefits of networking multiple PCs is that you save money on hardware. The PCs do not need separate printers, for example. Instead of purchasing two inexpensive printers, buy a better printer and share it between two PCs. In addition to printer sharing, you can also share files.

TIME SAVER

Networks make for more accurate file integrity. Instead of keeping two Address Book data files on each PC, for example, keep just one and the other PCs on the network can access it. When you make a change to the Address Book, all PCs connected to the network will know about the change. With separate Address Book files on each of the PCs, you won't know which are current.

CAUTION

Networking is easier than ever with Windows and today's networking hardware. Nevertheless, networking is still fairly technical and, if problems arise, can be difficult to fix if something goes wrong. For a more complete coverage on networking, check out Sams Publishing's *Absolute Beginner's Guide to Networking* for one of the best introductions to practical networking that you'll find.

Many of today's games let networked users compete against one another. Your children will think you're grand if you network your PCs and set up a few of these multi-player games between the machines.

Some Network Specifics

Several types of networks are available depending on your needs. Although nobody agrees on the single best network for all uses, a home or small business network consisting of the following elements is probably your best beginning:

- **LAN (Local Area Network)**: A network of PCs located in one place, such as a building, as opposed to a *WAN* (*Wide Area Network*) that connects two or more PCs via telephone lines or satellite.

- **Peer-to-peer**: Each PC connected to the network is considered a peer—that is, equal—with other PCs. The opposite of a peer-to-peer network is a *client/server network*, in which you dedicate one PC (the *server*) as the master PC where all networked files are stored and served to the *server* PCs connected to the network. A client/server network is often more efficient than a peer-to-peer network, but the server PC must be used only as a server.

- **Ethernet-Based Network Interface Card (NIC)**: The expansion card located inside each PC that enables PCs to communicate with each other. The Ethernet system is the most common and efficient for small businesses and home-based networks.

- **10BASE2 Coax Cabling**: The cabling between the networked PCs that resembles cable television wire.

- **Connectors and Terminators**: Each PC requires a *T-connector* so that the network cable can run to the PC and then pass through to the next PC on the network. The final PC requires a terminator plug to inform the network that no more PCs exist.

You can take this list to your PC store and start buying *or* you can take advantage of some instant networking products on the market that package all these components together. One of the most popular is *Network in a Box* from LinkSys. Several other networking products exist as well. These all-in-one packages provide all the necessary Ethernet peer-to-peer hardware you need, as well as the cabling and connectors. Purchase one kit for each PC you want to network, install the network cards into each PC's empty expansion slot, run the cabling, and you're in business.

The instructions with the networking kits explain some of the problems you'll encounter as you set up your network. Even the simplest network can be tricky to set up, but you're fortunate that, starting with Windows 95, Windows offers strong support for local area networks. Although your networking software setup, combined with Windows, may take a while to configure (again, the networking kit's instructions should be able to help with all problem scenarios because these kits are designed for networking newcomers), you'll soon be sharing files and printers. You'll be glad that you've pumped new life into that second PC that you couldn't figure out how to get rid of.

JUST A MINUTE

To load or save a file on a networked PC, instead of selecting a disk drive on your PC, you'll first select one of the networked PCs and *then* select a disk drive on that PC. After you select a folder, you'll be able to save or retrieve the file.

24

Summary

This hour explained how to use the Windows Address Book program to work as the central messaging center for your computer. The central repository of information in Address Book prevents you from having to keep the same information stored several places in Windows.

Microsoft Fax integrates your fax/modem to work with all Windows applications that print. Instead of going to the printer, the fax documents will route through Microsoft Fax so that you can send the document to a recipient within the Address Book or to a new recipient whose fax number you enter. One of the most interesting features of Microsoft Fax is the recipient analysis that Microsoft Fax makes. If the recipient is running Windows, the recipient receives your fax as a normal Windows document file instead of as a fax. That way the recipient has more flexibility in working with the file than if he received the document as a paper fax.

To really communicate with other PCs, especially the other PCs in your own building, consider a peer-to-peer network. The network enables you to communicate with other users on your network (faster than e-mail over the Internet), share files, and share peripheral devices.

24

Q&A

Q How do I copy my old phone dialing program's address book to Address Book?

A Try the File menu's Import | Address Book command. Address Book imports from these formats (and possibly more depending on the release date of your Windows): Eudora Pro, Eudora Light, Microsoft Exchange Personal Address Book, Microsoft Internet Mail for 3.1 Address Book, Netscape Address Book, and a special format called *comma-separated text files*, in which you can store data from most programs by using the File | Save As command.

Q I don't know whether I'm faxing to a recipient running Microsoft Fax under Windows. Do I fax, or send my file as e-mail?

A As long as you have a recipient's fax number, go ahead and fax the document. If the recipient is running Windows, your copy of Windows will know that right away and, instead of sending a fax, it will automatically send a document as if it were e-mail. If the recipient has a standard fax machine, your Windows system will know that, too, and send the document by using a standard fax signal.

Q What is the best way to run cables from room to room?

A Technically, running network cabling is safer than electrical cabling so you don't have to worry much about electrical shock. (Don't share conduit with electrical wires, however, because you'll probably violate safety codes, put yourself in danger, and even cause interference with the network from radiant signals in the electrical wires running along with the network cable.)

If you must run cabling from an attic down to rooms, consider calling an electrician for help. Electricians know all about running wires and cables through walls and around attic areas. They have the fishing tools needed to pull cable from hard-to-reach locations as well. In addition, they have the proper crimping tools to attach network connectors to the wire they run through the walls.

Glossary

10Base2 coaxial   A type of cable used in many networking environments that sends the network signal through a shielded wire resembling cable television wire.

8086, 8088, 80286 (286), 80386 (386), 80486 (486)   Pre-Pentium CPU incarnations from the first IBM-PC.

A

A-B box   See *switchbox.*

Access time   The average speed of a disk drive when locating data on the disk's platter.

active matrix   One of the most readable laptop monitor screen specifications.

ActiveMovie   A Windows program that plays video files.

AMD   Advanced Micro Devices, a manufacturer that competes against Intel.

America Online (AOL)   One of the most popular online services.

analog signal   A continuous signal that rises and falls gradually, such as the spoken voice. Your PC cannot work with analog signals but requires digital signals.

AOL   See *America Online.*

application program   A program, such as a word processor, that does specific work.

artificial intelligence   The capability of computers to learn.

AT&T WorldNet   A nationwide Internet service provider.

AutoComplete   The capability of some software programs to complete the typing of a word or phrase after you've typed only the first portion.

AutoPlay   The process that starts a CD-ROM installation or program execution (if you've already installed the program) when you insert a CD-ROM into a drive.

B

backup   A copy of your hard disk drive's contents.

backup file set   (Also called a *backup job* in some Windows versions) A predetermined list of files to back up that you can create.

backup set label   A descriptive name that labels a particular backup.

banks   The rows of memory inside your system unit.

baud rate   The maximum number of bits transmitted over the modem in a second.

beta release   The test version of software that companies release to users for feedback.

binary data   Compressed data such as programs and graphics as opposed to text files.

BIOS (Basic Input/Output System)   ROM-based instructions that describe how your PC interacts with its devices.

bit   One-eighth of a byte of storage.

Boolean expression   Combined words and phrases that help you perform searches, such as locating only articles that contain a certain item you're looking for.

boot disk   The disk drive that contains your PC's initial startup information.

booting   The process of turning on or restarting your PC.

browser   A program that enables you to traverse Internet Web pages.

bug   A computer error.

bulletin board systems (BBS)   A non-Internet–based computer system that you can dial from your PC and retrieve software updates by phone.

bus   A data connection on which data flows to or from a peripheral device.

byte   One character (alphabetic, numeric, or a special character) of storage.

C

cable modem   A modem that transmits and receives data over your television cable.

cache   A temporary storage location between the RAM and the CPU.

caret   Another name for your text cursor (also called the *insertion point*).

CD Player   A Windows program that enables you to control CD audio music.

CD-ROM   A storage device that accesses compact disc-based information and also plays audio CDs. New CD drives are now available that enable you to record onto the discs.

CD-ROM caddy   A plastic box you insert into some older CD-ROM drives that holds the CD-ROM.

cell   In a spreadsheet, a rectangle formed by the intersection of a row and column that holds a number, formula, or text that you enter.

Chat rooms   Areas of interest, sorted by topic—such as *PC Support, Teen TV, Religious Talk, Windows Troubleshooting, Politics,* and *Movies*—where you can talk (by typing) to others connected to the same chat room area.

chip puller   A tool with which you can easily remove integrated circuit chips.

client/server network   A network of PCs in which one PC, the *server*, is not used as a typical PC but dedicated to storing and offering access to files and printers to the other PCs, the *clients*, on the network.

clip art files   Files that contain collections of scanned drawings and photos you can use in your own publications and Web pages.

Clipboard   A special area of memory that temporarily holds data.

close   The process of quitting a program or getting rid of an open window.

CMOS (Complementary Metal-Oxide Semiconductor)   Memory that holds information about your PC hardware.

common dialog box   A dialog box that appears across several programs in the same manner for consistency.

compiler   A program that encrypts and compacts another program so it can be distributed without users being able to modify it.

CompuServe   An online service.

Control Panel   A window on the Windows desktop from which you can modify your PC's configuration.

controller card   An expansion card that enables you to control disks and CD-ROMs.

convention   Naming standards for files and PC devices.

CPU (Central Processing Unit)   An integrated circuit chip that processes the data flowing in and out of your PC. Also called a *microprocessor*.

crash   The failure of a disk drive.

CRT (Cathode Ray Tube)   See *monitor*.

cursor   Items on your screen, such as vertical bars or arrows, that show where the next text character will appear or where the mouse is currently pointing.

Cyrix   A manufacturer of microprocessors that competes against Intel.

D

data   Raw facts and figures. The singular for *data* is *datum* but the data processing industry often uses *data* in both the singular and plural.

database   A program that enables you to manage, view, and report large amounts of data.

default   A command or location that the PC will assume if you don't enter overriding information.

defragment   The process of removing the empty gaps left on a disk drive by deleted disk files.

desktop   The background screen on which program and data windows appear in a graphical user environment.

desktop PC   A PC that is small enough to fit on your desk.

desktop publisher   An application program you can use to polish writing and create newspaper- and magazine-like publications.

dialog box   An onscreen message box with multiple controls used for input.

differential backup   A backup in which you save only changes you've made to your disk since your most recent full-disk backup. Also called an *incremental backup*.

digital camera   A camera that stores digital pictures for input into a PC.

digital signals   Signals that rise and fall in distinct, discrete steps so a computer can read and write them.

DIMMs (Double Inline Memory Modules)   A small board that contains two rows of memory chips (usually nine chips reside on each row).

DIP memory (Dual Inline Packages)   Memory chips used in older pre-486 PCs.

DIP switches   Switches on an electronic circuit board that determine data flow and configuration values.

directory   See *folder*.

disk   A removable, magnetically coated disk enclosed in a plastic case that you insert into floppy disk drives (also called *diskettes*, *floppy disks*, *floppy diskettes*, and *floppies*).

Disk Defragmenter   The Windows program that defragments your PC's disk drives.

disk drive   A high-speed computer storage device that enables you to store and retrieve information.

DMA channel   A value that specifies which data path a device takes when exchanging data with the CPU.

dot pitch   The measurement between two pixels on a monitor.

dot-matrix   A printer that uses a rectangular print head comprised of pins that strike a ribbon in different combinations forming characters on the paper.

download   Retrieving data from a remote computer.

drive bays   Expansion slots in your system unit where you can install disk and CD-ROM drives.

driver   A software routine that tells Windows how to communicate with specific hardware.

DriveSpace   The Windows program that compresses your disk drive to give you more space.

drop-down list box   A special Windows control that works like a scrolling list but consumes much less screen space.

DVD (Digital Video Discs)   Disc-based storage drives that read and write several gigabytes worth of data and have the capacity to hold an entire movie on one DVD disc.

E

EDO (Extended Data Out)   High-speed RAM memory.

EIDE (Enhanced Intelligent Drive Electronics)   A new disk drive standard that allows for faster drives than drives that use the older ISA interface.

EISA (Enhanced Industry Standard Architecture)   An advanced expansion slot that accepts both the ISA standard and the faster EISA standard.

electronic spreadsheet   See *spreadsheet*.

e-mail (electronic mail)   Mail transferred between recipients over modems, network connections, and the Internet.

Encarta   Microsoft's CD-ROM–based multimedia encyclopedia.

Energy Star compliant   An energy-saving standard designed for PC equipment (also called *MPR compliant*).

ergonomic   Designed for human comfort or safety.

Ethernet   The most efficient and most common networking technology for PC networks.

event   Something that occurs in Windows, such as a mouse movement, keyboard click, or window closing.

expansion cards   Printer circuit cards that enable you to expand your PC's capabilities by adding items such as modems, sound, and new disk drive controls.

expansion slots   Locations inside your system unit into which you can insert expansion cards that add functionality to your PC.

Expedia   An Internet travel site that lets you plan trips and book car, hotel, and airline reservations online.

Explorer   The name of the Windows utility program that enables you to view and manage disk drives and folders.

extended CDs   Audio compact discs that contain digital information you can read from a PC such as the music's lyrics and the cover art.

F

field   An area on the screen where you enter information such as a name. Also called a text box.

file   A collection of related information stored on a disk or tape drive.

filename   The name given to a file.

filename extension   A filename's three-letter suffix that indicates the nature of the file.

fixed disk   A disk inside a disk drive, such as a hard disk, that you cannot remove from the drive.

flat-rate pricing plan   A monthly online service payment plan where you pay one monthly fee no matter how much (or how little) you use the service.

floppy disk   See *disk*.

floppy disk drive   The device that holds the disks you insert and communicates the disk's data to and from your PC.

folder   A collection of related files (also called a *directory* in pre-Windows 95 terminology).

font   A character's style or design.

footprint   The desktop or floor space that a PC or peripheral device takes up.

force feedback joystick   A joystick that jolts, jars, and shakes in response to the game in progress.

format   To prepare a new floppy disk or hard disk for use.

fragmented disk drive   A disk drive with gaps left by deleted files.

FrontPage   Software that helps you design and create Web pages.

FTP (File Transfer Protocol)   A standard that enables you to transfer files to and from other Internet-connected computers.

G

gigabyte   Approximately one million characters of storage.

GPS (Global Positioning Satellite)   Hardware that returns your current longitude and latitude.

graphical environment   An operating system, such as Windows, that displays information using both text and graphics.

graphical user interface (GUI)   See *graphical environment*.

H

hardware   The physical components of your PC.

header   The Inbox's one-line display that shows incoming messages' sender, subject, and date received.

heat sink   A device that removes heat from an electronic component.

home page   A Web page that displays when you first connect to the Internet. Also a term used for Web pages that individuals and companies design for the Internet.

home-brew PCs   The name applied to PCs that you assemble yourself.

host drive   The drive used to organize your compressed disk drive.

hot link   See *hotspot*.

hotspot   An area of the screen linked to another location that you can click to view different information. Also called a *hot link* or a *hypertext link*.

HTML (Hypertext Markup Language)   The language behind Internet Web pages.

I

icons   Small pictures on the screen that represent data, programs, windows, file types, and commands.

Inbox   The Outlook Express folder that holds your incoming e-mail. Other e-mail programs, such as Windows Messaging and Microsoft Exchange, also use the Inbox folder for incoming messages.

incremental backup   See *differential backup*.

information   Meaningful data grouped together in a manner you can use to make decisions.

infrared interface   A peripheral's wireless interface to the PC. Some keyboards use an infrared interface so that you don't have to attach the keyboard to the PC with a cable.

inkjet printer   A printer that shoots ink onto paper to produce the output.

input devices   Peripheral devices, such as a keyboard and mouse, that send information to your PC.

installation routine   The procedure needed to put software onto a PC.

integrated circuit chip (IC)   A small device located inside your PC's system unit that is so compact, it can house millions of electronic parts in an area the size of a matchbook.

Intel   The company that designs the most popular CPUs used inside PCs.

interlaced   Specifies the way a monitor's pixels overlap each other for clarity.

Internet   A world-wide system of interconnected computers.

Internet Explorer   Microsoft's Web browser provided free of charge from the Internet and with most major Microsoft software.

Internet Phone   Software that enables you to talk to other users on the Internet.

I/O   A computer abbreviation that stands for *Input/Output*.

I/O address   The memory location mapped to a specific peripheral device.

IRQ   An *interrupt request* number specifies the CPU signal value that refers to a particular peripheral device. When a CPU issues that signal, such as the IRQ for a modem, that device knows that the CPU wants its attention.

ISA (Industry Standard Architecture)   A hardware interface for expansion cards and disk drives.

ISDN modem (Integrated Services Digital Network)   A modem that transmits data over an ISDN line that offers faster performance speeds than regular analog lines.

ISP (Internet Service Provider)   A company that supplies Internet access to individuals and companies.

J

JAZ   A type of high-capacity removable disk drive.

jewel case   A thin, square plastic case that protects CD-ROMs from dust and scratches.

jumpers   Connectors that connect two pins together out of a series of three or more pins.

K

K56Flex   Along with *X2*, one of two modem standards capable of transmitting data at speeds as high as 56KB.

keyboard   The most frequently used input device with alphabetic, numeric, and special characters that you type to get data into your PC.

kilobyte (KB)   Approximately one thousand characters and exactly 1,024 characters.

L

LAN (Local Area Network)   A set of networked computers located within close proximity of each other and linked together without modems or other longer-distance connections.

laptop   A small PC that travels easily.

laser printer   A printer that uses a laser beam to burn toner ink onto paper to produce the output.

legacy hardware   Old, often outdated computer hardware that doesn't necessarily conform to today's standards and requirements.

license   The right to run software.

lithium ion   A type of laptop battery that is easier to keep charged to full capacity than other kinds of batteries.

logical disk   See *partition*.

M

mailing lists   Free (usually) subscription-based Internet services that send you any and all new messages and files posted to the mailing lists you choose as e-mail.

mainframes   Computers that several hundred or thousand users can share at one time. Mainframes are used by banks, universities, and large companies for their data processing.

master   Your boot drive.

mathematical operator   Special symbols inside formulas that perform calculations.

MCA (Micro Channel Architecture)   An IBM-developed expansion standard that improved upon previous expansion board standards.

media   Disks, tapes, paper, and other items on which data appears.

megabyte (MB)   Approximately one million characters (also called a *meg*).

megahertz (MHz)   Represents the speed of your CPU in millions of instructions per second.

memory   Storage inside your computer system.

microcomputers   Small desktop and laptop computers based on a small CPU-integrated circuit chip.

microprocessor   See *CPU*.

Microsoft Bookshelf   A multimedia-based program that offers complete reference books online.

Microsoft Network   See *MSN*.

MIDI files   Sound files that can contain complete reproductions of musical instruments.

millisecond (ms)   One-thousandth of a second.

minicomputers   Computers about the size of a refrigerator that work in a multiprocessor environment and generally support more storage and memory than PCs.

mini-tower   A PC whose case is a small, upright box that sits on the floor, or possibly on your desk if you have adequate vertical room.

MMX   Multimedia instructions embedded directly into some of the newer Intel Pentium processors.

modem   A device that enables your PC to communicate with other computers over phone lines.

monitor   The television-like video screen that shows PC output, also called a *CRT*.

monochrome monitors   Monitors that display one color only.

motherboard   The board inside the computer system that holds your memory and CPU.

mouse   A palm-sized device with two or more buttons that users roll around the desk to move a selection pointer (see *cursor*) around the screen.

MS-DOS   The pre-Windows operating system that uses a text environment and requires that you enter commands.

MSN (*Microsoft Network*)   Microsoft's entry into the online service market.

multimedia   The collection of sound, graphics, and video that come together on today's PCs.

multitasking   The process of doing two or more operations at the same time (or appearing to perform two or more tasks at the same time).

My Computer   A window on the Windows desktop that contains a description of your computer's hardware and files.

N

nanosecond (ns)   One-billionth of a second.

Netscape Navigator   A strong competitor to Microsoft's Internet Explorer Web browser.

network   Two or more computers connected together for file and peripheral sharing.

network interface card (NIC)   The card that you must install in an empty expansion slot to make your PC network-ready.

newsgroups   Discussion areas that hold files and messages related to specific topics.

non-volatile   A system on which the contents are not erased when the power goes off.

OCR software (Optical Character Recognition)   Software that converts scanned text to text files that you can edit with your word processor.

Oil Change   Software that automatically updates your PC's programs from Internet-based updates.

online   The state of a printer that is ready to print. This term is also used when you're connected to an online service or to the Internet.

online service   A dial-up computer service that offers news, sports, special interest, and possibly Internet information.

open   The process of starting a program, loading a data file, or displaying a window.

operating environment   The way your PC's operating system works with its users.

operating system   A system program that manages your PC's resources, such as memory and the modem.

orientation   The direction of the printed output on paper.

OS/2   IBM's operating system designed to compete with Windows.

Outbox   The Outlook Express folder that holds your outgoing e-mail that has yet to be sent. After Outlook Express sends the message, the Sent Items folder holds a copy of the message. Other e-mail programs also use the Outbox folder for outgoing mail.

Outlook 97   A program that comes with Office 97 that manages contacts, e-mail, and schedules.

Outlook Express   A Windows program that manages both your e-mail and newsgroup access.

output devices   Peripheral devices that send information from your PC to you, such as a printer and monitor.

OverDrive   A speed-up chip for Intel CPUs.

P

page preview   A full-screen view of a page of output that enables you to see how a printed page will look before you print to paper.

Paint   A Windows program with which you can draw color pictures.

parallel   A type of port connection (most often used for a printer).

parity   A memory-checking scheme used to determine if a memory location has the correct contents.

parse   To sift or sort through something, such as a list of commands that your PC must process in a given order.

partition   An area on a hard disk that acts like a distinct and separate disk, but is really just part of a single, larger disk. Also called a *logical disk*.

pass-through connector   A connector to which you attach two devices, enabling the data for one device not to interfere with the other device's data.

patch   A small program update that fixes a minor bug, but one that does not add any significant features.

path, **pathname**   The specific location of a file.

PC (Personal Computer)   A microcomputer (desktop or laptop) that conforms to the IBM-PC standard started by IBM in the early 1980s. Today's PCs primarily run the Windows operating systems.

PC card   A small expansion card (about the size of a credit card) that extends a laptop's capabilities (also called a *PCMCIA card*).

PC compatible   Software and hardware that run on computers that conform to the IBM-PC standard as opposed to a different standard, such as the Macintosh.

PCI (Peripheral Component Interconnect)   A hardware expansion connection that automatically adjusts its own hardware settings, such as IRQ, I/O address, and DMA channel values.

peer-to-peer   A set of networked PCs in which all are used and no one PC is dedicated to the sharing of files to the other PCs.

Pentium   The name of the latest Intel CPU that powers many of today's PCs. Several versions of the Pentium exist, such as the *Pentium Pro, Pentium Pro/MMX*, and the *Pentium II*.

peripheral device   A device, such as your floppy disk drive, printer, or monitor, that gets data to and from your PC's CPU.

photo CD   A CD-ROM drive that can read and display images from a CD with photographs stored on it.

PIM (Personal Information Manager)   An application program that enables you to store and organize your appointment book, calendar, and contact information.

pixel (*picture element*)   One dot on a monitor that, along with the other dots, comprises the picture and text displayed.

Plug and Play   The Windows technology that enables automatic detection and installation of software drivers for the new hardware that you attach to your PC.

port   A connector on the back of your PC into which you plug an external device, such as a printer.

PostScript   A special printer language that some desktop publishing software accesses to produce special effects on paper, such as printed watermarks on the background of the page.

PostScript emulation   Capable of supporting the PostScript standard.

power strip   A strip of electrical outlets, often with a power button, into which you can plug your PC and peripheral devices. Power strips often act as surge protectors.

power supply   A box inside your system unit that regulates electrical current coming into your PC and distributes that current to the devices in the system unit.

presentation program   A program that enables you to create custom overheads and handouts for audience presentations.

print job   A set of printer output.

printer subsystem   The routines that control all printing from within Windows.

Prodigy   An online service.

program   A set of instructions, stored in a file with a filename, that tell the computer what to do.

programmer   Someone who writes computer programs.

programming language   A computer language that programmers use to write programs.

PS/2 port   A popular, round port connector on the back of some system units for mice.

Q

query   A request to a database that results in returned data that meets a specific criteria.

queue   The list of print jobs waiting to print.

R

RAM (Random Access Memory)   Volatile short-term memory storage that holds data and programs as you use your PC.

read-only Web page   A Web page that contains frames and other advanced HTML code that cannot be changed.

record   A single entry of related data in a database.

Registry   A database of Windows system and program information needed for proper Windows operation.

resizing handles   Small boxes on selected images that you can use to drag or resize graphic images.

resolution   A printer and monitor measurement that dictates how clear the output appears.

ribbon cable   A flat data cable on which data flows to and from a storage device.

ROM (Read-Only Memory)   Non-volatile memory, whose contents are never erased, that contains start-up instructions for your PC.

root   The top-level folder on a disk drive.

S

ScanDisk   The Windows program that checks your disk drive for problems.

scanner   An input device that reads printed material and sends that material to the PC in electronic form.

screen savers   Programs that constantly change your screen's output when you're not using the monitor.

scrollbars   Bars you can click to adjust the information showing on the monitor.

SCSI (Small Computer System Interface)   A high-speed peripheral interface that enables you to chain together up to seven devices on one expansion card connection.

SDRAM (Synchronous Dynamic RAM)   The fastest RAM available today.

search engine   A routine that searches for data based on the criteria you enter.

sectors   Pockets on the disk where data and programs reside.

secure connection   Connection in which information you supply is encrypted on your end before being sent and then decrypted on the receiving end.

Sent Items folder   The Outlook Express folder that holds all messages you have sent over the Internet.

serial   A type of port connection most often used for a modem or mouse.

SIMMs (Single Inline Memory Modules)   A small board that contains a row of memory chips (usually nine chips reside on the board).

SIP memory (Single Inline Packages)   Memory chips used in older pre-486 PCs.

slave   Your non-boot drive.

snail mail   A term applied to regular postal mail.

software   Programs, applications, and data.

SoundBlaster-compatible   A standard followed by most sound cards that enables software compatibility.

spool   The process of sending printer output to a temporary disk file while Windows routes the data to the printer.

spreadsheet   A program that manages numbers and performs calculations in a grid-like manner (also called *electronic spreadsheets* or *electronic worksheets*).

Start button   The button on the Windows taskbar that you click to access programs and setup information.

Start menu   The Windows menu that appears when you click the Start button on the taskbar.

startup disk   A floppy disk you can make that will enable you to restart your PC if you ever lose your boot disk.

subdirectory   See *subfolder*.

subfolder   A folder that resides inside another folder (also called a *subdirectory*).

sub-woofer   A speaker that boosts your PC's low-end bass sounds.

suite   A collection of software programs that work together.

supercomputers   Extra-large and fast mainframes, super-cooled by ultra-cold liquid gases that run the most powerful applications needed by military and space exploration personnel.

surge protectors   A power outlet that keeps electrical current steady despite normal fluctuations on the line.

SVGA (Super Video Graphics Array)   A screen resolution that displays high-quality color graphics.

switchbox   A device with which you can switch between two printers. (Also called an *A-B box*.)

system   A set of interrelated parts that work together to accomplish a specific goal. Your PC is a system of components.

System Monitor   A program that checks your PC's resource levels.

system program   A program that manages other programs, such as your operating system.

system unit   The device that holds your PC's memory, internal disk drives, expansion cards, power supply, and CPU.

T

taskbar   The strip at the bottom of Windows 95 where the Start button resides as well as buttons that represent windows currently in use.

terminator   A plug that you must attach to the last PC on an Ethernet-based network that uses 10Base2 coaxial cable.

thread   A set of postings that go together, such as a question and an answer.

thumbnail sketches   A small preview of a picture or printed page.

toner cartridges   Storage drums that hold laser printer dry ink powder (the *toner*).

touch-screen monitor   A monitor that displays information and also accepts input as you touch the screen to point to screen objects.

towers   PC cases that are taller than mini-towers (often as tall as three feet high) and provide the maximum expansion room possible.

trackball   A device used in place of a mouse with a rolling ball atop a base with two or more buttons. As you roll the ball, the mouse cursor moves on the screen.

tree-structured folders   The organization of a PC's folders and subfolders.

U

undo   A feature that enables you to reverse a recent activity within a program.

unformatted disk   A disk that has not been formatted.

uninstall   The process of removing software from a PC (also called *deinstall*).

uninterruptible power supply (UPS)   A power supply that continues to supply power after the electrical source is turned off.

URL (Uniform Resource Locator)   The location of a specific Web page.

USB (Universal Serial Bus)   A new connection standard that enables you to plug other USB devices into a USB connection without having to worry about IRQs, DMA channels, and I/O addresses.

utility program   A program that enables you to manage your operating system and free disk space, or check your system for errors.

V

VESA Local (Video Electronics Standards Association's Local Bus)   A video card interface that supports more efficient video cards than previous standards (also known as a *VL-Bus*).

voice modem   A modem with which you can talk and send data with a single phone call.

volatile   The contents are erased when the power goes off.

VRAM (*Video RAM*)   RAM memory on a video adapter card that determines the card's resolution and screen capabilities.

W

wallpaper   The graphical background on the Windows desktop.

WAV files   The most common Windows-based files that hold sound.

wavetable   A sound standard (compatible with the SoundBlaster standard) that indicates a sound card is capable of advanced sound reproduction.

Web   An Internet system of graphical screen pages that displays text, graphics, and other controls (also called the *World Wide Web* and *WWW*).

WebTV   An Internet Web connection now available on some televisions that enables you to watch regular television or surf the Web from the same source.

wildcard characters   Characters that represent other characters in search criteria.

Windows   An operating system with a graphical user interface.

Windows Exchange   A pre-Windows Messaging program used by earlier versions of Windows to manage e-mail.

Windows Messaging   A program used by earlier Windows versions to manage e-mail.

wizard   A step-by-step software guide that walks you through a procedure, such as the installation of a program.

Word   Microsoft's word processing program that is currently the most popular on the market.

word processor   An application program that you run to create documents.

WordPad   A simple-to-use Windows-supplied word processor.

worksheet   See *spreadsheet*.

WORM drives (Write Once Read Many)   CD drives with which you can write data to a CD, but after that data is written, you cannot change the data. (A full WORM disc becomes a CD-ROM because you cannot alter the contents.)

WYSIWYG (Pronounced *wizzy-wig*)   Stands for *what you see (on the screen) is what you get* (on paper).

X–Z

X2   Along with *K56Flex*, one of two modem standards capable of transmitting data at speeds as high as 56KB.

ZIF (Zero Insertion Force)   An integrated circuit socket that provides a lever you can press to easily remove the chip from the ZIF socket.

Zip   A type of high-capacity removable disk drive.

INDEX

X-Y-Z